Students and E

# A
# *Troubled*
# *Eden*

❧❧

# A Troubled Eden

## NATURE AND SOCIETY IN THE WORKS
## OF GEORGE MEREDITH

*Norman Kelvin*

❦

Then soon was heard, not sooner heard
Than answered, doubled, trebled, more,
Voice of an Eden in the bird
Renewing with his pipe of four
The sob: a troubled Eden, rich
In throb of heart . . .

**OLIVER AND BOYD**
EDINBURGH AND LONDON

OLIVER AND BOYD LTD.

Tweeddale Court
Edinburgh, 1

39A Welbeck Street
London, W. 1.

First published by Stanford University Press 1961
First British edition 1961

Quotations from letters of Henry James, copyright ©
1948 by William James and Margaret James Porter;
reprinted by permission of Paul R. Reynolds & Son,
599 Fifth Avenue, New York 17, N.Y.

Printed in the United States of America

*To the memory of my mother*

# *Preface*

In the course of this study I have considered the larger part of Meredith's poetry and narrative writing, both of which are voluminous. I have not tried to touch on everything Meredith has left us. The major phases of his career receive full attention here, but certain stories and poems are given only passing notice and some are not mentioned at all. One novel, *Diana of the Crossways*, which is the object of concentrated attention in most studies of Meredith, is used here primarily to illustrate themes or to provide points of comparison when other novels are discussed. For my own purposes, a more extensive treatment of *Diana* has been unnecessary.

Aside from the impossibility of discussing in any meaningful way all that Meredith wrote, my reason for selectivity and emphasis in a study that covers a half century of Meredith's work is that some stories and poems seem to me to exhibit better than others his major themes and their development. References to *Rhoda Fleming* (1865) or the unfinished, posthumous *Celt and Saxon* (1910), for instance, would have allowed me to add details to my discussion of Meredith's understanding of nature and society, but they would not have enlarged the critical scope of that discussion or helped me shed new light on Meredith's worth as an artist. Meredith's achievements—his perceptions and the forms he gave them—are, I believe, fully evident in the works I have stressed.

I wish to thank the Trustees of the George Meredith estate for kindly permitting me to quote from Meredith's letters and manuscripts. Similarly, my thanks are due to the Yale University Library (Frank Altschul Collection) and to the New York Public Library (Henry W. and Albert A. Berg Collection) for allowing me to cite important manuscript materials in their possession. It is a pleasure, in this connection, to thank also the staffs of both libraries for their kind and generous assistance. I am indebted to Charles Scribner's Sons for permission to quote from *The Letters of George Meredith* (volumes XXVIII and XXIX of the Memorial edition of *Works*), collected and edited by William Maxse Meredith; from *The Letters of Henry James*, selected and edited by Percy Lubbock; and from *The Ordeal of George Meredith*, by Lionel Stevenson. I want to thank also Paul R. Reynolds & Son for their permission to quote from *The Letters of Henry James*. I am glad to record, too, that the Pageant Book Company has allowed me to use excerpts from *The Concept of Nature in Nineteenth-Century English Poetry*, by Joseph Warren Beach; and that Holt, Rinehart, and Winston, Inc., have permitted me to quote from *Understanding Poetry*, by Cleanth Brooks and Robert Penn Warren.

I am happy to acknowledge the many personal debts of gratitude I have incurred in the writing of this book. Professor Jerome H. Buckley guided me through the many stages of composition and gave unstintingly of his time and energy; indeed, the idea for this book grew out of my discussions with him. Professor Susanne H. Nobbe, by generously sharing with me her authoritative knowledge of Meredith and of nineteenth-century novelists in general, led me to many valuable substantive additions. Professor F. W. Dupee read closely what I wrote and held up a standard of critical excellence that was for me an elusive ideal; moreover, his suggestions led me to enlarge the scope of this study. Professors Alice G. Fredman, James Gutmann, Fritz Stern, and Marshall E. Suther, Jr., offered important criticisms of the manuscript and showed me ways to improve its content and organization.

Professor Walter Metzger gave me invaluable assistance by reading Chapters II and III; his sound and judicious advice led to many significant changes. Professor Robert K. Webb graciously permitted me to read the manuscript of his book, *Harriet Martineau: A Radical Victorian* (since published by the Columbia University Press) and imparted to me, in conversation, helpful ideas on nineteenth-century British political and social history. Professor Rudolph Binion gave freely of his time and attention; he read the manuscript with scrupulous care and made suggestions that brought clarity and ease to many a sentence in need of them.

In personal correspondence, Professor Lionel Stevenson was kind enough to share with me his expert knowledge of Meredith and to clarify a number of points of information without which I could not have proceeded with this study. Dr. Mark Jupiter assisted me in preparing certain materials, and Cary Lee Stone edited the manuscript with imagination and discretion. My father, Mr. Abraham J. Kelvin, assisted me by typing materials and by otherwise aiding in their preparation for my use. My final word of gratitude must be reserved for my wife, Phyllis; my debts to her are too varied and numerous to be cited here, but suffice it to say that her help made the writing of this book possible.

# Contents

# Contents

# A
# Troubled
# Eden

# Introduction

In Jacob Loewenberg's *Dialogues from Delphi,* two men, named
Meredy and Hardith, discuss a number of aesthetic questions. At one
point, Meredy (who, the author assures us, has not been tenden-
tiously characterized) says, "Any novel by Meredith is a sort of com-
pendium of society; it is conceived to throw reflection upon imposing
persons whose farcical behavior is disastrous to themselves and their
world. . . . His novels are designed to kindle a thoughtful vision
of human fate." Elsewhere Meredy observes, "Natural life . . . is
simply the raw material for the good life, for out of this material may
be fashioned civilized individuals and civilized societies. In the last
analysis, morality is synonymous with civilization, presupposing as
it does an original state of nature susceptible of conscious transformation. . . . [The artist] creates a new dimension of nature . . .
by forcing the facts of nature to echo or to image his own visions and
passions."

Meredy's reflections lead us to our subject. There are many ways
of viewing George Meredith's novels and poems, but Meredy's suggestion is that they be seen as a rendering into art of certain ideas
about nature and society. Meredith regarded himself as a speculative philosopher at large in the world of form, and no ideas were
more meaningful to him than those concerning nature and society.

The variety of Meredith's conceptual interests, within the two
areas described, has given rise to the suspicion that the novel and
poem were, for Meredith, merely vehicles for carrying messages. At
his worst, he justifies this suspicion. At his best, he obliterates any
ground for it; he demonstrates that it is because of his achievements

in form—his triumphs of style and technique—that his ideas have power and meaning.

Nature and society *are* the controlling themes in Meredith's works, but they alternate in ascendancy. His first important novel, *The Ordeal of Richard Feverel* (1859), is successful because it converts a view of nature into a pattern for tragedy. His work of the '60's, on the other hand, reflects the fact that Meredith had turned his attention to society. What he saw—or thought he saw—was that society is a battleground. The war imagery that took hold of his imagination in this period persisted in his writing to the very end. Most significant is the fact that his concern with battle influenced the structure of his works during the '60's, just as his conception of nature had influenced the pattern of *Richard Feverel*.

The '70's brought new forces, from within and without, to bear upon Meredith's work. "Rationalism"—for some men a creed for action and for others a provision for a self-image—became, for Meredith, a new source of inspiration for the form of his art.

The '80's witnessed a further shift in his career. Meredith had begun his literary life as a poet, but his *Poems* (1851) were poorly received. For the greater part of the next thirty years, he relegated his poetic ambitions to second place, giving precedence to the writing of novels.* By the end of the '70's, however, he had written his best novel, *The Egoist* (1879); it was only a moderate success with the public, but Meredith probably knew it was a masterpiece and felt free, as a result, to pursue the poetic ambitions so long kept in check. During the '80's he published no fewer than three volumes of poems, which are in large part a return to the theme of nature. This is not to say that ideas concerning nature are absent from the novels that appeared during the three previous decades, but the novel, despite *Richard Feverel*, is a form that almost insists upon first place being given to an author's conception of society. So it is that Meredith's interest in nature did not become ascendant again until he was ready to devote himself fully and freely to poetry.

Though Meredith lived until 1909, and published one volume of poems, *A Reading of Life*, as late as 1901, the dramatic conclusion to his career occurred in the 1890's. In the novels and poetry belong-

---

* Ironically, however, Meredith's finest poetic work, the sonnet sequence *Modern Love*, belongs to this period. It was published in 1862.

ing to this decade, he not only attempted a last clarification of his ideas about nature and society but strove to reconcile their opposing claims. Once more his triumph was not in the realm of creed-making or system-building but in that of form. However well his last efforts to harmonize the demands of nature and society may fare as argument, they stand up as poetic vision. And it is as such that we today read, enjoy, and learn from the works these efforts produced.

With his view of nature and society as our subject, a word may be said about Meredith in relation to his times and his contemporaries. Regarding nature, Meredith's was a minority voice among novelists and poets of the Victorian period, though his philosophical kin are to be found among men who accepted and spiritualized Darwin's theory of evolution. Matthew Arnold, Tennyson, John Stuart Mill, and Thomas Hardy were more representative of the literary temper of the times. They warned men that nature is no friend and alleged, in different ways, that man's destiny is dependent upon a power beyond nature. Meredith, like his friend Swinburne, like the Italian nationalist Mazzini, and like some Darwinists, saw nature as an active and benevolent principle that reveals to man his kinship with the rest of creation and that teaches him how to order his private, public, and political life. Meredith's faith in the benevolence of nature not only withstood the trials of a long life but inspired the form and the theme of much of his work, just as a distrust of nature influenced the work of Tennyson, Arnold, and Hardy.

As for society, Meredith's views about it changed perceptibly over the decades. In 1848 and '49 he was one, heart and soul, with the enthusiasts for the revolutions sweeping Europe. In the '60's, he was most similar to Harriet Martineau, to his hero Mazzini, and to the Tennyson of *Maud*. He conceived of war as an instrument by which nature corrects social wrongs and by which social character is molded. Later in the decade he adopted the social philosophy of the *Fortnightly* group, a philosophy stemming from John Stuart Mill and having as its main tenet a belief in liberal reform as opposed to both conservative restraint and revolution. Though he differed with it at significant moments, this liberalism largely characterized Meredith's social creed for the rest of his life. Mixed in with it, however, was a conservative element that had been present in his thought as early as the late '50's. Meredith numbered among his friends many con-

servatives—as well, of course, as liberals—and it is likely that from
time to time both groups had reason to believe he shared their view-
points and values.

It can be seen that Meredith relates to his period eclectically. His
political, social, and philosophical thought cannot be identified with
any single school or movement. His searching curiosity, and his
readiness to commit himself on many issues, led him by turns into
a number of differing intellectual camps. But this is not to say that
he lacked integrity. Not only were his convictions, varied as they
were, soundly held, but ideas that seem strange bedfellows when
regarded abstractly manage to exist together exceedingly well within the controlling forms of his art.

# 1

# *The Turning Point*

## 1859

### PATTERN FOR TRAGEDY

The year 1859, that *"annus mirabilis* of English literature"[1] and of nineteenth-century cultural development in general, has great significance in the personal history of George Meredith. When *The Ordeal of Richard Feverel* appeared, in June 1859, Meredith moved at a leap to a position of first importance among the novelists of the day. In the opinion of one critic, *Richard Feverel* shares with George Eliot's *Adam Bede*, published the same year, "the credit of endowing English fiction with artistic and intellectual self-respect."[2] Meredith had already published two short narratives, *The Shaving of Shagpat* (1855) and *Farina* (1857); but these, both fantasies, were a false start* and—except that they are early indications of his love for the exaggerated and the fabulous—do not anticipate the themes and forms that were to occupy Meredith throughout his subsequent career. *Richard Feverel* placed Meredith on the road he was never to leave again.

Many of the epochal works of 1859 are studies of nature, or society, or both, and *Richard Feverel* reveals a new richness when it is seen as a novel in which ideas about nature are central and in which ideas about society scurry round the periphery, seeking a way to enter into the heart of the story.

* Gordon Haight (pp. 11–12) has discovered that a rather favorable review of *Farina,* which appeared in the *Westminster Review* (October 1857) and which for years has been attributed to George Eliot, was actually written by Meredith himself.

The story concerns Sir Austin Feverel, his son Richard, and various other figures, of whom Lucy Desborough, who becomes Richard's wife, is the most important. Sir Austin has withdrawn from the world in bitterness because his wife deserted him, as Meredith's wife, Mary Peacock, deserted her husband two years before *Richard Feverel* was published. Sir Austin regards himself as a "scientific-humanist"; and he plans—in his bitterness—to bring up his infant son Richard in accordance with a strict System, one which will scientifically prepare the boy to cope with a world full of sham, hypocrisy, and vice. The chief object of the System is to ensure Richard's marrying the proper girl, one whose love will not become a deception and a poison, ending in desertion.

Sir Austin, at first, succeeds fairly well with his educational scheme. Richard's boyhood is given over to healthy sports, carefully selected companions, and a diet of reading that excludes such enervating and sentimentalizing stuff as poetry. But when Richard reaches young manhood, he falls in love with Lucy Desborough, who is the niece of a farmer and who, though as lovely and loyal as the System requires, is damned by the fact that she has not been personally chosen by Sir Austin—that she represents a gesture of free choice on Richard's part. Sir Austin not only refuses at first to receive the couple, who have married without his consent, but devises a scheme, in the name of science, to "test" Richard by keeping him apart from his bride for a time. The object of this experiment is vague, but Sir Austin still has enough power over Richard—the boy loves his father—to maneuver him into circumstances which separate him from his wife.

Soon, however, the scientific-humanist's carefully contrived arrangements begin to collapse. Richard, kept by Sir Austin's agents in London, is seduced by Bella Mount, a lady who represents vice as well as bewitchment and the need for compassion. Just at this time, Sir Austin decides the "testing period" is over, and he is now ready magnanimously to receive Richard and Lucy at Raynham Abbey, the estate of the Feverels. But Richard, full of self-loathing and shame, has decided he cannot return to Lucy until he is cleansed. To the annoyance of Sir Austin, Richard coldly asks him to receive Lucy alone at Raynham Abbey for the time being. Sir Austin refuses, the parting between father and son leaves the breach unhealed, and Richard departs for the Continent, seeking he knows not what. So matters stand until Richard, afloat in the Rhineland on sentimental dreams, including the dream of liberating Italy on horseback, receives the joyful, cleansing, and resurrecting news that Lucy has had a baby. Sir Austin, full of contrition by this time, has had her and the baby installed at Raynham Abbey. All that is needed to complete this happy domestic situation is Richard's return, and Richard sets about making his own amends by hurrying to England as fast as he can. However, he makes a fatal mistake. He stops for his mail at his London club before going down to Raynham Abbey. There he finds a letter from a repentant Bella Mount, informing him that her reprobate husband, Lord Mountfalcon, was attempting to seduce Lucy (on the Isle of Wight, where she had been left) while Richard was being maneuvered and enticed to stay in London. Nothing will do now but that Richard must challenge Lord Mountfalcon to a duel, and so insulting is Richard that even that modern and practical nobleman has no choice but to agree. At the same time he tells Richard's friend and second, Ripton Thompson, that he will gladly forget the matter in exchange for the most formal and perfunctory apology. However, circumstances contrive to keep Ripton from imparting these sensible tidings to Richard. Richard has a few wild, feverish tender hours in the arms of Lucy, in the bosom of his family at Raynham Abbey, and then with notice to no one leaves in the dawn to meet Lord Mountfalcon near Dieppe. The Raynham household, getting the explanation from Ripton Thompson, pursues Richard, but arrives in France only to find him near death from a bullet wound. Now the tragedy approaches its end. Lucy, under the shock of having had her husband back for a few hours only to face the possibility of losing him again, breaks down and dies. Richard, successfully passing his own physical crisis, awakens to a world that will henceforth be barren and meaningless for him.

It would seem that the villain in this tragedy is Sir Austin's System, or perhaps science in general. This is not quite so. The problem is not that Sir Austin is a scientist who has devised an inapplicable system for shaping his son, but that Sir Austin's "scientific humanism" is a contradiction in terms[3] and a mask for his real motives. The System in itself is not, up to a point, such a terrible thing. It makes Richard into a lover of the natural and a hater of the sham and the artificial. Moreover, it develops his sensibility so that he can distinguish between them. The System also deserves the residual credit—the credit not assignable to chance—for the fact that Richard falls in love with Lucy, a girl whom Meredith describes as "a daughter of earth," and therefore a happy choice for a young man. Meredith acknowledges that the System has been designed to guide Richard toward just such a girl as Lucy. After describing Richard as an "arrow," capable of flying fast and far with Lucy, Meredith (pp. 121–22) says: "Then truly The System triumphed . . . and could Sir Austin have been content to draw the arrow to the head, and let it fly, he might have pointed to his son again, and said to the world, 'Match him!' "

The cause of the tragedy is not the System[4] but Sir Austin's character, two entities that are quite separable. This becomes clear when we realize that the real trouble does not begin until *after* the System has done its work and ought to be dropped. Sir Austin's tragic fault is his inability to see that after Richard marries Lucy—albeit without his, Sir Austin's, permission—the System is no longer applicable. This fault leads to the episode called "Nursing the Devil," in which Sir Austin searches strenuously for reasons to repudiate the marriage he should acknowledge as his own success.

What the episode reveals is that Sir Austin's scientific humanism is a mask for egoism and that his primary drive is wounded pride. When Lady Blandish, a good friend of Sir Austin, pleads with him immediately after Richard's marriage to accept the fact and thus save the boy from the "consequences," he answers (p. 351): "That I should save him, or any one, from consequences, is asking more than the order of things will allow to you, Emmeline, and is not in the disposition of the world."

It is an absurd answer, one which uses an irrelevant scientific principle to deny the humanistic goal of increasing human well-being in a situation in which free choice, from a rational viewpoint, is possible. Sir Austin is using scientism to further the purposes of the most irrational of human motives, wounded egoism.

Although authors are notoriously poor explicators of their own novels, certain comments Meredith made to Samuel Lucas regarding the connection between the System and Sir Austin's egoism are worth noting: "The moral is that no System of the sort succeeds with human nature, unless the originator has conceived it purely independent of personal passion. That was Sir Austin's way of wreaking his revenge."[5] Actually, these words contradict an earlier part of the same letter to Lucas, in which Meredith says that the System *did* succeed— through "the young fellow's luck in finding so charming a girl"—and that the tragedy does not occur until his father "strikes down . . . [the] fabric" of his own success. Nevertheless, the analysis of Sir Austin is consistent with the story. All his actions, good or bad, have been dictated by "personal passion," which is clearly another name for egoism. This, of course, makes his persistent image of himself as a "scientific-humanist" continuously and richly ironic.

The irony is well rendered at the moment when Sir Austin, ignorant of the details of the Bella Mount incident and of what it has done to Richard, decides that his scientific experiment—keeping Richard separated from Lucy—ought to be ended (p. 479):

> Sir Austin Feverel had come to town with the serenity of a philosopher who says, " 'Tis now time." . . . He had almost forgiven his son. His deep love for him had well-nigh shaken loose from wounded pride and more tenacious vanity. . . . But the world must not suppose him soft; the world must think he was still acting on his System. Otherwise, what would his long absence signify? . . .
> The Aphorist read himself so well, that to juggle with himself was a necessity. As he wished the world to see him, he beheld himself: one who entirely put aside mere personal feelings: one in whom parental duty, based on the science of life, was paramount: a Scientific Humanist, in short.

The sequel is the explosion of reality upon this egoist-scientist. Richard departs for the Continent, and the train of events leading to the conclusion rapidly transpires.

If we ask the moral meaning of Sir Austin's character and of its effect upon others, the answer is that Sir Austin, a mechanist-theorizer reinforced in his folly by egoism, is incapable of dealing with a real boy in a concrete situation. With regard to his self-image—which does not, of course, involve egoism—Sir Austin stands in the Cartesian-Newtonian tradition. At one point he asserts (p. 134), "Man is a self-acting machine. He cannot cease to be a machine." These words put us in mind of Ralph Crum's estimate of Newton's cultural and historical significance. Crum says that one of the effects of the publication of the *Principia Mathematica* was to strengthen "the position of

Descartes . . . that man himself has been formed by mechanical means . . . and that he acts and reacts according to a complicated system of springs."[6]

Clearly the moral meaning of *Richard Feverel* is that human life is something other than the action of a complicated system of springs. That "something other" is spiritual, irreducible, and unpredictable. The one thing we can say about it, according to Meredith, is that it derives both its energy and its spirituality from its relation to earth. In the scene in which Richard first meets Lucy, his awakening love for her is described as an organic part of the woodland processes going on about the young pair. (It is worth noting again that Meredith, during this scene, describes Lucy as a "daughter of earth.") Later in the novel, when the news reaches Richard that he is a father, he marches out into a Rhineland forest, and there, amid the quiverings, noise, and flashing of a thunder and lightning storm, he experiences the spiritual rebirth he had been vainly seeking for months.[7] Again, a natural scene has been both a context and a contributing source to the awakening of spiritual energy in a human being. There are echoes here of Wordsworth and Goethe, but Meredith, in *Richard Feverel*, through his vivid sense of motive and personality, has transformed the Romantic nature creed into something of his own.

The most important way in which Meredith's nature philosophy finds expression as art is in the very pattern of the tragedy. In nature, according to Meredith and most of the Romantics to whom he was indebted, the life history of an individual goes from birth to seed-time to fruition to death and then to rebirth in some form— usually in the form of the next generation.[8] For Meredith, the last stage of this process has a spiritual meaning akin to the meaning resurrection has for the Christian. Significantly, therefore, the tragedy in *Richard Feverel* stems from a disordering of this natural, joyful, and affirmative cycle.

If we look closely at the novel we see that all the stages in the natural cycle are present but that at the end something extraordinary—the disarrangement of the *order* alluded to—takes place. The early chapters of the story are devoted to Richard's infancy and boyhood; his approach to manhood is signaled by a chapter titled "The Blossoming Season"; fruition comes with the marriage of Richard and Lucy and the birth of their child. Richard suffers a spiritual death. Then, in the Rhineland scene, which occurs in a chapter titled "Nature Speaks," he is reborn to the present and the future. Thus, the natural cycle is complete, and were the story to end here the moral would have been that the round of nature's processes brings ultimately joy and fulfillment. But the story does not end here. Nor is "rebirth" followed by another period of "seed-time." It is followed by death—Lucy's physical death and Richard's second spiritual death. The pattern and cycle of nature are in violent disorder, and this disruption of nature is, in *Richard Feverel*, the very source and meaning of the tragedy.

As a tragedy based on a conception of nature, *Richard Feverel* is meaningful and successful. But if we ask, is this not also a story about society and does not the tragic ending derive also from a conception of society, we enter upon difficulties rather than easy answers.

OUTSIDE THE ORDER

Society, as an idea, does not govern the structure of *Richard Feverel* as the idea of nature does. The novel makes statements *about* society, takes a position with regard to certain social institutions, but it never integrates these assertions into an over-all vision of ordered or disordered reality.

The most important social attitude in *Richard Feverel* is a commitment to the Carlylean doctrine of work. Austin Wentworth, a cousin of Sir Austin and a man who can best be described as "the hero as minor character," is an apostle of work. Austin not only is reminiscent of a Carlylean hero,[9] but is modeled upon the Christian socialist leaders Charles Kingsley and F. D. Maurice. Austin's efforts to establish in South America a community of English workingmen, a community made up of the poor and unemployed, recalls the efforts of the Christian reformers to establish in England cooperative workshops for the unemployed. Austin, though always a secondary figure in the story, is Richard's hero. It is possible to argue that Richard's "social" tragedy is that Lucy's death shatters him before he has an opportunity to devote himself to manly and purposeful work. But since Meredith is very hazy about Richard's work in the world, to insist upon the social implications of the tragedy is to reach for implications beyond those clearly realized by Meredith himself.

A second and related social idea in the novel does derive from the image, however vague, that Richard presents. Richard is heir to

a title and an estate. There is some desultory talk about his someday
going into Parliament and working for the betterment of the nation
as a whole. (One of the objects of the System, we might add, was
to train him to be a proper "leader of men.") Given Richard's background and aspirations, however faintly the latter may be delineated,
and given certain biographical facts concerning Meredith, there is
good reason to believe that the characterization of Richard was in
part, at least, inspired by the Young England Movement.

This movement was begun by a group of youthful men in Parliament who were mostly the sons of the landed aristocracy. The leaders were George Smythe and Lord John Manners. Fearful of revolution, these two believed that the way to avoid it was to promote
closer ties between the upper classes and the lower. Aristocracy and
poor were to combine against radicals and manufacturers, their common enemy and the sappers of the structure of English society. Thus
the upper classes were to be leaders of a feudal, organic society in
which they would play a paternal role. In 1842, Disraeli, though
nearly twenty years older than Smythe and Manners, temporarily
joined them and provided their movement with a forceful and articulate voice. He soon deserted the Young Englanders, however, and
by 1845 they had ceased to function as a group, though Manners, for
one, persisted in most of his original views.[10]

In 1846, Meredith, who was then eighteen and had been without
direction since his return in 1844 from school in Germany, was arti-
cled to R. S. Charnock, a lawyer more interested in literature than
in law. Although Meredith never seriously pursued his own study
of the law, his clerkship gave him entrée into a circle of intellectuals
led by Charnock.[11] Charnock belonged to the Arundel Club, of
which Lord John Manners was also a member.[12] It seems highly
likely that Meredith, in daily touch with Charnock and his literary
friends, often heard the name and ideas of Charnock's eminent club-
fellow discussed and debated. And strengthening this probability
is the fact that Meredith in later years, referring to the period of his
association with Charnock, told Edward Clodd: "I had no stomach
for the law, so I drifted into journalism, my first venture being in
the form of a leader on Lord John Manners, which I sent to the
*Standard*."[13] Add to this the fact that the second most prominent
member of the Young England Movement, George Smythe, "fought
in the last duel on English soil, 1852,"[14] and the possibility that Mere-

dith had the leaders of the Young England Movement somewhere in view when he came to create *Richard Feverel* takes on an even deeper interest. A last fact worthy of note is that one of the aspirations of the Young England Movement was to "assert the ideal significance of the territorial aristocracy,"[15] and that this is precisely the class to which Richard belonged.

## CONSERVATIVE LEANINGS

Meredith's interest in the Christian socialists and the Young England Movement does not throw additional light on the structure of *Richard Feverel*, but it helps explain his mind and temperament during the 1850's and the '60's as well. The generation of critics writing after Meredith's death in 1909 created for the public a monolithic, liberal-radical Meredith, one who was always on the side of "progress" and radical democracy. Meredith was such a person in 1848, and showed signs of becoming one again near his death. But in between—in his most fruitful years—his political and social ideas varied from decade to decade, and seldom, if ever, did he show any real commitment to the democratic radicalism which his enthusiasts, during the two or three decades after his death, insisted he believed in. *Richard Feverel* tells us that in 1859 Meredith's hero was not a radical born of the people, like George Eliot's Felix Holt, but an aristocratic and cultivated gentleman who would lead the people though not identify with them. The phase in Meredith's career which followed the publication of *Richard Feverel*, and which has perplexed Meredithian critics and students, in this light becomes clear.

From 1860 to 1868 Meredith contributed weekly articles to one Tory paper, *The Ipswich Journal*, and occasional pieces to a second, *The Morning Post.** Some critics have found it difficult to understand why Meredith, the putative democratic radical, should have chosen to write for Tory papers, but there is really nothing puzzling about

---

* In later life he was deeply annoyed when the facts about his period of Tory journalism were brought to light. According to J. A. Hammerton (pp. 11–16), Frederick Dolman made the findings and presented them in an article in the March 1893 issue of the *New Review*. Curiously, Dolman's findings were allowed to pass from sight, and in 1909 an unnamed critic, ignorant of Dolman's research, announced publicly his intention of unearthing Meredith's contributions to *The Ipswich Journal*. This caused Meredith to remark to Clodd ("Recollections," p. 21), "Some ghoul has threatened to make search for these articles; may the Commination Service be thundered in his ears."

the episode.[16] Meredith was always inclined toward the conservatives and the aristocracy. His leaning in their direction was more marked during the late '50's and in the '60's than it was in subsequent years, but it never actually ceased. Partially it was caused by a contempt he felt for a long time for the commercial classes and their values,[17] a contempt he shared with other men of letters, notably Tennyson. Partially it was the result of the difficult life situation which was shaping Meredith the man. Son of a tailor; handsome, sensitive, and of an aristocratic bearing; financially straitened; deserted by his wife; responsible for the upbringing of his son, he learned in the late '50's to rely for his share of life mainly on his talent as an artist. It was easy enough for him to feel a kinship between the artist, born with talent, and the aristocrat, born to high position. But the feeling made life a risky business at best, and no doubt the equation lay buried in the deeper recesses of Meredith's mind and character.

On the surface, his talent and his personal bearing had a certain value—the first had produced *Richard Feverel* and both were gaining him friends among the well-born, particularly in the circle of which Lady Duff Gordon was the center. But the life he led was without safety, and therefore, during the very period in which he engaged in Tory journalism, he developed other forms of protective fantasy as well. Happily for us, these for the most part produced richer and more meaningful works than his *Ipswich Journal* leaders.

With the '60's a new theme appears in Meredith's novels and poems. It is a preoccupation with war and battle in general—war that begins with Meredith's personally embattled situation and extends to the international scene. And a new figure emerges in his works. It is the soldier, the armored knight, the man whose heroism and self-regard are not dependent on wealth or the vagaries of class acceptance and rejection, as was the case with the naked artist even in the democratic nineteenth century. Surely the soldier, who willingly exposes himself to death, is safe from the rejections, the deceptions, the pains and terrors that Meredith, the artist and the man of no background, knew only too well in the dubious life that his talent was opening for him.

## 2

# Society Is a Battleground

### THE 1860's AND AFTER

When Meredith was old and famous, literary pilgrims came to pay him homage, carry away anecdotes, or merely flatter themselves with his conversation. On one occasion, Richard B. Haldane, a frequent visitor at Box Hill, brought along Sir John French, a military hero of the Boer War. Meredith soon got into an argument with Sir John about the disposition of troops at the Battle of Magenta. " 'No one with any military knowledge,' " the General declared, " 'could have imagined that at that stage a whole division could have been brought up to the point where you say they should have been.' " " 'General,' " Meredith retorted, not the least bit chastened, " 'I have observed that cavalry leaders, however distinguished, are bad judges of the operation of mixed troops.' " Haldane decided "that the moment was opportune for summoning the motor car that was to take French back to Aldershot."[1]

This anecdote is often quoted to illustrate the aging Meredith's continuing irreverence toward authority. But the interest in military affairs that gave rise to Meredith's impertinence lay deeper and had a more enduring character than has generally been recognized. Actually, that interest began in the '60's, and immediately found expression in the imagery, themes, details, values—and even overarching forms—that are elements and aspects of Meredith's work.[2] It even influenced his choice of experiences to be deliberately sought. In 1866, when fighting broke out in Italy, Meredith urged the editor of *The Morning Post* to send him to the front lines as a war correspondent. He got the assignment, and his collected dispatches from the theater of battle are most revealing of his values and attitudes during this period.

Before he left England, Meredith finished and published *Vittoria*, the action of which takes place in Italy during the uprising of 1848. Among other things, the novel is a virtuoso piece devoted to a display of military terminology and tactics and of the skills belonging to a good soldier. Even more to the point, its over-all pattern of events is the actual pattern of the 1848–49 war in Italy.

The writing of *Vittoria* and the departure for Italy in 1866 do not, however, mark the commencement of Meredith's concern with military matters. A few years earlier, the American Civil War was being fought. Meredith was a zealous friend of the South. When the Confederate raider *Alabama* was about to leave Cherbourg harbor to battle the waiting *Kearsarge*, Warren Adams of Saunders and Otley, who was Meredith's employer at the time, "rushed over to Cherbourg, interviewed Captain Semmes of the . . . *Alabama* on the very eve of its fight . . . and obtained the log and captain's journal" for publication.[3] Meredith was commissioned to write an introductory chapter and a closing one, and the latter in particular is as revealing of his values and of the quality of his imagination as anything he wrote during this period.

### THE SQUIRE OF LOW DEGREE

But the real beginning of Meredith's attachment to military themes and situations occurs in *Evan Harrington* (1860), the first of his novels of the '60's. The war theme of *Evan Harrington* is not immediately apparent because the novel is a comedy and because it contains autobiographical elements deriving from a period in Meredith's life in which actual military combat played no part. The point, however, is that *Evan Harrington* draws upon Meredith's own early experiences in "society" and that by 1860 Meredith was no longer vague concerning what society was to be in his work. Society, in *Evan Harrington*, is a battleground, as the form and details of the story make abundantly clear.

The story concerns Evan Harrington, who, like Meredith, is the son of a tailor. Evan is in love with Rose, daughter of Sir Franks and Lady Jocelyn of Beckley Court. Rose was openly modeled on Janet Duff Gordon, daughter of Sir Alexander and Lady Duff Gordon.

Meredith had been in love with Janet during 1859 and 1860, but though she was pleased to have him—whom she called "my Poet"[4]— write poems declaring his love and though she spent much time with him, she evidently did not encourage him to believe they could ever marry. Indeed, during the very period in which she was seeing a great deal of Meredith, who was her neighbor in Esher, she must have been making the acquaintance of Henry James Ross, who was to become her husband in 1860. Meredith did not attend the wedding, but his subsequent letters to Janet are singularly free of reproach or of any hint of his own love other than a good-humored envy of her husband's happiness. One reason, of course, why Meredith did not protest was that his first wife, Mary Peacock Meredith, who had left him three years earlier, was still living. Indeed, it is difficult to see what he had ever hoped for from Janet. Being so very poor at the time, he does not seem to have contemplated a divorce action.

Yet two facts persist. The first is that Meredith loved Janet. The second is that Janet, daughter of aristocrats, married a man of substantial wealth at a time when Meredith, son of a tailor, was nearly penniless. We do not know what feelings he had when he discovered that his natural charm and wit could win him a place at the Duff Gordons' dinner table but were not enough to make his hosts take seriously any idea he might have had of becoming their son-in-law. Nor do we know if he ever suspected Janet herself of regarding his origins and his unpromising financial condition as the real barrier to their union. But we do know that the central characters of *Evan Harrington* were inspired by the Duff Gordons and by Meredith's image of himself, and that the novel was written in 1860, during the period of Janet's engagement to Henry Ross. If we can say little about the Duff Gordons, about the meaning their world had for Meredith, about the sense he had of himself in relation to this world, we can speak freely of the Jocelyns, of the world of Beckley Court, and of Evan Harrington's relation to this world.

Evan, though deeply in love with Rose when the novel begins, tries manfully to mask his passion. Having agreed to take over the family tailor shop in order to pay off the debts that his father, the great Mel, left behind when he died, he considers it dishonorable even to visit Beckley, where Rose, ignorant of his background and

situation, might respond to his love. In brief, Meredith depicts Evan
as too honorable to plan, calculate, and maneuver himself into the
proximity of the girl for whom he would gladly die. Instead, Evan
remains passive, even protesting, while his fantastic sister Louisa
(who is married to an impoverished Portuguese count) does the dig-
ging and sapping, and, aided by chance, finally clears the way. Evan,
innocent of any deception or even expectation, finds the Jocelyns,
who believe him to be of aristocratic origin, insisting that he be their
guest at Beckley Court.

*Evan Harrington* was appearing serially in *Once a Week* during
1860, and Meredith was writing the novel as he went along, barely
keeping up with his deadlines. His editor, Samuel Lucas, and many
of his readers complained that *Evan* was moving too slowly. Meredith, though he partially defended himself by delivering Lucas a
lecture on novel writing, acknowledged that there was some justification for the complaint and promised that the story would move
more swiftly once he had gotten Evan and the Countess installed at
Beckley Court. Indeed, it took him twelve chapters to get Evan in-
vited to Beckley, which then remains the scene of the novel, with
few interludes, until the end. Actually, these beginning chapters do
not drag for the reader who has learned to enjoy Meredith, *pace*
Lucas and his subscribers. But Meredith was acutely responsive to
the charge, as his letters accompanying the chapters he sent to Lucas
reveal. He admitted that he *was* having difficulty but explained his
purpose at length. In an early letter he said: "My work is at present
a study: the incidents shape and are dependent on character: consequently they have to be thought over and worked with some labour."[5]
Later, in response to some complaint not made clear, he added: "Remember that in Smollett conduct is never *accounted* for. My principle is to show the events flowing from evident causes. To *naturalize*
them to the mind of the reader." But in his next letter, he admitted:
"Your advice is good. This cursed desire I have haunting me to show
the reasons for things is a perpetual obstruction to movement." Then,
after he submitted Chapter Six, he wrote: "I sent a chapter (partly
re-written) called 'My Gentleman on the Road.' I particularly wish
your opinion of it. I stress small incidents; but they best exhibit
character." And Meredith, apparently after receiving a glum reply
from Lucas, could only repeat: "Doubtless in a 'Serial' point of view,

there may be something to say; but I fancy I am right in slowly building up for the scenes to follow. . . . 'On the Road' is rather long. . . . It developes the character of the hero partly: the incidents subsequently affect him." And in the last letter in the series, written perhaps after Evan had arrived at Beckley but while the readers, apparently, were still complaining, Meredith said: "I maintain that the story is true to its title,* and that I avoided making the fellow a snob in spite of his and my own temptations. Hence probably the charge of dullness: but this comes of an author giving himself a problem to work out and doing it as conscientiously as he could. The ground was excessively delicate."

Interesting as these letters are for the light they throw on Meredith's method and on his theory of the novel, they leave us with unanswered questions. Why this constant reiteration that he needs "to show the reasons for things," to account for incidents in "character," to move cautiously over "delicate" ground? Why does he need to prevent Evan from becoming a snob? And why the fear that he might make him one? Meredith was intent to the point of anxiety on "proving" beyond any doubt that Evan had every expectation of becoming a tailor and forgetting Rose, that he never would have presumed to solicit an invitation to Beckley, and that it was, indeed, "incident"—i.e., Countess Louisa's maneuvering plus accident—that landed him, protesting and still pure, in the very house in which Rose lived. Janet Ross, who seems to have been given to proprietary feelings when it came to Meredith, referred to *Evan Harrington* in later years as "*my* novel."[6] Since Meredith wished her to regard it as such, he was determined that it should not contain the image of an upstart aggressively pushing himself into a world in which he was not wanted: into her world.

But it was not only what Janet Ross or he himself might think of Evan's motives that made him construct the novel so cautiously. There is another reason, more integral to the structure of the story, though not entirely separable from Meredith's reasons for writing it. Once inside Beckley Court, however he got there, Evan finds that Rose loves him. But the upper-class world, suspecting his origins, fights with every cruel and underhanded means available to push

---

* Meredith's subtitle for *Evan Harrington* was *He Would be a Gentleman*.

him back to the tailor's shop. It was essential to Meredith's conception of Evan's character that Evan show himself of unassailable integrity throughout the comic but savage fight that ensues. Just as he
could take no initiative to get to Beckley, so he has to remain passive
in the war that is declared against the Harringtons. Giving offense
to no one, challenging no one, ever ready to withdraw should Rose
wish it, eager to comply with the desires of Rose's parents, Evan can
flash out only when insulted, and then only as honor requires.

But the fight that swirls around him is bitter, and someone has
to take the initiative in his behalf if he is not to be crushed. It remains for the vulgar Louisa, who, like her aristocratic enemies, will
use any weapon at hand, to assault when necessary. Louisa, indeed,
carries the war, and it was a war that Meredith dearly wished to
write about in this novel. In the end, he has it both ways. Evan
remains true to the character we glimpse in the early "incidents,"
while a war in which the upper classes are mercilessly pilloried is
carried on by the snobbish daughter of a tailor who is every bit as
bad as her enemy. Evan remains free to repudiate his sister when
he finds out how low her tactics have been, and Meredith, meanwhile,
has been free to cause Louisa to bring out the low behavior of the
aristocrats, behavior for which he can then, with grim satisfaction,
thoroughly baste them.

Thus, *Evan Harrington* is indeed the story of a battle, and Beckley Court is the battlefield.[7] What we know of Meredith's relationship with the Duff Gordons also suggests that Beckley is a symbol of
the society that had both accepted and rejected Meredith just before
*Evan Harrington* was written. And Evan, merely by entering society,
becomes a beleaguered knight.

This reference to knighthood is not casual. The key to *Evan Harrington,* considered as the story of a war in which society is the
battlefield, is the medievalism of its imagery and of its over-all pattern. Early in the novel, Evan goes home for his father's funeral.
His mother tells him of the debts his father left behind; Evan will
have to become a tailor to pay them off, she adds, if he wishes to
do the honorable thing. He retires to his room in agony. The image
of Rose, lost forever should he become a tailor, tortures him. Yet
he sees the point of honor his mother has raised. He gazes at the
wall, and there, significantly, hangs a picture of Douglas and Percy
doing battle. Then, says Meredith, describing Evan's tormented rev-

erie (p. 86), "There were the Douglas and the Percy on the wall. It was a happy and a glorious time, was it not, when men lent each other blows that killed outright; when to be brave and cherish noble feelings brought honour; when strength of arm and steadiness of heart won fortune; when the fair stars of earth—sweet women—wakened and warmed the love of squires of low degree."

Meredith may be gently satirizing Evan here, but when Meredith uses a comic interlude to help delineate a *hero*, the comedy is a cloak thrown over his own most earnest feelings. Evan is dreaming of a world in which "natural" virtues, of the kind Meredith felt he himself possessed, were the values cherished by society; in which lack of money and the misfortune to have been born of "low degree" do not prevent a gifted man from winning a lady who is herself a triumph of privilege and cultivation, of money and breeding. He is dreaming, in brief, of a better democracy than the kind in which Meredith might dine with the Duff Gordons but not marry one of them. Like Carlyle and Tennyson, and indeed like many medieval romancers, Evan saw a superior form of social justice, a true democracy of talent, in a society which raised a man of faithful heart to the highest degree. But for us, Evan's vision of himself as a knight who hopes to be rewarded for his manly virtues is only half convincing. We see that it is both an accurate expression of the moral sensibility of youth and a naïve symbol of the struggle in which Evan and Meredith himself were engaged. It is accurate because it suggests the power of youth's belief that there are better standards than money and birth for judging a man's worth; it is symbolically naïve because it does not convey the psychological experience of battling for status in Victorian society.

Inadequate as it is, the image of Evan as a knight appears again later on. By then Evan has won Rose—only to decide he has to give her up in order to shield his sister from the consequences of an atrocious act, the forging of an injurious letter bearing the signature of Ferdinand Laxley, a young aristocrat who has previously been Evan's hopeless rival in love. Rose, though heartbroken, now pledges herself to marry Ferdinand.

Though Evan has deliberately made the sacrifice by taking upon himself the Countess's crime, he is dimly aware that the whole concatenation of events had its origin in the facts of society—particularly in the fact that he is the son of a tailor. He needs an outlet for his frustration and ruefully reflects that he may at least get the satisfaction of fighting Laxley, once the latter hears about the infamous letter, which Evan has led people to believe is his own work, not his sister's. Meredith says (p. 457):

[Evan] took a stick, and ran his eye musingly along the length, trifling with it grimly. The great Mel had been his son's instructor in the chivalrous science of fence, and a *maître d'armes* in Portugal had given him polish. In Mel's time duels with swords had occasionally been fought, and Evan looked on the sword as the weapon of combat. Face to face with his adversary—what then were birth or position?

Clearly, however much this passage, too, is a reverie of Evan's, we are not supposed to find anything ridiculous or archaic in the great Mel's having trained Evan in the "chivalrous science of fence." (As we saw in *Richard Feverel,* and as we shall see again many times, the duel was an institution which fascinated and troubled Meredith, and he seldom took it lightly.) It is evident that Evan's skill with the sword is not the least of his accomplishments and is meant to be indubitable proof that he has every right to consider himself the equal of the aristocrats. It is as if Meredith were not quite sure that courage and "steadiness of heart" were sufficient for a tailor's son to claim the respect owed a gentleman; actual training in a gentlemanly skill seemed needed as well. But why Meredith had him instructed in a skill really irrelevant to the life of a *nineteenth*-century gentleman is puzzling unless we realize that resentful as Meredith was when he thought about society, he was also discomfited and intimidated, and thus ultimately evasive.

Dickens provides an interesting contrast here. In *Great Expectations* (1860–61) we meet a boy who also wants to be a gentleman, and for the same reason that Evan does: so that he may marry a girl who has been brought up a lady. But aside from the general broadening of his experience, the only "training" Pip receives is instruction in table manners, kindly offered by his friend, Herbert Pocket. This is realistic, as is the fact that Pip goes off to London, not to a country house, to fledge his wings. Indeed, the whole conception of a country house as the scene of social conflict between a poor boy and the aristocracy is somewhat out of touch with the realities of the Victorian world. London, not a country house, was the place in which a boy whose father kept a shop might hope to win acceptance for his natural abilities, if only because the people from whom he would seek acceptance had risen from shops themselves. In his own case, what recommended Meredith to the Duff Gordons was the fact that he was an interesting if unsuccessful writer. It is likely that Lady Duff Gordon, an intelligent and perceptive woman, recognized that he was a man of talent; had Evan been one, his story might have gained a dimension of actuality it now lacks.

But here we face a paradox. Unrealistic as his fundamental conception is, Meredith does use realistic detail in constructing this novel. He was concerned about being as accurate as possible in his depiction of life in a country house. Moreover, his presentation of the various members of the upper class, of the parvenu Countess, and of Evan himself rests largely on comic analysis. And to explain motives, even if many of them are overlooked, is to write realistically. What is unrealistic has already been suggested: the moralistic conception which refuses to penetrate social reality, which prefers to transform a nineteenth-century country house into a medieval castle and a tailor's son into a "squire of low degree." These images and devices are not intrinsically inadequate, but they are inadequate as Meredith uses them. Since he makes them account only for "birth" and "position," on the one hand, and "natural virtue," on the other, thus rendering them incapable of conveying any real range and variety of psychological experience, they are ultimately incapable of producing the moral impact for which he designed them.

It is not only in his conception of Evan in relation to Beckley Court that Meredith uses medieval imagery. After Evan tells Lady Jocelyn that he is the author of the false letter, he prepares to get himself and his kin off the premises as quickly as possible. His sister, however, cannot believe that he has been mad enough to ruin himself, and she refuses to leave. Evan, for the first time, becomes firm with her, and she finally realizes that the Battle of Beckley is indeed ending in defeat for her. Meredith says (pp. 465–66), in a succinct comic passage which, despite its brevity, holds worlds of meaning for this novel: "The Castle of Negation held out no longer. Ruthless battalions poured over the walls, blew up the Countess's propriety, made frightful ravages in her complexion. Down fell her hair."

The Countess, in this passage, has become a comic microcosm of Beckley Court itself. With the phrase "Down fell her hair" Meredith neatly suggests that her masquerade is over, that she is no longer even a caricature of elegance and breeding. But he has done something more. He has anticipated the end of the novel. What has really fallen has been the Countess's false pride. And just as she is "the Castle of Negation," so is Beckley, which has tried so hard to deny Evan's claim that he, one of nature's noblemen, has a right to love Rose. In the end, though the Battle of Beckley is itself lost, Evan does marry Rose, and when he does the false pride of the society symbolized by this country house falls as did the Countess's hair, signifying the same sudden collapse of unwarranted pretensions.

One final image, which does indeed summarize the situation, occurs near the end of the novel. Meredith says (p. 532): "This, if you have done me the favour to read it aright, has been a chronicle of desperate heroism on the part of almost all the principal personages." He then describes them, engaged in their heroic deeds, as "the Countess de Saldar, scaling the embattled fortress of Society," and "Rose, tossing its keys to her lover from the shining turret-tops," while Evan is "keeping bright the lamp of self-respect in his bosom against South wind and East." The imagery of this passage catches up the central idea of *Evan Harrington*, the idea of a fortress besieged.

Without placing too heavy a stress on Meredith's experience with the Duff Gordons, we can see now some of the meaning of his use of chivalric imagery in *Evan Harrington*. He wanted to write a novel about Janet Duff Gordon. He also wanted it to be about the efforts of a tailor's son to enter society in order to win Janet. To his mind, it was inevitable that the central situation, indeed the over-all form, of such a story should be a battle. However, he did not want to write about what defeat in this battle would do to the tailor's son. Hence, he not only caused his hero to win but used knightly metaphors in such a way that they permit us to see only the action of the story and the expression of sentiments which are exclusively noble and brave. He so used them that they mask as much as they reveal.

Both the uniqueness and the limitations of *Evan Harrington* become clearer when we think of two other novels of 1860 that present boys of the lower classes who want to become gentlemen. We have already seen how differently Dickens conceived Pip with regard to the question of the training necessary for gentlemen. Another detail of *Great Expectations* also provides a revealing comparison. When

Pip first meets Herbert Pocket, that young gentleman challenges him to a fist fight. Poor Herbert, though brave and schooled in the science of boxing, is badly knocked about by Pip, who is untutored, uncouth, but vastly more robust. Meredith would not have seen the point of allowing gentlemanly training coupled with courage to suffer so complete a defeat, even at the hands of natural ability and strength.

In the first part of George Eliot's *The Mill on the Floss,* efforts are made to turn Tom Tulliver, a miller's son, into a gentleman. Tom, unlike Evan and Pip, was not born one of nature's noblemen. He has limited intelligence and limited capacity for making moral discoveries. Nevertheless, he, too, wants to be a gentleman. When sent to study with Mr. Stelling, a clergyman with a reputation for cultivating and polishing his scholars, Tom dimly grasps only one precept, that "all gentlemen learned the same things."[8] This insight gives him just enough motivation to mislearn a smattering of Latin.

Such is Tom Tulliver. It is noteworthy that this quasi-boor, aspiring to be a gentleman, has, like Evan, a taste for things military. We see his fascination with weapons and we are told he has a great love for "fighting stories," a love which Eliot implies is quite natural in a youth who is all boy and who shows little promise of real manliness. Meredith either would have winced at the association of military fervor with juvenility or would have repudiated it. He would not, in any case, have been party to the belittling of an enthusiasm which was decidedly his own.

### THE FAINT THIN LINE

War imagery appears again in Meredith's next major work, the sonnet sequence *Modern Love* (1862). The poems in the sequence are so rich in meaning, however, that it will be necessary to place the battle images within a larger pattern rather than to emphasize them as a dominant theme.

The sonnets tell of the death of love between a husband and wife and of the fatal results of their efforts to revive love. The wedded pair are doomed by character and by passion—i.e., nature—to endless conflict and misery. War imagery is employed to dramatize this situation. In the first stanza, or sonnet, the couple lie upon their marriage bed, miserably isolated from each other, both wishing for "the sword that severs all" (I, 133).[9] Similarly, the concluding lines of *Modern*

*Love,* which have prompted much critical comment,[10] are vividly suggestive of the action of battle:

> In tragic hints here see what evermore
> Moves dark as yonder midnight ocean's force,
> Thundering like ramping hosts of warrior horse,
> To throw that faint thin line upon the shore!
>
> (L, 155)

Norman Friedman tells us that the "ramping hosts of warrior horse" are the irrational impulses of the blood divided from the brain and that the "faint thin line" is the chosen few who have reached the "shore" of personal integration, who have learned to balance blood, brain, and spirit, Meredith's spiritual triad.

My own reading of these lines is similar but not the same. The "ramping hosts" are indeed the irrational drives of mankind, but they are "thundering" through history, conceived of as an evolutionary process. The "faint thin line" is composed of men who have emerged somewhat wiser and better from both personal and historical struggle. I believe this historical, or evolutionary, reading is necessary to explain the force and movement of the imagery; to explain why the "faint thin line" *emerges* from the ranks of the warrior horse.

Not to be taken for granted is the fact that the driving, irrational forces that have been pushing man forward since primitive times are warlike. They are presented in the image "warrior horse"—which suggests that man has had to battle his way forward, has had to engage in combat with unnamed antagonists who have assaulted him from within and without. Thus, when we return to the fact that the poem is about the failure of a marriage, we see that the reason for the failure is that the husband and wife have not battled their way to the "shore." Still caught up in a conflict within themselves, they have turned their "dark" passions outward upon each other, and though sensitive and perceptive, have approached each other as barbarian aggressors. They are not individuals transformed by reason and capable of passion without destructiveness, the definition of love for the "faint thin line."

A way of emphasizing the use of conflict imagery in *Modern Love* is to compare the poem with Browning's "James Lee," a dramatic monologue spoken by a wife. Certain passages of *Modern Love* are also dramatic monologues, though it is the husband who speaks in them. The significant difference, however, is that James Lee's wife, in telling of the decline of her husband's love, in searching for an understanding of him and herself, gives no intimation of conflict. Not only are there no battle images in the poem, but they are unimaginable: the tone and mood of "James Lee" exclude them. The poem is marked instead by resignation to the passing of love and by sensibility to earthly sorrow:

> Nothing endures: the wind moans, saying so;
> We moan in acquiescence: there's life's pact,
> Perhaps probation—do *I* know?
> God does: endure His act![11]

The transiency of love is a divine mystery and man must simply acquiesce in it. A combative mood and pose would be egregiously wrong. There is, in the poem, a vision of free will and hope, but it is conveyed in the metaphor of key and lock rather than in any image suggesting that to try to do something about the frailty of love is to engage in conflict. James Lee's wife says, at last:

> Your soul's locked fast; but, love for a key,
> You might let it loose, till I grow the same
> In your eyes, as in mine you stand: strange plea![12]

Love, in Browning's poem, is a single entity: something to be given or withheld. In Meredith's work, love is more complex. It has many pseudonymous forms—lust, false purity, egoism—and these must be discovered and defeated. It was failure to rout out these false forms that made the husband and wife enemies. The central situation in *Modern Love* is conflict: with oneself and with one's mate. The central situation in "James Lee" is submission to loss, submission made more painful by a vision of what might have been, but submission nevertheless.

When we consider how often it has been said that Meredith and Browning had similar outlooks, the difference in their approach to an unhappy marriage is all the more intriguing.[13] There is, of course, Browning's Christianity to account for part of the difference. But the main explanation is a difference in temperament beneath superficial similarity, plus the fact that Browning had not experienced what Meredith had. *Modern Love,* written soon after Mary Peacock Meredith's death, was in part at least torn from flagellant memory.

But if the source of *Modern Love* is remembered pain, its form is the result of studied and triumphant craft. The fifty sixteen-line stanzas (or sonnets) which make up the poem tell a story which moves successfully both on the level of narrative interest and in the mode of dramatic conflict and disclosure. Cecil Day Lewis has described *Modern Love* as follows: "Its movement can best be traced as a series of impulses and revulsions proceeding from the conflict within the husband's mind, which swings wildly from jealousy to generosity, from pity to indignation, from hysterical egotism to civilized sympathy, from regret to cynicism, from cursing to blessing. . . . [The poem's] dramatic shape, no less than its individual parts, is created by the straight conflict between instinct and intelligence, without the mediation of any accepted moral code."[14] Day Lewis, at a further point in his discussion, cites these lines:

> Then each applied to each that fatal knife,
> Deep questioning, which probes to endless dole.
>                     (L, 155)

He says: "It is an irony to which *Modern Love* does full justice, that the exercise of intelligence, upon which an equal married relationship must depend, is also one of the forces most calculated to wreck it: partly because conscious analysis, 'that fatal knife, Deep questioning,' cuts both ways and is a terribly risky instrument to use upon the living tissues of a relationship so deeply rooted in instinct."[15]

The generalization contained in this passage is questionable. It seems as if Day Lewis doubts that understanding is a good thing in a love relationship. Certainly it would be better to say, if we speak generally, that some people can stand truth and others cannot, but that everybody ought to take as much as he can tolerate. The real point of *Modern Love* is not that analysis, by definition, cuts both ways, but that the "fatal knife" was being employed for the wrong purposes and was thus damaging two people who, to judge from their description, could have assimilated a great deal of understanding if only the motives behind the search for it had been correct. The tragedy in *Modern Love* is that analysis has become the instrument not of understanding but of the dark, irrational passion which has no name but whose motive is destruction.

The first stanza sets the scene. Husband and wife, their love dead, lie awake on "their common bed":

By this he knew she wept with waking eyes:
That, at his hand's light quiver by her head,
The strange low sobs that shook their common bed
Were called into her with a sharp surprise,
And strangled mute, like little gaping snakes,
Dreadfully venomous to him.

(I, 133)

Already established is the husband's keen, and vexed, responsiveness to the wife he loves, despises, pities, and scorns—each in turn as the story develops. But it is with the words "Dreadfully venomous to him" that we come upon the central theme. Whatever else he feels toward his wife, the husband is ensnared by her beauty and by the memory of love. "Passion"—nature itself—remains a constant while other feelings change. Thus the husband says:

Cold as a mountain in its star-pitched tent,
Stood high Philosophy, less friend than foe:
Whom self-caged Passion, from its prison-bars,
Is always watching with a wondering hate.
Not till the fire is dying in the grate,
Look we for any kinship with the stars.

(IV, 135)

Besides noting the precise and brilliant imagery of this passage, we find in it a conception of fate. Not until youth is over can we be philosophers, can we look for "kinship with the stars." The passion of erotic love is man's fate during the greater part of his life. This theme—man's essential haplessness—is advanced in Stanza VIII (p. 136):

But no: we are two reed-pipes, coarsely stopped:
The God once filled them with his mellow breath;
And they were music till he flung them down,
Used! used!

Love, besides being man's fate, has an ambiguous quality: it heals or destroys depending on the circumstances. Between this husband and wife, it is a destructive force, and for the husband in particular, a deadly potion:

Her gentle body near him, looking up;
And from her eyes, as from a poison-cup,
He drank until the flittering eyelids screened.

(IX, 137)

Although love between husband and wife is in ruins, the husband's

eagerness for his wife is unabated. It is the result of his "passion" and
is indeed a desire for poison.

Much, though not all, of the tone of *Modern Love* is bitter. Besides saying that love is a fated and fateful passion, the poem says
that love is transient. Here the husband speaks:

> . . . Prepare,
> You lovers, to know Love a thing of moods:
> Not, like hard life, of laws. In Love's deep woods,
> I dreamt of loyal Life: — the offence is there!
> (X, 137)

Soon after the above stanza we become aware of one of the
extraordinary aspects of *Modern Love*. The poem is a sonnet sequence which deals directly with "society": many of the most ironic
and poetically skillful lines portray the husband and wife keeping
their heads up in society while their hearts drown or lie dead within
them. Yet interwoven with this "modern" social phenomenon, a
ruined marriage in which appearance and passion are equally productive of pain, is the theme of nature. Husband and wife, in their
happy days, had a favorite woodland spot. It is here, toward the end
of the poem, that the husband finds his wife with the man she has
taken for her lover. Also, in a last attempt at reconciliation, the husband and wife walk in the woods, and just before the final tragedy
they meet at the seashore. But nature, in addition to being thus a
context for this social tragedy—a wrecked marriage—is also a voice
in the poem. She speaks the truth, which is bitter. She is ambigu-
ously called a "friend" of man. She is honest with him, but she gives
him no relief (indeed, later we are told she can be cruel). Fairly
early in the poem, the essence of her creed, minus the suggestion
that she can be cruel, is given:

> "I play for Seasons; not Eternities!"
> Says Nature, laughing on her way. "So must
> All those whose stake is nothing more than dust!"
> .   .   .   .   .   .   .   .   .   .   .
> . . . Upon her dying rose
> She drops a look of fondness, and goes by,
> Scarce any retrospection in her eye;
> For she the laws of growth most deeply knows,
> Whose hands bear, here, a seed-bag—there, an urn.
> Pledged she herself to aught, 'twould mark her end!

> This lesson of our only visible friend
> Can we not teach our foolish hearts to learn?
> (XIII, 138–39)

The imagery is not sentimental: it converts bitterness into irony and irony into serious questioning.

Since love, by its nature, is transient, and passion is a kind of fate whose direction the individual cannot control, it would be crude for an intelligent, sensitive husband to blame his wife in a situation such as the one the poem presents. Yet in the complexity of life, not to blame does not mean to be free of cruelty. The husband says:

> I bleed, but her who wounds I will not blame.
> Have I not felt her heart as 'twere my own
> Beat thro' me? could I hurt her? heaven and hell!
> But I could hurt her cruelly!
> (XIX, 141)

Social compulsion—the image society has of this couple and constrains them to cope with—leads to one of the most effective of the sonnets, in which society supplies the situation, and nature, mingled with Christmas season associations, supplies much of the imagery. Again it is the husband who speaks:

> 'Tis Christmas weather, and a country house
> Receives us: rooms are full: we can but get
> An attic-crib.  Such lovers will not fret
> At that, it is half-said.  The great carouse
> Knocks hard upon the midnight's hollow door,
> But when I knock at hers, I see the pit.
> Why did I come here in that dullard fit?
> I enter, and lie crouched upon the floor.
> Passing, I caught the coverlet's quick beat: —
> Come, Shame, burn to my soul! and Pride, and Pain—
> Foul demons that have tortured me, enchain!
> Out in the freezing darkness the lambs bleat.
> The small bird stiffens in the low starlight.
> I know not how, but shuddering as I slept,
> I dreamed a banished angel to me crept:
> My feet were nourished on her breasts all night.
> (XXIII, 143)

All the pain and frustration inherent in this incident indicate that the husband requires solace. His wife unfaithful, he begins an affair with another woman, who is known throughout *Modern Love* as the

"Lady," as distinguished from the wife, who is "Madam." Speaking to his "lady," the husband once more suggests in bitterness that passion, the dark side of nature, is beyond man's control:

> O Lady, once I gave love: now I take!
> Lady, I must be flattered. Shouldst thou wake
> The passion of a demon, be not afraid.
>
> (XXVII, 145)

Then, in what he ironically calls a sonnet to his lady's eyes, the husband sums up the meaning of human life and of love as part of the human condition:

> What are we first? First, animals; and next
> Intelligences at a leap; on whom
> Pale lies the distant shadow of the tomb,
> And all that draweth on the tomb for text.
> Into which state comes Love, the crowning sun:
> Beneath whose light the shadow loses form.
> We are the lords of life, and life is warm.
> Intelligence and instinct now are one.
> But nature says: "My children most they seem
> When they least know me: therefore I decree
> That they shall suffer." Swift doth young Love flee,
> And we stand wakened, shivering from our dream.
>
> (XXX, 146)

Through her instruments, passion and transiency, nature causes man to suffer. Nowhere else in Meredith's work is nature, "our only visible friend," depicted as so inherent a source of tragedy. Perhaps the hardness of Meredith's vision of nature here is one reason why so many critics have called *Modern Love* one of his best works.

As the narrative continues, the husband and wife, after deceptions, jealousy, and cruelty, make a foredoomed effort at reconciliation. Mechanically, the wife announces she is going to bed, and intimates, apparently for the first time in many a day, that the husband is to follow her. The attempt fails miserably. The husband, early the next day, says:

> If I the death of Love had deeply planned,
> I never could have made it half so sure,
> As by the unblest kisses which upbraid
> The full-waked sense; or failing that, degrade!
> 'Tis morning: but no morning can restore

What we have forfeited. I see no sin:
The wrong is mixed. In tragic life, God wot,
No villain need be! Passions spin the plot:
We are betrayed by what is false within.
                                   (XLIII, 152)

Not only are these lines terse, concise, and endowed with a kind
of accuracy of feeling—a technical accuracy which makes the tone
and mood accurate—but they point up the philosophical dilemma
which leads to tragedy in *Modern Love* and was, moreover, to occupy Meredith for the greater part of his career. "I see no sin" signifies that Meredith deprives himself of the traditional explanation
for human suffering. These words point forward to a long period,
beginning in the '70's, during which Meredith, with results that had
a complicating but enriching effect upon his art, struggled hard to
embrace the rationalist view of the human situation. And when Meredith says, "No villain need be! Passions spin the plot: / We are betrayed by what is false within," he is unwittingly acknowledging the
dilemma and the contradiction to which exclusive faith in nature
leads. "Passion," after all, is nature; and in this poem—which Day
Lewis (along with many others) has called Meredith's best[16] and in
which he sees Meredith revealing himself for the first and last time
in his poetry—nature, taking the form of human life, is tragic. The
affirmative victory of the "faint thin line" belongs to the future. For
the present, we are betrayed by what is false within: the forms that
passion takes, the inescapable facts of human "nature." Meredith was
to struggle with this ambivalent character of nature, to exonerate her
and separate her from man's wrong-doing and error. In this poem,
however, the character of nature is clearly ambiguous. In the guise
of "passion," nature is hardly the beneficent mother she becomes
elsewhere in Meredith's work.

At this point in the poem, intelligence and sensitivity, finely mixed
with passion and a sense of being fated, prevent the wife from carrying the charade any further:

She sees through simulation to the bone:
What's best in her impels her to the worst:
Never, she cries, shall Pity soothe Love's thirst,
Or foul hypocrisy for truth atone!
                                   (XLIV, 153)

But cruelty and passion are really spent, and we approach the conclusion to this tragic marriage. The husband and wife, filled with emptiness, dead memories, and a determination to be honest, walk together. The stanza which describes them at this juncture is one of the finest in *Modern Love*. Swinburne said of it, in 1862, "A more perfect piece of writing no man alive has ever turned out."[17] And M. S. Henderson calls it "the resting-place and the bridge, between the passion of the past and the pitifulness of the future."[18] Whatever else may be said of it, this particular stanza is a triumphant, lyrical realization in poetry of Meredith's responsiveness to nature, as well as a perfect interlude before the tragedy:

> We saw the swallows gathering in the sky,
> And in the osier-isle we heard them noise.
> We had not to look back on summer joys,
> Or forward to a summer of bright dye:
> But in the largeness of the evening earth
> Our spirits grew as we went side by side.
> The hour became her husband and my bride.
> Love, that had robbed us so, thus blessed our dearth!
> The pilgrims of the year waxed very loud
> In multitudinous chatterings, as the flood
> Full brown came from the West, and like pale blood
> Expanded to the upper crimson cloud.
> Love, that had robbed us of immortal things,
> This little moment mercifully gave,
> Where I have seen across the twilight wave
> The swan sail with her young beneath her wings.
> (XLVII, 154)

The swan in particular, among the other inspired images and the graceful rhythms of this stanza, arrests our attention. It is the lovely bird of death.

The wife, misinterpreting her husband's confession, believes that he still desires his Lady. Madam perversely decides she must nobly yield her husband to this other woman, and nothing he can say will change her conviction. In vexation and perplexity the husband cries out—in lines which reverberate beyond the limits of the poem:

> Their sense is with their senses all mixed in,
> Destroyed by subtleties these women are!
> More brain, O Lord, more brain! or we shall mar
> Utterly this fair garden we might win.
> (XLVIII, 154)

It is not an idle or comic cry of exasperation.  The wife, convinced she is doing the right thing, takes poison, calling her husband to her as she dies.  Then Meredith ends, drawing together the varied meanings which have made the characters complex and which have never really been separable:

> Thus piteously Love closed what he begat:
> The union of this ever-diverse pair!
> These two were rapid falcons in a snare,
> Condemned to do the flitting of a bat.
> Lovers beneath the singing sky of May,
> They wandered once; clear as the dew on flowers:
> But they fed not on the advancing hours:
> Their hearts held cravings for the buried day.
> Then each applied to each that fatal knife,
> Deep questioning, which probes to endless dole.
> Ah, what a dusty answer gets the soul
> When hot for certainties in this our life!
>
> (L, 155)

It was not only the innate character of passion that caused the tragedy.  It was something derived from both nature and society which "condemned . . . this ever-diverse pair" to live in a common trap.  The tragedy was caused, also, by intelligence gone wrong— seeking analytically for answers and explanations, holding on to the past instead of embracing the present and future.  The result of it all is warfare, decreed by nature (passion) and caused by an intermingling of nature and perverted intelligence ("what is false within" and the probing of the "fatal knife").

Meredith, as Day Lewis observes, laid himself bare in *Modern Love*.  The conflict is not cloaked in military imagery until the very last lines of the poem, when Meredith once more draws his armor about his bruised self and distracts us with a vision of the future.  In its best passages, in its moments of painful revelation and self-confrontation, *Modern Love* is an interlude, one which ends before the poem itself concludes.

### THE IMAGE OF THE SOLDIER

It remains true that for the most part, during the '60's, it was the military figure and not the naked soul that attracted Meredith or at least emerged from his imagination.  We can ask why this should

have been so, and the answer is that the military figure is the one
who, in the course of his customary activity, symbolically resolves
the contradictions and breaks through the frustrations that beset
Meredith at the time. A soldier is expected to suffer pain: he
measures his professional competency by his ability to keep going
in spite of it. This combination of activism and stoicism appealed
to Meredith, both before and after he had tried naked self-confrontation in *Modern Love,* as the virtue which would see him through
his own ordeals. A soldier, too, by performing specific acts of heroism, wins respect from society, from those whose birth and station
are superior to his own. Finally, the kind of conflict a soldier engages
in is neat and definite. The issues are clearly drawn, the conflict itself
is not endless and baffling. The right application of skill and courage
not only can terminate it, but can do so in victory. Victory itself, with
its accompanying exaltation of spirit, is a concrete and imaginable
goal that does not raise difficult questions of self-knowledge.

Here, perhaps, was the greatest appeal for Meredith of the image
of the soldier. The soldier *did* need courage, skill, endurance, loyalty,
even a kind of practical intelligence. All these Meredith admired,
either believing himself to have them or confidently hoping to ac-
quire them. A soldier did *not* need self-awareness, and however much
Meredith may have respected self-awareness, there were large areas
in which he was markedly lacking in this complicated, ambivalent,
and subtle virtue. Nowhere in his novels, poems, or letters did he
ever fully face the effect which his origin as a tailor's son had upon
his pride, his attitude toward society, or his feelings about tradition.
Nowhere did he ask himself the meaning of his departures from the
"radicalism" that was presumably his dominant attitude. (What
makes questioning all the more appropriate in this area is that many
of his conservative affirmations were shallow rather than profound.)
And nowhere did he face the contradictions in his ideas about women.
His later novels are constructed around bold, independent heroines
who are partially reminiscent of Mary Peacock. His second wife,
Marie Vulliamy, whom he married in 1864, was quiet and self-
effacing, the antithesis of the heroines he was to create after his
marriage to her. And the daughter of his second marriage, Mariette,
found in Meredith an anxious, conventional father, ever fearful that
liberty would lead to license.[19] Though these contradictions are not
remarkable, they have, in Meredith's work, the peculiar ability to

make themselves uncomfortably felt, to draw attention to their troubled existence just beneath the surface of his writing. In concealing them in the image of the soldier, he felt he had muffled them and prevented their crying out. Contradictions, however, cannot be ordered to lie still and pretend they do not exist.

The other meaning of Meredith's interest, during the '60's, in military matters lies in certain historical events of the period. These were the American Civil War and the struggle in Italy for national liberation and unification.

### TOURNAMENT AT SEA

Meredith believed that the American Southerners were fighting for the same principles as were the Italians. Both, in his view, were struggling to rid themselves of an oppressive tyrant. If there is any contrast at all in his approach to the conflicts, it is in the fact that he was able at times to assume an air of detachment when discussing Austria's determination to keep control of the Italian states but was never able to comment on the American Civil War in other than fervid, partisan terms. He makes an interesting comparison with Harriet Martineau, that redoubtable woman who could be as enthusiastic about war as Meredith and who also saw a common theme linking the American Civil War and the Italian wars of unification. But Miss Martineau regarded the North as the champion of liberty and was as energetic in her condemnation of the South—the slaveholding power—as Meredith was in his praise of it. Slavery was not an issue for Meredith. In his view, the war was being fought because the South, a cultivated society of gallant gentlemen and their ladies, was asserting its right to be free of the heavy-handed direction of the coarse and commercial North. Meredith was not being bold or different; he was expressing the prevalent British upper-class view of the American war.[20] However, neither was he being sycophantic, attempting to please his Tory employers on *The Morning Post*. *Richard Feverel* and *Evan Harrington* help us, if indirectly, to understand that his admiration for the South arose out of his conviction that a good society is one built upon manly, aristocratic values, a society in which gentlemen (but not snobs) govern in the interest of everyone.

For Meredith, the Southern leaders were the incarnation of the best aristocratic traditions. Not only were they prepared by birth and position to lead, but they were, in this war, actually leading. The spectacle of a nation being led by its "best," by its hereditary aristocracy, was edifying. It seemed to suggest that such things might be possible in England, too. Meredith did not wish to examine this possibility too closely; he was not quite sure *what* the English aristocracy ought to do, in what specific activities it ought to lead. This, however, only made the American situation more attractive. The issues across the Atlantic were more clear-cut for him than were those "at home," whether that phrase be taken to mean what was going on in his own heart or in his own society. Given Meredith's tendency to see war as the objectified, simplified projection of all complex and subtle problems, there was for him a beautiful logic and a robust appreciation of reality in the course of action the Southerners had taken when they could no longer tolerate the tyranny of the North.

Meredith's great opportunity to express just what this war meant to him came when he was assigned to write a description, for Captain Semmes's book, of the fight between the *Alabama* and the *Kearsarge*. He made that battle as symbolic of the entire conflict as he possibly could. In his narration, the *Alabama* is brave but beleaguered. It is pitted against a foe that is materially stronger; the *Kearsarge* did, in fact, carry heavier guns. But the *Alabama's* crew possesses unmatchable courage and loyalty, profound gallantry, and magnificent chivalric capability.

The last of these virtues is the most intriguing, for once shaped and identified by Meredith's imagination, it caused the Southern ship to undergo the very same transformation that had changed Evan Harrington, a poor boy of the nineteenth century, into an outnumbered but undaunted knight of medieval tradition and myth. In Meredith's mind, the *Alabama*, too, became the warrior of a simpler time, "when to be brave and cherish noble feelings brought honour; when strength of arm and steadiness of heart won fortune," despite the foe's material superiority.

Meredith begins this transformation quite early in his account of the fight. Referring to the townspeople who crowded the shore as the Confederate raider prepared to leave Cherbourg harbor and meet the waiting *Kearsarge*, he says: "All Cherbourg was on the heights above the town and along the bastions and the mole. Never did knightly tournament boast a more eager multitude of spectators."

And a bit further on, Meredith, with true partisan zeal, shifts his point of view to deckboard, almost identifying with the men of the *Alabama*: "Now and at last, our day of action has come! was the thought of every man on board. The chivalrous give and take of battle was glorious to men who had alternately hunted and fled for so dreary a term. They trusted for victory; but defeat itself was to be a vindication of their whole career, and they welcomed the chances gladly." And then, as the *Alabama* gets under way, actually engages in the battle which was to be fatal for her, Meredith, with mingled pride and melancholy, observes: "The *Alabama* entered the lists when she should have been lying in dock. She had the heroism to decide upon the conflict, without the strength to choose the form of it."[21]

The recurrent image of knightly combat is unmistakable: "Never did knightly tournament boast a more eager multitude of spectators," "The chivalrous give and take of battle," "The *Alabama* entered the lists." These words convey to us once more the strong suggestion that Meredith found the style and vocabulary of realism too limited for his purposes, even when he was engaged in writing contemporary history. They suggest that when depicting or praising heroism, he found a more congenial mode for his ideas and feelings in the usages and imagery of a world antithetical to his own.

Regarding praise of military heroism, there is an interesting parallel between Meredith and Carlyle. During the '60's, they stand together—and apart from other Englishmen of letters—in their extreme glamorization of war. Out of similar sentiments sprang similar visions of glory. Meredith, even when he disagreed with Carlyle, was always more sympathetic toward him than were many of his contemporaries. He cited Carlyle's knowledge of the spirit as reason for his own abiding affection and admiration.[22] To these we may add Carlyle's unqualified praise of the soldier and his bold readiness to see in the soldier the embodiment of all important manly virtues. Meredith never acknowledged this as a reason for the high regard in which he continued to hold Carlyle after others had begun to repudiate the aging prophet, but his own work is better evidence for it than any explicit declaration he might have made.

The other aspect of Meredith's descriptions of battle scenes—his tendency to slip the demands of contemporary realism—was to undergo change. Perhaps he became aware of this tendency. In his next major work to have war as its theme, he made a forceful attempt to write about battle in more modern terms. That work was *Vittoria*, published in 1866.

But if his intention was to write more realistically, he succeeded only in part. The tone of the novel is imitation romantic, and the details pertaining to soldiers are often colored by the small-boy wonder that Meredith could never wholly suppress. Nevertheless, he did manage, at significant moments, to shift his point of view, to probe the savagery of war, to see even that an army, like Austria's, could have the unglamorous function of gluing together an empire that was not intrinsically glorious and that would otherwise fall apart.

*Vittoria* concerns the Italian uprising against Austria during 1848–49, and the action of the novel faithfully follows the actual course of events of that war. Though most of the characters are freely invented, Mazzini, Meredith's idol,[23] appears briefly at the beginning and then, though off stage, continues to make his presence felt throughout the story. The other characters are Vittoria, an opera singer destined to play an important part in the uprising; Count Carlo Ammiani, an Italian patriot who eventually becomes Vittoria's husband; Barto Rizzo, leader of the radical underground; a number of other Italians who play lesser parts in the war; various members of the Austrian army and aristocracy; and certain English men and women whom the reader first met in *Sandra Belloni* (1864), a novel covering an earlier part of Vittoria's life, passed in England.

We learn at the outset of *Vittoria* that a new opera is to be performed at La Scala on the fifteenth of March, 1848. Vittoria, the prima donna, has agreed to sing a revolutionary song at the close of the performance. This song is to be a signal to the Milanese to rise up and touch off a war of national liberation throughout the Italian states. As matters turn out, there are complications and delays, including incidents which lead some of the conspirators to suspect Vittoria of treason. However, the uprising does take place, signaled by Vittoria's inflammatory song, and the revolt spreads.

From that point to the end of the novel, Meredith weaves his characters into the fabric of history itself, involving them in a chain of actual events that includes everything from the Smokers' Strike of 1848 to the last futile uprising of Brescia in 1849. The over-all pattern of the novel is therefore the actual pattern of the war, and Meredith's historical scrupulosity accounts for the episodic and uneconomical structure of *Vittoria,* just as it tells us something about his intentions in writing the story. While the characters are conscientiously, even laboriously, drawn to suggest their individuality, the theme of the novel is not really so much the fate of any one of them as it is the course of the war. What happens in the beginning, middle, and end of *Vittoria* is controlled by what *did* happen in Italy between 1848 and 1849, not by the requirements of a plot proceeding from "character," requirements which Meredith strove so hard to meet in *Evan Harrington.*

These considerations bring to mind Dickens's *A Tale of Two Cities* and Stendhal's *The Charterhouse of Parma.* Dickens and Stendhal, too, followed the course of a war, but they never became so fascinated with military history as to lose sight, Dickens of his characters and plot, Stendhal of the grim, comic confusion of war. In *Vittoria* Meredith demonstrates no such virtues, but gives us instead a richness of military detail, detail that indicates not only the continuation of the theme of war in his work, but new departures in his expression of this theme.

The first change we note, as we read *Vittoria,* is the relative absence of medieval imagery. This change can be partially explained by the fact that the 1848–49 uprising was for Meredith inherently idealistic and so did not require transformation. Indirectly, it can also be explained by the goal Meredith explicitly set for himself at the beginning of the novel. He declared that he was not going to be partisan, that he would "deal equally with all." And he added (I, 12) that he would approve of "strong devotion, . . . stout nobility, . . . unswerving faith and self-sacrifice," whether on the part of the Italians or the Austrians. Although the desire to be impartial would not in itself have prevented him from transforming battle scenes into medieval tournaments, it kept the tone of the novel flat and sober— for long stretches at least. And this tone, designed for a more serious study of men at war than Meredith had previously attempted, precluded the *limited* use of medieval imagery he had made before. It required him either to demonstrate an ability like Tennyson's to use knights as large symbols of manliness or to abandon such figures altogether. Though he did not entirely keep to it, he chose the latter path.

There was nothing in Meredith's intentions that prevented him from displaying his inveterate passion for armed conflict. Such passion could always be attributed to one of his characters. Then, too, when Meredith analyzed motives or situations he could, and did, freely confess himself fascinated by much of what he "objectively" analyzed. Examples are numerous. One occurs early, before the uprising. Count Serabiglione, who is not a partisan and not to be trusted, praises Vittoria's voice. He exclaims to her (I, 125), "But, three good octaves! . . . It is precisely the very grandest heritage! It is an army!" And Vittoria, thinking of the coming revolt and the part she is to play in it, answers, "I trust that it may be!" Meredith was quite unaware of the extravagance of this imagery; he thought it quite brilliant and meaningful. For him an army was potentially a thing of beauty in itself.

Later, Laura Piaveni, one of the most passionate of the insurgents and also one of the most beautiful and charming of women, speaks of the coming uprising (I, 134): "We have plenty of arms in the city. Oh, that we had cannon! I worship cannon! They are the Gods of battle!" We may ask: what manner of author is it who depicts one of his heroines as thinking reverentially, adoringly, of cannon? Clearly, it is an author who, though he is unaware of his own sexual symbolism, wants us to see that the heroine has subordinated not only her fortune but her femininity to the patriotic cause. Laura is not an Amazon; she is a worshiper. And for Meredith, the nation that was struggling to deliver itself out of political slavery was the embodiment and symbol of perfect liberty. Like Swinburne, but with less awareness of what he was doing,[24] Meredith could make the nation an object of religious worship for his characters. The cannon Laura yearns for are weapons to be used in a holy war, and she, in her strange passion, sacrifices her femininity only to become something better—a sexless, holy crusader.

Count Ammiani is another whose reflections and observations are thoroughly colored by the military facts of life. At one point, he overhears a friendly but heated disagreement between Laura and Vittoria. As he listens he observes (I, 136) that "Laura spent her energy in taunts, but Vittoria spoke only of her resolve and to the point." Then, says Meredith, "It was, as his military instincts framed the simile, like the venomous crackling of skirmishing rifles before a fortress, that answered slowly with its volume of sound and sweeping shot." It does, indeed, require military instincts to conceive of a debate between two heroines as an exchange between skirmishing rifles and defending cannon! But Meredith was not attempting to render Count Ammiani absurd, as we are likely to suspect today. He was, rather, suggesting that there is something heroic about a man whose imagination is in military harness. He was telling the reader that Count Ammiani, like Laura, was unconsciously subordinating his tenderer feelings to his more warlike at every possible and impossible moment, because that, in a word, is what total war, religious-patriotic war, requires.

Vittoria, as we might guess, has a full share of military fervor and instincts. Meredith, in fact, apportions to her his own special enthusiasm: his keen admiration for swordsmanship and for fathers who train their sons, as did the great Mel, in this skill. Significantly, Vittoria's admiration is revealed during an early love scene between her and Carlo Ammiani (I, 152):

> "You are a good swordsman?" she asked him abruptly.
> "I have as much skill as belongs to a perfect intimacy with the weapon," he answered.
> "Your father was a soldier, Signor Carlo."
> "He was a General officer in what he believed to be the army of Italy. We used to fence together every day for two hours."
> "I love fathers who do that," said Vittoria.

Since this intimate exchange takes place before the couple become engaged, what Vittoria is doing is taking Carlo's measure—not as a man, but as a potential fighter for Italy's freedom. Though we smile (unhappily without Meredith's leave), we recognize that she, too, is making a sacrifice. She is narrowing the grounds for her choice of a husband to such an extent that serviceability to the nation becomes the *sine qua non*. Perhaps Meredith meant to suggest that this was one of the tragic consequences of sacrificing oneself to the nation, because Vittoria is not exactly happy in the marriage she ultimately enters into with Count Ammiani. If this was his intention, however, he hinted at it in the faintest manner possible, because, happy or not, Vittoria remains devoted to Count Ammiani to the day of his death, and thereafter transfers this devotion to their child, cherishing in his person the Ammiani name and tradition.

The treatment of character is not the only aspect of *Vittoria* that was influenced by Meredith's war-inspired sensibility. The depiction of an army gave this sensibility an even larger opportunity to express itself. Meredith converts an army into an organic entity; an aesthetic embodiment of motion, discipline, and color; and, finally, an instrument and symbol of power. In this novel, it was more appropriate to do so when the Austrian army was in view, and it is, indeed, in his descriptions of the Austrians that Meredith's attitude toward an army as a distinct, human phenomenon becomes apparent. Here, for example, is the way the Austrian troops are presented as they march through Verona on their way to Milan (I, 191):

Following . . . came a regiment of Hungarian grenadiers, tall, swart-faced, and particularly light-limbed men, looking brilliant in the clean tight military array of Austria. Then a squadron of blue hussars, and a Croat regiment; after which, in the midst of Czech dragoons and German Uhlans and blue Magyar light horsemen, with General officers and aides about him, the veteran Austrian Field-Marshal rode, his easy hand and erect figure and good-humoured smile belying both his age and his reputation among the Italians. Artillery, and some bravely-clad horse of the Eastern frontier, possibly Serb, wound up the procession. It gleamed down the length of the Corso in blinding sunlight; brass helmets and hussar feathers, white and violet surcoats, green plumes, maroon capes, bright steel scabbards, bayonet-points,—as gallant a show as some portentously-magnified summer field, flowing with the wind, might be; and over all the banner of Austria—the black double-headed eagle ramping on a yellow ground. This was the flower of iron meaning on such a field.

Again Meredith has juxtaposed an image of gentle beauty with one of harsh power, as he did when he compared Vittoria's voice to an army. This time, however, he has done it with subtle effect, because we can believe that a body of men so colorfully caparisoned might well appear at first like a "portentously magnified summer field, flowing with the wind." And the concluding sentence, making its abstract point at the same time that it appeals to our senses, delivers its impact with accuracy and force.

Another side of the matter is Meredith's feeling about the military detail he piled up so assiduously throughout the passage. We get the unmistakable impression that he took great satisfaction in distinguishing the various military units, in describing their uniforms, equipment, and general appearance. We feel he did this with the air of a seasoned general appreciatively estimating the fighting potential of troops on review. Indeed, as we read this passage we detect the same pseudo-professionalism, the same desire to be taken as a military expert, that prompted Meredith to argue so presumptuously with Sir John French nearly forty years later.

If the Austrians provided Meredith with an opportunity to display his knowledge of technical military detail and his admiration for disciplined troops, the Italians offered him the chance to depict the fury and chaos of war as it is fought by an army of street fighters who insist on being seen and felt as individuals, rather than as parts of a pattern. Their passion—their individual passion—rather than their aggregate ability to create pageantry and a sense of the presence of power, marks them as warriors. It also allows Meredith to describe aspects of warfare hitherto absent from his writing. Barto Rizzo, leading the Milan uprising, is portrayed in a manner that shows this vividly (II, 391):

[Barto Rizzo] bounded by them, mad for slaughter, and mounting a small brass gun on the barricade, sent the charges of shot into the rear of the enemy. He kissed the black lip of his little thunderer in a rapture of passion; called it his wife, his naked wife; the best of mistresses, who spoke only when he charged her to speak; raved that she was fair, and liked hugging; that she was true, and the handsomest daughter of Italy; that she would be the mother of big ones—none better than herself, though they were mountains of sulphur big enough to make one gulp of an army.

Barto Rizzo is performing the act of adoration that Laura Piaveni, equally ardent but a lady and a member of the upper classes, could only dream of carrying out. Yet Barto is not a hero of this novel. What was only excessive passion in Laura's *words* is a sign of mental unbalance in Barto's *action,* as we learn further on in the story.

Since this is the most vivid instance of the Italians in action, they come off second best when compared with the Austrians. It is as if Meredith did not quite approve of the unbridled zeal of untrained partisans, or at least felt that they made a less meaningful impression upon the observer than did their enemies. Knowing that Meredith's sympathies were, in reality, with the Italians, and that he thought himself to be exercising exemplary restraint in writing *Vittoria* from an "objective" point of view, we may wonder why he did not find the passion of men like Barto Rizzo at least as worthy of admiration as the discipline and skill of the Austrians. The answer is in the statement of aims that Meredith provides at the beginning of the novel, where he tells us that he will approve of devotion, nobility, unswerving faith, and self-sacrifice wherever he finds them. Though he does not say that he will approve of these virtues only when he finds them all in one person, he makes it clear, in the course of the story, that the degree of *nobility* present gives color and strength to the other qualities. By "noble," Meredith does not simply signify birth and position. He means courageous; capable of devotion, unswerving faith, and self-sacrifice; and, most important, *capable of submitting one's passions to the governance of intelligence.* Because Barto Rizzo cannot do the latter, he cannot be considered noble, and if not noble, he cannot be regarded a hero. Since he does, however, have some of the virtues of a hero, he cannot be portrayed as simply inconsequential. So Meredith, to solve the problem of characterization—to get rid, so to speak, of Barto's claim to be taken seriously even though he lacks nobility—declares him mad.

We understand through implication why Meredith lacked enthusiasm for Barto. But we learn through explicit statements what it is about the real heroes that distinguishes them from ordinary men. The way, for example, in which Meredith describes Mazzini tells us why he is the perfect hero, the superb leader in a cause that depends upon military action. Mazzini, Meredith says (I, 9–10), had "an orbed-mind, supplying its own philosophy, and arriving at the sword-stroke by logical steps." And most important of all, in Mazzini's character the "passions were absolutely in harmony with the intelligence." As zealous as Barto Rizzo for Italian liberty, he will never be guilty of irrational, abandoned action, even when it might through chance lead to victory. He makes only those moves that are sanctioned by his splendid tactical intelligence, which never loses its grasp of the larger plan. He has, in short, a noble mind.

The Austrian officers, whenever they can be individually distinguished, fairly glow with nobility and heroism. Meredith, pretending to lean over backwards in the interest of fair play, was really

keyed up with admiration for these sterling soldiers. On one occasion, however, it takes close reading to see what he is getting at.
Describing the Austrians hurling themselves into battle, he says (II,
390), "On they came, officers in front of the charge, as usual with
the Austrians." Succinct, written with an air of false casualness—
Meredith playing the quietly observant but thoroughly experienced
military authority again—this line puts the Austrian officers into that
select company to which Mazzini belongs and from which Barto
Rizzo is excluded. But how so? Are they not guilty of folly in exposing themselves in the front of the charge? Are they not allowing
their passions to govern their intelligence, an arrangement that destroys their claims to nobility? They are not. Their courage is of the
coolest and most logical order. They are not foolhardy but are acting
in accordance with the best (for Meredith) military theory, which
says that the way to win a battle is to regard junior officers as expend-
able; to have them provide example, inspiration, and guidance just
long enough to carry the charge of the main body of troops into the
enemy lines, after which superior brute force can finish the job.
Barto Rizzo is willing to die for the sake of one mad moment of
ecstasy. The Austrian officers know that if they die their death is
decreed by intelligence, by the master battle plan, just as Mazzini
knows that for him, survival is decreed. Intelligence commands that
Mazzini, being indispensable, not expose himself recklessly. The
orders the Austrians accept are different, but they originate, like his,
in governing brain; thus they, like him, are noble.

The only hero who is allowed to act on pure impulse without
forfeiting his patent is Count Ammiani. He is special because he
fights as much for his personal reputation, for the honor of his family
name and the tradition of his class—the Italian aristocracy—as he does
for Italy. Often the personal and class claims upon him conflict with
those of the war, and Meredith sees the resultant dilemma as a kind
of romantic tragedy. At such moments, Meredith betrays the weakness that dogs him whenever he attempts to resolve a conflict within
one of his characters which has its origins in the public world. He
transforms the character into a knight and reduces the political and
moral problems to a single, set question: what course of conduct does
chivalry require? Thus, when Vittoria commits the enormous folly
of warning Wilfrid Pierson, her former lover and now a free-lance

soldier in the Austrian army, not to be in Milan on the fifteenth of March, and when, as a consequence, Vittoria is denounced by certain of the conspirators led by Barto Rizzo, Count Ammiani can do nothing but flush with indignation at the ungentlemanly insult these accusers have been guilty of. Though he has not yet become Vittoria's betrothed, it is obvious to him that she has a noble character and thus could not have committed treason. The possibility that she is not a traitress, but guilty of a monumentally stupid error, never occurs to him. A true lady, the image of feminine perfection to a knight like himself, is apparently as incapable of injurious error as she is of outright deceit. Curiously, Meredith seems to condone Carlo's conception of a "noble" woman. All things considered, he seems to say, Barto Rizzo's suspicion of Vittoria, though she comes within an ace of destroying the uprising, is mean; and Carlo's refusal to believe her guilty even of error is generous, generous in a way that only true knights and their ladies can understand.

Carlo is forever risking his life to carry out some mission of personal importance that has nothing to do with the strategy of the uprising. Here, too, he is condoned, even somewhat admired. Meredith says in effect that for people who do not have conflicting interests intelligence ought to be the supreme guide, but that for people who do, who are caught between the obligations of personal honor and public duty, intelligence cannot even speak, let alone lead. It cannot, in short, say how the conflict ought to be resolved. However, since such conflicts persist in occurring, the thing to do, Meredith seems to believe, is to transfigure the divided hero in question, cast a special protective aura over him when he fights his personal battles, talk about him in battle as if he were living in an age in which individual combat could decide momentous public issues, and ignore the question of whether his erratic conduct has damaged the army of which he is a leader. We recognize that Count Ammiani is the upper-class mirror image of Evan Harrington, just as he is the brother-in-arms of Captain Semmes of the *Alabama*. Evan was transformed into a knight and thus permitted to escape the real social and psychological conflicts of the world in which he fought. Captain Semmes became a knight, as did his ship, and thus the loss to the South of the sorely needed *Alabama*, a loss for which Semmes was criticized in England and the South by more hard-headed naval experts than

Meredith, became the sad but necessary and glorious outcome of a personal affair of honor. Similarly, Count Ammiani ultimately dies by throwing himself, equipped only with a sword, upon a whole squad of Austrians; and though the war at that point is not quite over, and though the Italians can hardly spare a single competent leader, we are left with the peculiar feeling that he will not be greatly missed in the councils of his fellows in which the war in general is the main issue. He has, throughout, been tilting at the Austrians as if they were old, personal opponents, independent knights whom he had met before in other tourneys but who are now disguising their own individuality in the uniform of Austria. He is not intended as a Don Quixote, but that is only because when it came to knighthood and chivalry, Meredith's comic sense failed him utterly.

So far, Meredith's expressions of interest in war seem consistently to have embodied the sentimentalist's view of bloodshed. Obviously, "sentimentalist" is used here in a manner diametrically opposed to Meredith's habitual use of it. But we must add that Meredith's was an understandable sentimentality, perhaps even pardonable, because in *Vittoria* it is connected to the very real nineteenth-century issue of Italian nationalism versus Austria's desire to hold her empire together. Given this situation, and given nineteenth-century conditions, the question of whether warfare was morally "justified" seems rather remote. We cannot expect Meredith, writing in the 1860's of a war that took place less than two decades earlier, to challenge the meaning of war itself, as if he were writing in the 1920's of what happened between 1914 and 1918. His sentimentality, if such indeed it be, could only be shattered by history, and the portion of history which was to be the axe-head had not yet materialized.

Nevertheless, Meredith was not totally insensible to the fact that war, viewed in isolation from the higher objectives for which it can presumably be fought, appears ugly indeed. After all was said and done, he knew that the central fact of nineteenth-century warfare was not the experience of a Count Ammiani, but mass slaughter. Moreover, by the '60's he had become convinced that modern man was himself a battlefield, not where ignorant armies clashed by night but where a primeval savage wrestled with the rational man of the future. And though it was not his primary purpose, in writing *Vittoria*, to admit this conviction, he fashioned an occasion to do so.

This admission does not come until the end of the novel, until Meredith has depicted war, through more than five hundred pages, as acts of chivalry, colorful spectacle and pageantry, and the highest objective for the enthusiasm of beautiful women and cultivated gentlemen. It does not come, we might say, until the passion has been spent and the glamor dulled by two years of carnage. Nevertheless, it comes; and when it does it strikes a note which will be heard again and again throughout Meredith's career, though, curiously, never loudly enough to drown out its antithesis: the praise of soldiers and soldierly conduct.

The moment in *Vittoria* at which Meredith repudiates war occurs when he is describing a second march of the Austrian army, a march which occurs late in the novel, and late, therefore, in the war. This description (II, 596-97), or rather the observation it inspires, is in marked contrast to the earlier passage:

An Austrian foot regiment, marching to the drum, passed. . . . The fife is a merry instrument; fife and drum colour the images of battle gaily; but the dull ringing Austrian step-drum, beating unaccompanied, strikes the mind with the real nature of battles, as the salt smell of powder strikes it, and more in horror, more as a child's imagination realizes bloodshed, where the scene is a rolling heaven, black and red on all sides, with pitiable men moving up to the mouth of butchery, the insufferable flashes, the dark illumination of red, red of black, like a vision of the shadows Life and Death in a shadow-fight over the dear men still living. . . . This regimental drum is like a song of the flat-headed savage in man. It has no rise or fall, but leads to the bloody business with an unvarying note, and a savage's dance in the middle of the rhythm.

Had Meredith written this way at the beginning of *Vittoria*, he would have had to tell a different story, an anticipation of Stephen Crane, of Tolstoy, of the kind of war novel that claimed its place after 1918 and drastically changed the image of war in literature. He would have been obliged to write with greater irony, and thus might really have become the realistic war novelist he wished to be. As it is, *Vittoria* is "objective" in that it praises both Italians and Austrians, but, with the exception of the passage just quoted, it is heavily weighted on the side of heroics.

We do respond for brief moments to *Vittoria*, but these, beyond the one just cited, occur when Meredith succeeds in making us see Italy through the eyes of the patriots and in making us love Italy as they do. We do not respond during the scenes in which these patriots fight for Italy, because Meredith, as a rule, cannot make the agony and numbness of battle as convincing as the romantic yearning, between battles, for national independence. The one passage in which he shows he really knows what battle is like is quickly superseded by scenes describing the melodramatic antics of Count Ammiani, and it is with these that the novel ends. Since Count Ammiani represents that half of Meredith's vision which portrays the soldier as radiant hero rather than as flat-headed savage, *Vittoria* ultimately vindicates the claim that war provides man with one of his more exalted experiences.

REALITY AND ILLUSION

Soon after *Vittoria* was completed, Meredith finally got a firsthand look at war. His opportunity was provided by a new outbreak of fighting in Italy in 1866. Once more the Italians were attempting to oust Austria from a part of their land, and Meredith, having just completed an "objective" account of an earlier attempt, was eager to describe this latest struggle in a form that would allow free rein to his frankly partisan feelings. He was passionately pro-Italian, and he wanted to get as close to the fighting as possible and to tell the world how wonderful the Italian patriots were. He therefore urged the editor of *The Morning Post*, still his intermittent employer, to send him to the front as a war correspondent. To his immense pleasure, he got the assignment, and he immediately made his way to Italy, where he remained throughout most of the fighting. Actually, his assignment in Italy was to be painfully brief. The war that Meredith went to cover turned out to be a mere epicycle of the Austro-Prussian conflict, and Austria, even while suffering a major defeat at the hands of the Prussians, managed to rebuff the Italian attack with little difficulty. The final unification of Italy that Meredith had rushed off to describe did not take place.* In June he had arrived expectantly to witness great events; by September he was quietly making his way home.

As matters turned out, therefore, Meredith was once again obliged to write about the defeat of courage, stout nobility, loyalty, and self-sacrifice. The central situation for him—evoking from him the same

---

* Venetia, the territory fought over, was in fact joined to Italy after the war, but the union—the result of a plebiscite and of Bismarck's maneuvering—was in no sense an achievement of Italian arms.

response as did Evan Harrington's departure from Beckley, Captain Semmes's defeat by the *Kearsarge,* and Count Ammiani's last desperate leap upon the outnumbering Austrians—was the battle which took place on June 24th. It was indeed important; the Italians had pinned great hopes upon it. But they were defeated that day and never again in the war made an important stand. For Meredith, "the 24th of June" became the keynote of all the dispatches he was subsequently to send. At first he insisted that the battle had been a Pyrrhic victory for the Austrians. Later, however, when they disappointed his expectations by appearing stronger than ever, he fell back upon his old habit of resolving a difficult situation by transforming the participants into brave knights and their enemies. In a dispatch dated June 30th, he described the conduct of a certain General Durando during the action of the fateful 24th:

General Durando, perceiving that the Cerale division was lost, did all that he could to help it. Failing in this he turned to his two aides-de-camp and coolly said to them: "Now, gentlemen, it is time for you to retire, for I have a duty to perform which is a strictly personal one—the duty of dying." On saying these words he galloped to the front and placed himself about twenty paces from a battalion of Austrian sharp-shooters which were ascending the hill. In less than five minutes his horse was killed under him, and he was wounded in the right hand. . . . I called on Durando, who is now at Milan, the day before yesterday. Though a stranger to him, he received me at once, and, speaking of the action of the 24th, he only said: "I have the satisfaction of having done my duty. I wait tranquilly the judgement of history."[25]

Whether Meredith, in describing the actions of General Durando during the battle, was recounting fact or legend is not important to us. What matters is that his imagination was so taken with the idea of an important general transforming a public situation into a personal one. In his earliest dispatches, those written before the 24th, Meredith had struck an entirely different note. He had prided himself on his knowledge of military tactics. He had even treated the readers of *The Morning Post* to an account of the disposition of Italian and Austrian troops, an analysis of the tactical problems which these dispositions raised, and a professional-sounding estimate of what movements the opposing armies were likely to make. This undoubtedly was the manner and tone he had hoped to employ throughout the reporting of what he confidently expected to be a war leading to an Italian victory. Faced, instead, with the task of writing about heroes who were gradually going down to defeat, he suddenly found that their tactical problems—the analogues of the psychological and social problems of a civilian—were uninteresting to him, and that what was really important was the moral image these heroes presented; what was really at stake was private rather than public issues.

It is the last of these "discoveries" that makes Meredith's use of chivalry so weak, so much less meaningful than Tennyson's, for example. Tennyson could suggest that the knights of the Round Table were, in their individual adventures and battles, grappling with questions that had large ethical meaning; Meredith, when he transformed his characters into chivalric figures, invariably made them indifferent to responsibilities transcending their personal concerns. Thus, General Durando heroically—not foolishly—attempted to throw his life away after the very first battle in a war that was presumably being fought for Italian liberation and not for the sake of providing him an opportunity to display his courage and love of honor. We get the uncomfortable impression that life is inadvertently imitating art, that General Durando is unwittingly following in the footsteps of Count Ammiani.

The extent to which Meredith's conception of heroism turned on his inability to deal profoundly with defeat—with what in nonmilitary life would be the failure of ambition—is revealed in a dispatch he sent on July 8th. After devoting the better part of his article to deeds of extraordinary courage performed by individual Italians on the 24th, he says:

Talking of heroism, of inimitable endurance, and strength of soul, what do you think of a man who has his arm entirely carried away by a grenade, and yet keeps on his horse, firm as a rock, and still directs his battery, until hemorrhage—and hemorrhage *alone*—strikes him down at last, *dead*! Such was the case with a Neopolitan—Major Abate, of the artillery—and his name is worth the glory of a whole army, of a whole war.[26]

Curiously, Major Abate's conduct, unlike General Durando's, needed no justification by Meredith. Though "beyond the call of duty," his heroism was in a direct line with it. Yet Meredith could not let the matter go at this, or, better, pursue to its bitter conclusion the thought that even purposeful heroism does not necessarily lead to victory. Instead, he fell into his familiar habit, in this case with highly confusing results, of altering the purposes for which the battle had been fought. Whatever Meredith meant exactly by saying Major

Abate's name was "worth the glory of a whole army, of a whole war," one implication certainly is that "glory" is as important as victory, if not more so. Thus Major Abate's short life, like Achilles's, was crowned with high reward, almost as if the gods had managed the Italian war in such a way as to keep a bargain with him. Or, his name, like Hector's, was declared triumphant and committed to eternity, worth more in that realm than the fate of Troy. What is ironic and confusing is that Meredith did not acknowledge Major Abate as the hero he actually was: a hero who died, like any good nineteenth-century soldier, in the service of his country.

If Meredith had drawn this moral, he would have been obliged to explore the difficult meanings, the obstacles to a heroizing imagination, posed by the death and defeat of a servant. He would ultimately have had to face the fact that the fortunes of servants are tied to their master's—in this case, the nation's—and that if the master wins no glory, neither do they. He would have had to concede that in defeat the worth of their heroism, though not diminished, is not easily defined; that to define it is indeed a large, serious, and modern problem. Instead he substituted the simpler notion that the death of such men in defeat can readily be conceived as glorious victory, and he invoked the spirit of Homeric Greece for support. But this was illogical. In that mythical time and place, the death of servants, under any circumstances, never mattered.

In short, Meredith, in the face of the Italians' defeat, lost sight of the purposes for which they were fighting and began to endow these patriots with the motives which sent the Greeks sailing to Troy. Writing again of the glorious 24th in the dispatch just quoted, he tells how one Italian dashes "at the Austrian flag-bearer, wrenches the standard out of his hands with his left one, has it clean cut away by an Austrian officer standing near, and immediately grapples it with his right, until his own soldiers carry him away with his trophy!" Significantly, Meredith concludes: "Does not this sound like Greek history repeated—does it not look as if the brave men of old had been born again, and the old facts renewed to tell of Italian heroism?"

Indeed, it looked that way to Meredith. But let us not labor the connection between his inability to explore defeat and his facile turning to heroes of old when he sought an image to express what was worth cherishing in heroic failure. Enough to say that it was itself the result of a failure. He had tried to relate fact to truth and to convert the first into the second. He succeeded only in producing superficial and misleading fantasy.

And this was generally his fate when he tried during the '60's to write about war. Preoccupied as he was with the theme, he nearly always failed to transform its hard, grim data into psychological and moral reality. Nevertheless, the motives which inspired his attachment to battle imagery and situations were not the kind that could be readily extinguished by disappointing consequences in his writing, consequences which in any case he did not recognize as bad. These motives remained alive, with varying strength, to the end of his career. Moreover, as time went on, their objectifications became increasingly diversified, even while remaining, for the most part, expressions of his sense of society. Whether he wrote directly about war or symbolically presented a civil situation in military terms, it was society in a larger sense that he delineated. And it should not surprise us to learn that he continued to do so long after the '60's. When that decade ended, his own battle with society had just begun.

In *Evan Harrington* and *Vittoria*, military and chivalric images were central. In subsequent works his use of such imagery was peripheral, even casual. For the most part, it tells us more about the categories into which Meredith's perceptions and preoccupations seem to fall than about the form and structure of any particular novel or poem.

### THE DUEL

One of these categories is "the duel." This institution troubled and fascinated Meredith, and for years exercised a strong grip upon his imagination. He saw it as a social phenomenon that required thorough investigation, and in the course of his work he turned it round and round, viewing it from every angle. Though it never again played as important a part in the pattern of a novel as it did in *Richard Feverel*, it occurred so often that it forms a distinct theme, or subtheme, in Meredith's writing.

We recall that Evan Harrington dreamed of challenging Ferdinand Laxley to a duel. In *Vittoria*, Captain Weisspriess, the bravest and most gallant of the Austrian officers,* hardly has time to sheathe

---

* A would-be seducer of Vittoria, he becomes, in a crisis, her protector. He wishes to avoid a meeting with Carlo, both for Vittoria's sake and because he admires Carlo. In the end, he even tries to intercept Carlo's capture at the hands of other Austrians, in order to shield him from death. But Carlo, ignorant of Captain Weisspriess's good deeds and intentions, remains his bitter enemy to the finish.

his sword from one end of the novel to the other. He is challenged so often by young Italian noblemen that he actually puts an advertisement in a Milan newspaper announcing that his fight with Count Ammiani will be his last! As matters turn out, he is right, for in a final scene Count Ammiani runs him through, before dying himself at the hands of other Austrians.

In *The Adventures of Harry Richmond* (1871), the first of Meredith's novels of the '70's, the duel appears again. One of the earlier episodes of the story concerns the life of Harry Richmond as a boy at Rippenger's School. Heriot, a friend of Harry's and a school hero, has an enemy in Boddy, usher and school villain. Heriot and Boddy become rivals for the love of a girl, and Harry, who was away from school while the tension was mounting, tells us how matters stood when he got back (I, 62):

On my return to school, I found it in a convulsion of excitement, owing to Heriot's sending Boddy a challenge to fight a duel with pistols. Mr. Rippenger preached a sermon to the boys concerning the un-Christian spirit and hideous moral perversity of one who would even consent to fight a duel. How much more reprehensible, then, was one that could bring himself to defy a fellow-creature to mortal combat! We were not of his opinion; and as these questions are carried by majorities, we decided that Boddy was a coward, and approved the idea that Heriot would have to shoot or scourge him when the holidays came.

So much for the morality of boys. Later in the novel the situation recurs, but with different actors. Harry, grown, is in love with a German princess. He too has a rival, a German prince, and once more rivalry in love suggests a duel. This time a fight actually takes place, and Harry, describing it, does not have the same air of innocence, humor, and detachment that he had when recounting the incident from his childhood concerning Heriot and Boddy (I, 341):

The "cliquetis" of crossed steel must be very distant in memory, and yourself in a most dilettante frame of mind, for you to be accessible to the music of that thin skeleton's clank. . . . We exchanged passes, the prince chiefly attacking. . . . I touched him on the arm and the shoulder, and finally pierced his arm above the elbow. I could have done nearly what I liked with him; his skill was that of a common regimental sabreur.

Harry offers to continue the duel with pistols. The prince accepts, and Harry falls wounded in turn. He concludes his account, "A silly business on all sides."

Silly it may be, but there is a tone of secret pleasure in his description of the incident. It is Meredith's old tone of the professional evaluating the fine points of a military performance. Writing this passage for Harry Richmond's delivery, Meredith floated on the same sensation of *expertise* he had experienced when arguing with Sir John French, when describing the armaments of the *Alabama* and the *Kearsarge*, when speculating, in his first dispatch from Italy in 1866, on the course of battle. Meredith wants us to know that Harry's manliness consists not only in his ability to dismiss dueling as childish but in his ability to practice what he belittles.

The next reference to a duel in Meredith's works occurs at the beginning of *Beauchamp's Career* (1875). Nevil Beauchamp, the hero, has decided to send a challenge to the "Colonels of the French Imperial Guard" because scurrilous attacks upon England have appeared in French newspapers. Beauchamp is a junior officer in the British navy and hardly more than a boy at the time; also the incident occurs in the 1850's, a period in which unfriendly comments about the British did, in fact, make regular appearances in French newspapers.

It is clear that Meredith intended Beauchamp to look comical at this point. The "mature" Meredith is ascendant. Yet this is the second instance (Richard Feverel's dream of liberating Italy on horseback was the first) in which Meredith has ridiculed a boyish hero for responding too passionately to a historical event which Meredith himself felt quite strongly about. The conclusion is unmistakable. When Meredith adopts a corrective attitude toward one of his younger heroes for excessive warlike zeal in the name of honor, he is correcting himself.

Discussion of the duel next occurs in *The Tragic Comedians* (1880). The novel is based on the lives of Ferdinand Lassalle and Helene von Dönniges, and Meredith tries to remain faithful to historical outlines and to the characters of the persons with whom he deals. Thus Lassalle, as a socialist, was hardly likely to have a high opinion of the aristocratic institution of dueling. Sigismund Alvan, the character based on Lassalle, speaks as follows (p. 28):

I desist and I decline the duel. I have done it, and proved myself a man of metal [sic] notwithstanding. To say nothing of the inhumanity, the senselessness of duelling revolts me. 'Tis a folly, so your nobles practise

it, and your wiseacre sanctions. No blood for me: and yet I tell you that
whatever opposes me, I will sweep away. How? With the brain. If we
descend to poor brute strength or brutal craft, it is from failing in the brain:
we quit the leadership of our forces, and the descent is the beast's confession.

The prose is more vigorous but the sentiment is oddly like Head-
master Rippenger's. Meredith's attitude toward the duel, already
modified in *Beauchamp's Career*, has changed even further. It is as
if Meredith has discovered that passion could transform a Rippenger
into a man, though the latter's principles remain unchanged.

While Meredith was still in his boyhood, English society had decided that the duel was unequivocally bad. Hence we have the odd
spectacle of Meredith slowly advancing toward a private position
which is essentially the one the public and the institutions of England had reached a generation before. But even *The Tragic Comedians* did not bring Meredith quite up to that point. Alvan dies in
a duel, and there is something ineluctably heroic in his behavior.
He is, after all, a *tragic* comedian. It was not until Meredith wrote
*Diana of the Crossways* (1885) that he finally, and without res-
ervation, adopted the long-prevalent middle-class attitude toward
dueling.

Early in this story, Redworth, the hero, engages in conversation with Sullivan Smith, a comical and hot-headed Irishman who is
an act of pure but unwitting patronization on Meredith's part. Redworth and Smith are at a ball, at which Diana, the heroine of the
novel and also Irish, is the lovely object of everyone's attention.
Sullivan Smith has more patriotism than ego, and though intoxicated
by his countrywoman, quickly accepts the fact that he is not good
enough for her. He becomes her faithful watchdog and attendant, a
caricature of the knight who expects no reward. Smith fancies that
another man at the ball has insulted Diana, and he confides to Redworth that he is going to challenge the fellow. Redworth exclaims
(p. 38), "You don't mean to say you're the donkey to provoke a duel!"
He later adds, "If I'm struck, I strike back. I keep my pistols for
bandits and law-breakers."

Meredith makes clear not only that Redworth's views are dictated
by morality and intelligence but that his middle-class temperament

is a brave one, as brave as any. Truly significant is the fact that having once created Redworth and made him speak as he does, Meredith was finally released from a preoccupation that had held him fast for more than half his life. There are no significant references to dueling in any of the works that come after *Diana*.[27] The ghost of whatever it was that had troubled Meredith was finally laid.* The character of Sullivan Smith is, incidentally, further indication of what was happening to Meredith. Smith is the old chivalric hero made farcical, and Meredith was never again to take that figure seriously.[28] Redworth, on the other hand, is the first of a new kind of hero to appear in Meredith's novels—one who would never for the sake of pride cross swords or exchange pistol shots with another man, no matter what the provocation.

Yet what ceased to hold Meredith as an actual situation remained in his imagination as metaphor and epigram. Not only the duel, and its derivatives boxing and fencing, but battle in general supplied these figures of speech. In *The Egoist* (1879), Laetitia Dale, one of the wisest of the characters, complains of a certain Professor Crooklyn at a dinner given by Mrs. Mountstuart (II, 366):

Nothing more unfortunate could have occurred; he spoilt the party. Mrs. Mountstuart tried petting him, which drew attention to him and put us all in his key for several awkward minutes, more than once. She lost her head; she was unlike herself. I may be presumptuous in criticizing her, but should not the president of a dinner-table treat it like a battle-field, and let the guest that sinks descend . . . ?

Later in the novel, the principal characters are at another of Mrs. Mountstuart's parties. Sir Willoughby, the egoist of the title, draws Mr. Dale away from the table. Meredith then employs a singular phrase to describe the talk heard in the background. The majority of voices at the table are ranged in unison against one man's, Dr.

---

* A question comes to mind: Did Meredith, when he learned in 1857 or 1858 that his wife, Mary, was having an affair with the painter Henry Wallis, feel that he should have challenged Wallis to a duel? Having failed to do so, was Meredith nagged for years by a doubt as to whether his forbearance had been civilized or cowardly? On April 18, 1858, Mary bore Wallis a son. She and Wallis were in Wales at the time. Meredith, far from seeking the pair out, refused Mary's request to see him before she left England. There are, however, other ways of explaining Meredith's preoccupation with dueling, as we shall see.

Middleton's, and Meredith says (II, 579) that the debate sounded to the withdrawing pair like the "sharp snaps of rifles and the interval rejoinder of a cannon." This is precisely the simile that Meredith had used more than a dozen years earlier to describe the animated discussion that took place between Vittoria and Laura. The excuse for the image then was that the discussion was being overheard by Count Ammiani and that his "military instincts" supplied the comparison. But here it is Sir Willoughby and Mr. Dale who overhear the disputants. Neither of these gentlemen has instincts that could possibly be called "military." Clearly, it is Meredith himself who hears the snap of rifles and the boom of cannon at the dinner table.

In *Diana of the Crossways*, Meredith at one point wishes to describe witty dialogue. He abandons, for this purpose, cannon and rifles, and returns to swordplay. Diana, the heroine, inexplicably marries the ogrish Mr. Warwick, a Gilbert Osmond done in colored ink, and is compelled by his cruelty to leave him. During their separation (he eventually dies), she becomes famous for her dinners, at which, reputedly, the wit is always brilliant. At one of these dinners, the "wit" is produced by Diana and Whitmonby, a literary critic. Meredith goes to great descriptive lengths to demonstrate how really superb the wit is. (It is, in fact, quite terrible.) Then, the exchange between Diana and Whitmonby concluded, Meredith says (p. 323):

Whitmonby nodded twice, for signification of a palpable hit in that bout; and he noted within him the foolishness of obtruding the slightest allusion to our personality when crossing the foils with a woman. She is down on it like the lightning, quick as she is in her contracted circle; politeness guarding her from a riposte.

### THE SEXES

This scene reveals how frankly Meredith identified the pleasure of social colloquy with the sensation of combat, but it reveals, too, Meredith's sense that one of the primary battles of the world is the one that goes on between men and women. In the passage quoted above, Meredith has merely hinted lightly at the existence of this fight. Elsewhere in *Diana* he has occasion to muse about the institution of marriage, and his declarations concerning the battle between men and women become more direct (p. 402):

Marriages are unceasing. Friends do it, and enemies; the unknown con-
tractors of this engagement, or armistice, inspire an interest. It certainly
is both exciting and comforting to hear that man and woman are ready to
join in a mutual affirmative, say Yes together again. It sounds like the end
of the war.

This is one war which Meredith eventually believed or hoped could
be ended altogether and for all time. Matey Weyburn, the hero of
*Lord Ormont and His Aminta,* a novel of the '90's, says that society
could end the war by bringing boys and girls up differently (pp.
287–88):

> There's the task. . . . It's to separate them as little as possible. All the—
> *passez-moi le mot*—devilry between the sexes begins at their separation.
> They're foreigners when they meet; and their alliances are not always bind-
> ing. The chief object in life, if happiness be the aim, and the growing better
> than we are, is to teach men and women how to be one; for, if they're not,
> then each is a morsel for the other to prey on. . . . Some of them fall in
> love and strike a truce, and still they are foreigners. They have not the
> same standard of honour.

Besides establishing the hope of peace in some form in the
Meredithian universe, the passages just quoted from *Diana* and
*Ormont* are indicative of a large and important area of Meredith's
interests, one distinct from his commitment to art but which clearly
superimposed itself upon his activity as an artist. This is Meredith's
preoccupation with international relations, and particularly with
power politics, in the latter decades of the nineteenth century.

### DEFENSE OF ENGLAND

From the '70's onward Meredith became increasingly alarmed
about England's inability to defend herself if attacked. In *Beauchamp's Career* he took energetic note of "the harsher air blowing
from the continent toward England."[29] Moreover, "his opinions on
English politics came to be dominated by concern over the country's
lack of adequate defense and need of a large permanent army."[30] G.
M. Trevelyan, speaking of the years following the Franco-Prussian
War, says: "We were too ignorant of Germany to regard her as a
serious rival. Only eccentric intellectuals like Matthew Arnold and
George Meredith warned us that there was something in German
professors and their *geist* that was at once admirable and dangerous."[31]

National defense, and the subsidiary matter of conscription, became consuming issues for Meredith. In 1885 he wrote to his long-
time friend, Admiral Frederick Maxse:

From the Foreign point of view, our Government, in Foreign affairs, must
appear a table of imbeciles. But Diplomacy that is not backed by force is
a nerveless thing. Either we surrender our position universally, or we must
have men in arms—soldiers as well as sailors. Nothing, I suppose, but war
will push the English to this policy, so it seems that they will consent to
sink, unless a fit of the old national pride precipitates them helplessly into
the struggle.[32]

On March 18, 1878, he had written to William Hardman: "Press
for an army. Ultimately it will come to conscription, and the sooner
the better. The volunteering system gives us a scum of men no match
for the countries that bring their best into the field." Meredith was
still at it in 1905. In August of that year he wrote to a friend, "Join
. . . with others of your kind in urging your countrymen to the cause
of compulsory service. All the present muddle about our Army comes
from this cowardly endeavor to shirk this main question. Hence our
shivers when Germany frowns."[33]

Haldane, as Secretary for War, finally established a Territorial
Army, and Meredith's "theories about national defense were partially
put into practice."[34] But only partially, and not sufficiently to satisfy
Meredith. On July 3, 1908, he wrote to Frederick Greenwood: "As
to our country, if the people were awake, they would submit to be
drilled. The Territorial 15 days is ludicrous; and the fear of imposing
drill for at least a year seems to me a forecast of the national
tragedy."[35]

Meredith pursued the theme of national defense in his poetry.
"To Colonel Charles" (1887) is "a plea for steady, systematic arma-
ment, instead of laxity varied by fits of panic."[36] "England Before
the Storm" (1891) is another plea for preparedness in a threatening
world. "Trafalgar Day" (1896) declares Nelson a hero in the battle
for freedom. Says Meredith: if we must fight, let "Our Nelson be our
battlecry!"[37] And in "The Call" (1908), Meredith warns of the danger of war with Germany and of England's disinclination to heed the
danger. None of these poems has much merit. They deserve the
oblivion into which they have fallen. They are vigorous but didactic,
free of commonplace phrasing but too obviously contrived. Their
interest to us here is that they show clearly how indifferent Meredith

could be to the line between art and preaching when the issue at hand was England's defense.

IMPERIALISM

As J. R. Seeley made clear to his generation, closely allied to the question of national defense was the question of imperialism.* Meredith was often on the side of imperialism. In "The Voyage of the 'Ophir,' " a slight poem of 1901, he says that imperialism is good, so long as it "trusts to love" and means "strength to service vowed." These words recall Seeley's thesis that Britain has a moral obligation to continue to govern such dependent lands as India. Seeley would readily have adopted "strength to service vowed" as his motto.

A pertinent passage occurs in *Lord Ormont and His Aminta* (1894). The boys at Cuper's School are defending Lord Ormont, who, while in charge of the British cavalry in India, was reprimanded for disobeying civilian authority. The boys' opponent is Mr. Shalders, an usher (pp. 20–21):

> Mr. Shalders was cornered by the boys, coming at him one after another without a stop, vowing it was the exercise of a military judgement upon a military question at a period of urgency, which had brought about the quarrel with the Commissioner and the reproof of the Governor. He betrayed the man completely cornered by generalizing. He said—"We are a civilian people; we pride ourselves on having civilian methods."
>
> "How can that be if we have won India with guns and swords?"
>
> "But that splendid jewel for England's tiara won," said he, . . . "we are bound to sheathe the sword and govern by the Book of the Law." . . .
>
> "What if we find an influential Indian prince engaged in conspiracy?" . . .
>
> "We summon him to exonerate himself."
>
> "No; we mount and ride straight away into his territory, spot the treason, deport him, and rule in his place!"
>
> It was all very well for Mr. Shalders to say he talked to boys; he was cornered again, as his shrug confessed.

Shalders comes off second best, but we should note that Meredith was only keeping up with the times. Both middle-class and "radical" opinion had come round to favoring imperialism, as the career of Meredith's contemporary, Joseph Chamberlain, well testifies. Meredith's feeling for imperialism speaks of at least one remaining affinity with

---

* Seeley's book *The Expansion of England* was published in 1883 and made a deep and immediate impression.

his old friend Swinburne. Jerome H. Buckley, speaking of Swinburne in the latter part of the century, says: "Into his jingoistic propaganda the poet carried not a little of his old republican ardor; in tone, at least, the reactionary remained the radical. If he never achieved a theology as positive as his dogmatic imperialism, he seemed ultimately, of his own accord, at one with the high Victorians in his declared wish to live as if there were in life some moral or religious purpose."[38]

Except that Meredith was never particularly interested in republicanism, this evaluation would fit the underlying facts of his life, too. His own championing of imperialism, though not as ardent as his promotion of other causes he associated with the defense of England, was carried on in a tone of moral urgency. He, too, could embrace political ideals and programs with a fervor other men reserved for theological affirmations.

Meredith's feeling for imperialism provides, also, a parallel with Henry James. F. W. Dupee has said of James: "The story of his opinions and emotions was largely that of the many other active patriots whose concern for the fate of civilization, however real in itself, was strangely, as it seems now, untempered by any knowledge of the complex moral implications of world imperialism. On the one hand he had never had any love for Germany; and on the other he had constantly envisaged the British Empire as the necessary if sometimes bad core of the world order."[39] Meredith, though he had an intimate knowledge of German culture, came to regard Germany as a threat soon after 1870. And he would have been pleased to be called one of the "other active patriots." Then, too, his concern for civilization, different as it was from James's, was similarly "untempered by any knowledge of the complex moral implications of world imperialism."

But actually, when we sum up all that Meredith had to say about imperialism we see that the subject occupied a much smaller place in his thought than other questions relating to England's power. He did not, like the true writers of colonial fiction, make "clear to thousands of eager but ignorant people at home, as well as to bewildered participants in the struggle itself" the varieties of meaning that attached to imperialism.[40] He even warned England not to try to gain more territory than she could hold.[41] Ultimately, his interest in imperialism derived from his preoccupation with the defense of England rather than from any feeling for the glory of empire. Though he echoed Seeley in speaking of England's responsibility to rule dependent peoples, this was not a central moral precept for Meredith. It was a kind of auxiliary idea that would serve to justify a war if England's territories were threatened. The possibility of attack, principally upon the British Isles but by extension upon anything British, was the main force working upon Meredith's imagination and determining his response to the issues of the day.

### THE MANLY VIRTUES

Underlying nearly all we have said about Meredith's interest in battle situations and imagery, about his concern with preparedness and the international power struggle, is the fact that Meredith believed that military conduct was moral conduct. We saw that Evan Harrington's virtuous actions were rendered in military metaphors. Meredith could also imply that military virtues were literally the manly virtues and that they were the basis of civilization. He never stated the idea as baldly as did Carlyle, who in 1867 wrote:

That of commanding and obeying, were there nothing more, is it not the basis of all human culture; ought not all to have it; and how many ever do? I often say, The one Official Person; royal, sacerdotal, scholastic, governmental, of our times, who is still thoroughly a truth and a reality . . . is the Drill-Sergeant who is master of his work, and who will perform it. By Drill-Sergeant understand, not the man in three stripes alone; understand him as meaning all such men, up to the Turenne, to the Friedrich of Prussia;—*he* does his function, he is genuine; and from the highest to the lowest no one else does.[42]

But in various works Meredith echoed the spirit of this passage. At one point in *The Egoist,* Dr. Middleton delivers a kind of after-dinner speech (II, 551):

"We [English] . . . shine at our best . . . in a state of war. In a state of war we are at home, our men are high-minded fellows. . . . In the state of peace we do not live in peace: our native roughness breaks out in unexpected places, under extraordinary aspects—tyrannies, extravagances, domestic exactions: and if we have not had sharp early training . . . within and without . . . the old-fashioned island-instrument to drill into us the civilization of our masters, the ancients, we show it by running here and there to some excess."

War as positive / civilization
see 43     advancing.

In the poem "The Test of Manhood" (1901), Meredith asserts that the whole of human life is a war fought for the advance of civilization. The "test of manhood" is the ability to see that the struggle is going on and that each individual must play his part. Each must see

> . . . that it is a warfare but begun;
> Unending; with no Power to interpose;
> No prayer, save for the strength to keep his ground,
> Heard of the Highest; never battle's close,
> The Victory complete and victor crowned.[43]

The persistency with which Meredith's poetry turns humanity's struggle for spiritual advance into a military campaign has been noted by Hildegard Littmann. She points out that when Meredith speaks of the future, he says, "Yet there our battle urges." And, she observes, he assures mankind that God approves. She quotes:

> And the fair heaven reflecting inner peace
> On righteous warfare, that asks not to cease.

Miss Littmann also remarks that Meredith's idealization of the fighting spirit derives from his religion of action. Thus, she says, he urges John Morley, on the occasion of the latter's visit to the United States:

> Trim swordsmen they push forth: yet try thy steel
> . . . And bring the army of the faithful through.

Even the comic spirit, Miss Littmann adds, is conceived at times as a weapon forged for spiritual battle. In his "Ode to the Comic Spirit" (1892), Meredith speaks of this spirit as the "Sword of Common Sense" and "Captain of our civil Fort." As for peace, she says that Meredith insists it means laziness and corruption. She quotes his assertion that man is "a creature matched with strife." She tells us that in one poem he exclaims to his friend Morley, "Scorn fireside peace," and that elsewhere he practically exhorts mankind to fight against peace. He calls it "our lullaby word for decay."[44]

Certain bits of Meredith's biography add further color and point to this multidimensioned theme of war in his work. Speaking of Meredith in the later years of the century, Lionel Stevenson says that "the history of war was [a] favorite subject, and his conversation often turned to episodes in the lives of great commanders." In the '80's, Meredith edited "a series of 'Military Biographies' as part of his duties with Chapman and Hall."[45] In 1904, his lifelong friend

Leslie Stephen died, and Meredith wrote an essay in memoriam. One passage in it makes abundantly clear just how central to Meredith's conception of Stephen were the military virtues:

I have often said of this lifelong student and philosophical head that he had in him the making of a great military captain. He would not have been opposed to the profession of arms if he had been captured early for the service, notwithstanding his abomination of bloodshed. He had a high, calm courage, was unperturbed in a dubious position, and would confidently take the way out of it which he conceived to be the better. We have not to deplore that he was diverted from the ways of a soldier, though England, as the country has been learning of late, cannot boast of many in uniform who have capacity for leadership.[46]

Though Leslie Stephen was a renowned rower, walker, and mountain climber, not many men who knew him well would have pictured him in the role of a military captain—"notwithstanding his abomination of bloodshed." Meredith himself, in *The Egoist* (1879), had already cast Leslie Stephen in the role of Vernon Whitford, a quiet but manly scholar. The point is that to Meredith genuine "manliness" in any shape or disposition implied the potential military leader.

In a group of manuscripts, dating from the '60's or '70's,[47] there is a sketch of a short story that was never completed. It is nothing more than an outline of a battle, as it might appear in a communiqué. There are no notes to indicate how the characters were to be developed. On the other hand, the manuscript begins with a diagram of gun positions![48] Meredith's first impulse was to think not about the psychology of men in battle but about problems in military strategy. Perhaps nothing illustrates more vividly than this sketch how completely Meredith could identify with the military mind, how ready he was to imagine himself a strategist equipped with technical knowledge and able to speak in a tone of authority on military matters. The question is, did the moralist give rise to the strategist, or was it the other way around? Whichever the answer, this sketch shows the pleasure Meredith took in planning a battle, and it is a pleasure akin to the kinds that accompanied his other many-sided interests in war and military conduct.[49]

### NATURE AND WAR

In our discussion of *Richard Feverel* we saw that Meredith's earliest moral ideas derived from his conception of nature. Most of his in-

terest in war and battle—as themes and sources of imagery—derives
from his conception of society, i.e., his belief first made apparent in
the '60's that society is a battleground. Nevertheless, Meredith made
it clear that war is also a natural conception in the sense that nature
sanctions the just war. In *Sandra Belloni* (1864), a kind of prelude
to *Vittoria*,[50] Merthyr Powys, an Englishman who intends to spend
his life and fortune for the liberation of Italy, says, when speaking of
the plan to revolt against Austrian rule (II, 524), "We are merely
bondsmen to the re-establishment of the provisions of nature." A war
fought in the name of nationalism is "moral" because "natural."

There is a strong echo here of the Wordsworth who began to write
patriotic political sonnets in 1802 and who maintained (in the *Tract
on the Convention of Cintra*) that the moral basis of nationalism is
in accord with nature—essentially the doctrine of Mazzini many years
later. Meredith may have been quite aware of his debt to the tradition linking Wordsworth and Mazzini, and it is more than likely that
Merthyr's words are Meredith's idea of what Mazzini himself might
say. Mazzini, we recall, appears at the beginning of *Vittoria* and directs the revolt which Merthyr, in *Sandra Belloni*, anticipates. And
when we speak of Meredith's debt to the Romantic tradition, Carlyle,
too, deserves mention. Carlyle says that when Frederick I created
the Prussian army he proved himself "a son of nature" because "he
had the honesty to do what nature taught him." And he was rewarded. He was the victor in the Battle of Mollwitz.[51]

### THE POSSIBILITY OF PEACE

We could go on piling up instances culled from Meredith's work
in which he declares that nature at certain times sanctions war. But
the point has been made, and rather than pursue it further let us now
recall that Meredith did believe one battle—the battle between men
and women—could and should be ended. Meredith was not a purist
in his attachment to combativeness. Though so often in his work society *is* a battleground and though nature often decrees men must
fight, there is another side to his thought that cannot be ignored.
Meredith very often expressed the hope that peace among nations,
as well as between men and women, might become a reality. While
warning England to be powerful enough to retaliate if attacked, he
was aware that whenever war breaks out, human intelligence has

somewhere and somehow failed. On July 14, 1870, he wrote to his son Arthur: "It has looked recently as if we should have war between France and Prussia, and I fear it must come on . . . When men's brains are insufficient to meet the exigencies of affairs, they fight."[52]

A similar note is struck in a poem called "On the Danger of War" (1885). Meredith directs a plea to Wisdom and says:

> Avert, High Wisdom, never vainly wooed,
> This threat of War, that shows a land brain-sick.[53]

Only the "brain-sick"—those incapable of "wisdom"—want war.

In the "Ode to the Comic Spirit," the Spirit, which is "common sense" incarnate, attacks those who promote strife and war:

> These, that would have men still of men be foes,
> Eternal fox to prowl and pike to feed;
> Would keep our life the whirly pool
> Of turbid stuff dishonouring History.

Promoters of war, in short, are promoters of chaos in human society.

In "Foresight and Patience" (1894), the virtues named in the title hold a debate. Patience urges Foresight to "look back at the primitive times and see that man was really worse then, when 'yes' and 'no' always meant a fight." The reason, she adds, is that "foresight" was then unknown.

Another poem, "Cageing of Ares," was written in 1899 and dedicated to the council at The Hague. Meredith's tale, derived from the *Iliad,* tells how the Titans—Ephialtes and Otos—imprisoned Ares, god of war, and gave peace to their mother earth, Gaea, for thirteen months. Meredith describes mankind's joy while Ares is absent:

> Then did good Gaea's children gratefully
> Lift hymns to Gods they judged, but praised for peace,
> Delightful Peace, that answers Reason's call
> Harmoniously and images her law.

The important word is "reason," for it is reason that calls for peace. The word occurs also in "On the Danger of War":

> When nations gain the pitch where rhetoric
> Seems reason they are ripe for cannon's food.

Elsewhere, France in war becomes the "headless with the fearful

hands." Thus again a nation at war is described as bereft of reason—
that is, "headless."

A similar observation occurs in a letter Meredith wrote to G. M.
Trevelyan in 1900, commenting upon the Boer War: "I am rather
beaten to the ground at present by the slain, wounded and sick of
my friends under the brand of South Africa, in a war that a fore-
thoughtful or even commonly prudent policy might have steered us
clear of."[54] The worst aspect of the war is that it was unnecessary—
a consequence of lack of forethoughtfulness or of a "commonly
prudent policy." Again, Meredith is deploring, in different words,
the nonapplication of reason to an international problem.

Two years before his death, Meredith, in a letter to Dr. Ernst
Dick, put in final form his belief in the possibility of peace. His
theme is the disarmament conference then in progress:

> Ideals, after a long period of derision, are at last matter for belief, and
> have become the subjects for a striving to make them actual. This one of
> Disarmament calls for the general exercise of common humaneness and
> common sense. . . .
> We may hope that a time is at hand when without further bloodshed
> the energies of men will be directed to a more complete conquest of the
> elements, for the common weal. Battle enough for them in that region.[55]

We can compare this statement with the theme of William James's
essay "The Moral Equivalent of War," and we can note too that Meredith has again sounded his characteristic phrase, "common sense."
In Meredith's thought "common sense" is not the vague term it is
often accused of being today. It is a synonym to Meredith for *reason*
and as such has, he believes, a clear and definite meaning.

"Reason" is the basis of the antiwar theme in Meredith's thought
and writing. Meredith often rejects peace as the cowardly goal of a
commercial civilization, but he just as often praises peace and calls
it a reward for the use of reason. The contradiction does not represent
a contrast between two periods in Meredith's life. During the very
years he denounced pacifists and sang the praises of certain military
heroes, he urged his readers to recognize peace as the prize of reason.
But on his eightieth birthday, February 12, 1908—less than a year
after he wrote to Dr. Dick—he spoke in a very different tone when
reporters pressed him for words of wisdom that they might convey
to the world. He said that what mankind needed was "the spirit of

the soldier in every walk of life." He continued, "Life is a long and continuous struggle. It is necessarily combative. Otherwise we cease. Let the struggle go on. Let us be combative; but let us also be kind."[56]

These words fittingly conclude a writing career in which war figured so often as fact and symbol of man's condition and in which the soldier appeared so often as the archetype of all manliness, of virtues appropriate "in every walk of life." They do not, however, cast any final glow on the belief in peace which, especially after 1870, became an important part of Meredith's thought. Meredith never did provide us with a final statement to cap this half of the paradox, but the roots of his desire for peace were as deep in his mind and work as those of its antithesis.

It would be folly to try to resolve the contradiction. It existed. What we can do, however, is show that Meredith's faith in reason, the basis of his belief in the possibility and desirability of peace, first received major emphasis during a particular period—the 1870's—and that like his interest in war it was first expressed in a novel: made part of a view of society that is central to a story Meredith is telling. That novel is *The Adventures of Harry Richmond* (1871), and it inaugurates a period during which Meredith's regard for reason begins to equal, in its effect upon his imagination, his interest in war.

The '70's were rich years for Meredith. Not only *Harry Richmond* but also *Beauchamp's Career* (1875), the *Essay on Comedy* (1877), and *The Egoist* (1879) belong to this period. To all four, his concern for reason, though this concern was often an ambiguous one, made a large contribution as a source of ideas and as an influence upon form. Indeed, it brought about the rich culmination of his interest in form, for the '70's mark the height of his consciousness of the art of the novel, of the pains it requires and the rewards it offers.

# 3

# *The Rational Compromise*

## THE 1870's

In the debates of the 1870's, hardly anyone neglected to point out that "reason" was on his side. Christian and agnostic; Tory and Radical; idealist, positivist, materialist—each was bent on proving that his was the rational position. Only the celebrants of the sensual life seemed indifferent to the attempt, perhaps accepting the popular view of themselves as men ambitious to dethrone reason and therefore feeling it would be perverse to ask her for support. All others claimed to have won her special favor and were positive they had seen her nod approval on more than one occasion on which they had been arguing for their beliefs.[1]

The climate thus created in the '70's was highly congenial to Meredith. Though he had never courted reason in the manner of some expository writers, he had sent aloft petitions for her prosperity, crying, at one point, "More brain, O Lord, more brain!"[2] Now, as if to pay her the courtliest of all compliments and with the same stroke answer his own prayer, he set about conferring the blessing of rationalism on the world he himself was creating, the world of his novels. He did so in two ways: he began to apply more rational principles to its shaping, and he began to make reason—the consequences of its presence or absence—his theme.[3]

Meredith counted among his friends, many of whom were followers of John Stuart Mill, a large number of "rationalists" whose creed consisted of agnosticism, radicalism, and the general belief that "experience" is the only source of valid data for constructing true statements about the world or for reasoning out solutions to the problems of the individual and society. John Morley and Leslie Stephen were two of the closest of these friends, and they, along with Frederick Maxse, a naval officer turned radical politician, exerted a strong if indirect influence upon the expression of Meredith's own rationalist ideas.[4] Maxse was the model for the hero of *Beauchamp's Career* (1875), and Stephen for the hero (but not the protagonist) of *The Egoist* (1879). Morley, though his recognizable portrait is not to be found in Meredith's works, had more of an effect on the fate of rationalism as a *theme* in them than did anyone else. Without intending to, he made Meredith see that the clarity-loving rationalists, eager for empire, were challenging the autonomy of artists by denying them the right to regard truth as ambiguous.

### IN HARMONY WITH REASON

Before this happened, however, Meredith was to write about rationalism as if it were an uncomplicated virtue. In *The Adventures of Harry Richmond* (1871), he set the hero to discovering that "reason" is the beneficent link between the individual and society. Although we are not entirely convinced when the novel is over that this "discovery" is a truth, and though Meredith did not quite achieve the simplicity and order of structure he intended, *Harry Richmond* has strong, saving merits, among them an inspired conclusion, that prevent it from becoming just another of Meredith's ambitious failures.[5] Instead, it earns its place as the first of three consecutive works that together constitute Meredith's major achievement in the novel. With experimental vitality, but with increasing control of purpose and method, Meredith creates in the course of these stories a world in which society, conceived as a source of moral energy, is credible, profoundly envisioned, and skillfully differentiated from the individual will that it either aids or opposes.

As Lionel Stevenson observes of *Harry Richmond*, "The story had already been told in many familiar fictitious biographies—the slow, painful achievement of maturity by a youth who must conquer many illusions . . . about himself and the world."[7] What Meredith did, in retelling this "familiar" story, was to make "illusions" signify an absence of moral awareness, and "maturity" its presence. Harry Richmond, the first-person narrator, begins life as a boy for whom confusion, an active barrier separating his senses from reality, is a constant condition of existence. From infancy, he is torn between his fantastic, rootless father, who calls himself Richmond Roy, and his wealthy, no-nonsense maternal grandfather, who cannot bear the sight of Richmond Roy, blaming him for the death of Harry's mother. The effect of this division is to keep Harry in such a state of heightened emotion that he can, according to Meredith, distinguish neither actuality from hope nor right conduct from wrong.

Despite his confused feelings, however, Harry can travel only one path at a time, and during the first phase of his story, prompted by affection and admiration strong enough to lull his misgivings, he follows his father. Following him means sharing, or at least condoning, his delusions, hopes, and extravagant plans. The ostensible ground for all these is Roy's belief that he is the son of a king of England (presumably George IV); that his mother, an actress, was secretly married to his father; and that "Government" can and will be made to recognize his claims. All this Harry hears with covert enthusiasm. He is not reluctant to believe himself descended, once removed, from royalty. His father is a surrogate for his own imagination and makes it conveniently easy for him to dream the dream of mysterious royal parentage that Lionel Trilling has pointed out is not only the common heritage of all children but a motivating force for the hero of a certain kind of nineteenth-century novel.[8] It is a powerful dream. Most of what happens in *Harry Richmond*, including the hero's near marriage to a German princess, can be traced to it. But while Meredith exploits it as a force capable of generating events in the visible world, he simultaneously insists that its power is necromantic and that the world it touches loses substantiality, becoming a shadow-image destined for early extinction. He busily prepares Harry, who drifts somnambulistically in his father's adventurous but antic course, for the day when the world thus affected must end.

In the hands of Stendhal or Balzac, this would have meant, simply, preparation for a tragic resolution. In Meredith's hands it means preparation to be seized, at the last moment, by a rescuing moral. Before the illusory world that Roy has fashioned is dissipated, Harry renounces "adventure" as a way of life and, as a result, is swiftly cut loose from his father and brought safely into the snug harbor of reality. This equation of adventure with illusion is really Meredith's repudiation of what he took to be the romantic conception of existence. Thus, the first of the controlling ideas in the novel is that he who seeks experience for its own sake—i.e., adventure—is behaving irrationally, for he is, in effect, avoiding the two "reality" goals of life: to discover himself and to discover his proper relation to society. Since to be moral means, to Meredith, to be in harmony with oneself and one's society, especially the latter, it follows that he who irrationally seeks the irrelevant and consequently illusory life of adventure is immoral.

Nowhere, it must be said, does Meredith indicate that adventure might be converted into an act of self-creation, in the manner, for example, of Huck Finn or David Copperfield. The comparison with Dickens is particularly instructive. *David Copperfield,* though apparently sprawling, is actually organized by the theme of adventure. The occasions for adventure, while David is still a boy, occur at reasonable intervals along a winding road, and they consist, actually, of meeting new people, each of whom has an enormous influence on the hero's destiny. Thus, the appearance in sequel of Peggotty, Mr. Murdstone, Mr. Peggotty, Miss Murdstone, Mr. Creakle, Mr. Micawber, and Aunt Betsey, to name a few, has the effect of a series of dramatic disclosures. There is a promise of new developments, new risks to run, new triumphs and losses, whenever one of the characters named makes his entrance. We can say that "the spirit of adventure" in *David Copperfield* has to do both with whom we shall meet next and with what will happen next. In *Harry Richmond,* however, these are separated. Like David, Harry becomes involved with new people, but his relations with them are carefully distinguished from his "adventures." By the latter Meredith means Harry's wanderings over England and Germany, which have very little influence on the outcome of the story and are therefore indeed illusory, idle, and immoral peregrinations for a character who must be created from page to page. Significantly, Harry discovers himself when he reflects not upon the events that have occurred but upon the people closest to him. These are his father, Squire Beltham, Princess Ottilia (the German princess he almost marries), and Janet Ilchester (the girl he ultimately does marry). With the exception of the Princess these main participants in Harry's life were all "given" in the conditions of his childhood, and their entry into the story is in no way dependent upon Harry's adventures. As for the Princess, in some ways the most important of the four, Harry's meeting with her does occur fortuitously while he is searching in Germany for his

father, but since Roy had already discovered her and marked her for
his son's bride, the events leading to their encounter are anticlimactic.
These four, through direct or indirect influence, help Harry to get
over his romantic fever and youthful egoism (much the same thing
for Meredith) and to begin the life of reason in the "real" world.
They help him prepare for that life, and this preparation is the true
adventure of Harry Richmond.

The Princess Ottilia is the main agent in the process. She is,
perhaps not too incongruously, a symbol both of Roy's illusory dreams
of royalty and of Meredith's idea of perfect femininity. Though she
has beauty, her crowning grace is *mind*. The apt pupil of Professor
von Karsteg, a slightly feverish amalgam of German intellectualism
and nationalism, she has been led through his teachings to a worship
of reason as the guiding principle of action. She is susceptible in
precisely the degree Meredith is to the incantatory effect of words
like "reason" and "mind." Some of the Professor's opinions, admir-
ingly quoted by the Princess for the benefit of a rapt Harry, are of
course Meredith's own (I, 306):

> "You [the English] have such wealth! You embrace half the world.
> . . . All this is wonderful. The bitterness is, you are such a mindless
> people—I do but quote to explain my Professor's ideas. 'Mindless,' he
> says, 'and . . . neither in the material nor in the spiritual kingdom of
> noble or gracious stature, and ceasing to have a brave aspect.' He calls
> you squat Goths."

Actually, the explosive, ludicrous professor seems the last one
capable of inculcating a devotion to calm reason. Yet, whatever its
source, its existence in the Princess is credibly realized, and it effectively determines her relations with Harry. She wants to marry him,
but when she is reminded that the laws of the German Diet forbid
an heir to a throne to take a commoner for a husband, she is confronted with a dilemma. Truly in love with Harry, she also loves her
country, or rather, her duty.[9] The way in which she relates to her
country—her society—is meant by Meredith to be a triumph of mind
over irrational passion: "The laws of society as well as her exalted
station were in harmony with her intelligence. She thought them
good, but obeyed them as a subject, not slavishly: she claimed the
right to exercise her trained reason."[10] And by so doing, she breaks
through her dilemma: she agrees to give up Harry and wed a decent

German nobleman who, like herself, loves scholarship more than political power. Most significantly, Meredith gives every indication that she will never regret her renunciation of Harry or her acceptance of the man designated by the principle which is both society's chief agent and the chief spring of action in Ottilia's character: reason.*

Though Meredith has not given us a complete theory of the relation between the individual and society, he has told us, at least, that he does not believe civilization always breeds its discontents. It is a striking fact that during the '70's he persistently demonstrated in his novels that the right use of reason led to the free acceptance of most laws of society, English society included.[11] In *Harry Richmond*, Princess Ottilia, at peace with her tiny realm, serves as a pilot model for the hero who, Englishman and commoner, has a less obvious but similar adjustment to make.

But before Harry can fully profit from the Princess's example, he has to see the full implication of the quality in her he has already praised, her ability "to exercise her trained reason." He has to see that this ability enables the Princess not only to reconcile herself to her society but to dispel the illusory opposition between mind and heart. He says (II, 576): "I found myself possessed of one key . . . wherewith to read the princess, which was never possible to me when I was under the stress of passion, or of hope or despair; my perplexities over what she said, how she looked, ceased to trouble me. I read her by this strange light: that she was a woman who could only love intelligently—love, that is, in the sense of giving herself. She had the power of passion, and it could be stirred; but he who kindled it [had to] stand clear in her intellect's unsparing gaze."

In perceiving this, Harry advances a huge step toward his new life. He continues: "It is, I have learnt, out of the conflict of sensations such as I then underwent that a young man's brain and morality,

---

* To Meredith's mind, there is a clear antagonism between the rational and romantic view of life. Harry first learns about Ottilia's obligation through an official, Chancellor von Redwitz, who tells him about a parallel case, one concerning a Princess Elizabeth of Leiterstein. This princess readily gave up the commoner she intended to marry when the Diet forbade their union. She lived quite contentedly afterwards, and Redwitz remarks, in relating his parable, that there is no *romance* in it (II, 363-66).

supposing him not to lean overmuch to sickly sentiment, become
gradually enriched and strengthened, and himself shaped for capable
manhood." "Brain" and "morality"—so closely linked for Meredith,
as for many Victorians (even David Copperfield's Aunt Betsy Trot-
wood makes the connection)[12]—are about to teach Harry that an
"intelligent" love would mean for the Princess one that would not
create disharmony between herself and her country. He is ready to
accept the fact, as she already has, that they can never marry.

In accepting it, Harry is about to embrace the life of reason, and
though he cannot have the Princess, it will soon be time to reward
him. The prize is ready at hand, for Meredith has been preparing
throughout the novel for the day when Harry would be capable of
receiving it. The gift is the love of Janet Ilchester.

Janet, like Harry, is a favorite relative of Squire Beltham, and
while they were both children the Squire made it plain that he wanted
them to marry some day and become the joint heirs of his property.
But Janet, at that time, was not the girl to set a hero dreaming. She
was narrow in her sympathies and insensitive in her dealings with
Harry, particularly as these concerned his beloved father, whose
presence had been interdicted at Riversley Grange, the Squire's home.
In commenting on one dispute he and Janet have had over Roy,
Harry indicates in the strongest words just how unpleasant she could
be and how he regarded her (I, 108): "The meanness of the girl in
turning on me when the glaring offence was hers, struck me as con-
temptible beyond words." In addition, she was not very pretty; was,
in fact, emphatically plain. However, while Harry is off on the adventures that lead him to the Princess, and hence to self-discovery,
Janet grows gradually into a brighter figure. She becomes prettier,
and—more important—the obnoxious quality she exhibited as a child
becomes transformed into honest forthrightness of expression, firmness of will, and a capacity for deep attachment.* Most significant is
the manner in which this transformation reaches its apotheosis, for

---

* The figure of Janet has occasioned a variety of comment. R. H. Hutton, for
example, insisted that the childish and the mature Janet did not go together. He
said (p. 79): "As for [Janet] . . . there seems to be a real want of consistency
. . . between the rather repulsive picture of her as a child . . . and the picture
of her perfect courage and indomitable resolution as a woman; we do not say that
the two pictures might not be reconciled, but only that they *are* not." Lionel
Stevenson, while not concerning himself with Hutton's charge, has indirectly
shed light on the problem: "[Janet] was a realist, who naturally clashed with

it tells us that economy and interrelatedness of characters are two principles controlling the novel's structure. It is none other than the Princess Ottilia, or rather her influence, that completes the new Janet.[18] Through Harry, Janet becomes acquainted with Ottilia; soon acquaintance gives way to friendship, and then friendship, on Janet's part, turns into devotion and admiration. We learn what the Princess's influence on Janet ultimately becomes when, during the crisis preceding Harry's break with Ottilia, Janet is asked her opinion as to whether the Princess still wishes to marry. She replies (II, 592): "Oh, if you think a lady like the Princess Ottilia is led by her wishes . . ." And Meredith adds: "Her radiant perception of an ideal of her sex (the first she ever had) made her utterly contemptuous toward the less enlightened." The Princess, in becoming an ideal for Janet, plays the same role in her life that she plays in Harry's. In both, she is the moral touchstone, and Harry and Janet are actually converted to her image, giving up, in the process, their old irrational passions and wishes.

But for Harry the Princess is the *second* ideal: his father had been the first. Before Harry's conversion can be completed, that earlier guiding image must be exorcized. Actually the exorcism has already taken place before the final revelation of the Princess's character strikes Harry with its transfiguring force, as noted above. Recovering from an illness, with his thoughts turned to his father, Harry arrives at a painful but liberating realization (II, 541):

Must I say it?—He had ceased to entertain me. Instead of a comic I found him a tragic spectacle; and his exuberant anticipations . . . were

---

Harry's romantic notions because she never accepted the genteel conventions, whether as an uninhibited child or as a candid woman. As a portrait of Janet Duff Gordon she was probably a more objective achievement than Rose Jocelyn had been." (*Ordeal,* p. 185.) The clue lies in the last sentence. The earlier Janet Ilchester embodied Meredith's reproach to Janet Duff Gordon. Her "meanness" represented the cruelty with which he felt he had been used. The older Janet Ilchester, if this analysis is correct, is an act of forgiveness on Meredith's part and a reacknowledgment of the qualities in Janet Duff Gordon that had drawn Meredith to her in the first place. What Hutton was noticing was that qualities which ordinarily would exist simultaneously in a full characterization exist here only sequentially. In addition, the portrait of the mature Janet is much more fully developed than the earlier portrayal. Taking all these considerations together, we can see how Hutton was led to his strictures. Nevertheless, the two portraits, though subtly related, are reconciled, as a close reading of the novel will reveal.

examples of down-right unreason such as contemplation through the comic glass would have excused; the tragic could not. I knew, nevertheless, that to the rest of the world he was a progressive comedy: and the knowledge made him seem more tragic still. He clearly could not learn from misfortune; he was not to be contained. . . . I chafed at his unteachable spirit, surely one of the most tragical things in life.

In ceasing to find his father entertaining, Harry has indicated not only that he himself is capable of learning from experience, but that he no longer desires to court the romantic-tragic destiny that is clearly in store for Roy. Having become sane, sober, and rational, Harry prepares at this point to be a better follower of the Princess than he ever could have been as her lover or husband. And when we recall that a "follower" of the Princess must desire to live in harmony with the laws of society, we understand why Harry discovers that it is Janet, after all, whom he ought to and wants to marry.

The image of the mature Janet with which Harry falls in love tells us everything: "I had the vision of a matronly, but not much altered Janet, mounted on horseback, to witness the performance of some favourite Eleven of youngsters with her connoisseur's eye; and then the model of an English lady, wife, and mother, waving adieu to the field and cantering home to entertain her husband's guests."* Harry in this passage is doing precisely what the Princess did when she renounced him: dreaming in harmony with the laws of society—*his* society. If he marries Janet he will inherit Squire Beltham's estates and become a squire himself. He has already become, thanks to one of his father's more successful schemes, a member of Parliament.† What then is

---

* II, 660–61. In the novel, the passage does not sound quite as anticlimactic as it does out of context. Janet, when Harry has his "vision," is engaged to marry a worthless young lord, and a deep feeling of regret and loss accompanies the placid picture Harry paints for himself. Nevertheless, the fact that he does equate this plain, domestic image with his sense of loss indicates the profound change that has occurred in him.

† Meredith, in this connection, is guilty of unintentional irony. Struggling to throw off his father's influence, Harry says (II, 497): "Still I thought: can I never escape from the fascination?—let me only get into Parliament! The idea in me was that Parliament . . . would prompt me to resolute action, out of his tangle of glittering cobwebs." Considering the fact that it is strictly through Roy's efforts that Harry at this point finds himself a candidate (and is later elected), his view of Parliament as a means of escaping his father shows a definite want of feeling, a fact which Meredith gives no sign of having intended or recognized. Harry at this juncture is presumably capable only of noble, generous thought and feeling.

more *reasonable* than that he should dream of a wife whose virtues fit her for the life they would necessarily lead? Janet sits her horse well; she is interested in sports; the tenants will love her. She will be a homemaker; and the home is the center of existence for an English squire. She will entertain Harry's guests and thus make possible the large sociability which will be one of his chief pleasures as well as a political duty. Do we object that all this is very good but that Harry's "vision" of the girl he had come to want for his wife is hardly a romantic one? Just so; Janet is the bride decreed by reason, not romance.

The marriage takes place, and it almost seems as if the last thing said will be that Harry and Janet, like the Princess and her husband, are going to be supremely happy, proving that the reward for choosing the life of reason is not only happiness but happiness ever after. Fortunately, however, some saving instinct prevented Meredith from ending the novel on that distressing note. It told him that Roy had not yet been thoroughly accounted for.* It told him also that intertwined destinies cannot be treated separately. Responding, he brought *Harry Richmond* to a dramatic and symbolically meaningful conclusion, one that enlarges our understanding of Roy's tragedy at the same time that it joins his past to Harry and Janet's future.

As the newly-wedded couple approach Riversley Grange (now theirs, the Squire having died), they come upon a staggering sight. The Grange is going up in flames. Roy's last pitiful effort to produce a grand effect caused the fire, which proceeded from "an explosion of fireworks at one wing and some inexplicable mismanagement at the other." Harry says (II, 684): "The house must have been like a mine, what with the powder, the torches, the devices in paper and muslin, and the extraordinary decorations fitted up to celebrate our return

* When it became evident that the Princess and Harry would never marry, a fact Roy refused to accept until the very end, the poor man was subjected all at once to every other blow that reality had been waiting to deliver. He saw that "Government," which he believed had been bribing him over the years in a frightened attempt to get him to give up his claims, had never taken the slightest interest in him and that the mysterious money had actually come from Harry's Aunt Dorothy, who had always loved Roy, had, in fact, given him up only because she had not wanted to stand in the way of her sister. When Roy learned that he had been squandering the money of the woman whom he respected more than any other, and learned too that his hopes of being recognized as a claimant to the throne were dashed, his mind and spirit shattered. He had been nursed back to partial health just prior to the final scene.

in harmony with my father's fancy." The house ablaze, Roy rushes in, searching for Dorothy Beltham, his lifelong secret benefactor. But she has already been rescued. There is to be only one casualty in this fire, Richmond Roy himself.

The suggestion is apt. Roy's entire life had been a blaze, destined to end in cinders. His destruction of the house he was forbidden to enter during the Squire's lifetime reduces father and grandfather to a sad material parity: neither is to leave Harry anything but memories evoking pity. And Roy's attempt to rescue a woman who is not there is the final irony of a life spent in pursuit of illusion.

Of Roy's end Harry says, simply and starkly, "He was never seen again," and we can read this to mean that his like, too, was never seen again. For Roy represents Meredith's understanding, in the '70's, of romanticism, of an era and a kind of experience. Since Roy is credible we accept Meredith's underlying thesis, namely, that a romantic figure is a tragic figure because he will be destroyed by what is most appealing in him—his readiness to chart his course by the promise of a dream. Meredith is saying also that humanity can no longer afford romanticism. Nevertheless, what is really important about Roy's romantic-tragic death is that it rescues Harry from absurdity. Harry removed from his father's ways is Harry without an interesting future. There is really no suggestion at the end of the novel that his life is going to mean very much.* It will consist of rational compromise, of seeking the sensible way, in all departments of existence. Conflict, passionate error, and tragic ambition have all been eliminated. In the profoundest sense, the adventures of Harry Richmond have ended. Roy's death is not only the terminal point in his own life but it marks the end of the existence of Harry Richmond, a character in a novel. There can be no story after this, only an elaboration of the dubious moral, "Reason saves." That is why Roy's death was so necessary to prevent the conclusion from falling into absurdity. *His* life and tragedy, not Harry's adventures and rescue, constitute a meaningful statement about existence. Harry's career seems to imply that tragedy is

* Contrast with this the strong impression Dickens always gives that the way to become powerful is to grow up. Little boys in Dickens are helpless creatures to be used kindly or otherwise at the discretion of adults. Once a boy reaches young manhood, however, Dickens changes him into his own master, investing him with a force and independence that make credible any destiny that is indicated in the later pages of his story.

not a necessary condition of life. Live in harmony with yourself and your society, Meredith seems to be saying, and you will be safe. If we ask, safe from what? the logical answer would have to be safe from death, which is patent nonsense. Like many others, Meredith may have believed subconsciously that by repudiating romanticism he was banishing death. Only the death of Roy, coming at the very moment of the triumph of reason, reminds us, as it must remind Harry, of the limits of the power of "mind," thus putting the whole idea of rationality into some decent perspective. Roy's death is a triumph in its own right: the triumph of Meredith's artistic instincts over lesser ones.

### QUESTIONS OF THE DAY

Meredith may have been aware of how narrowly *Harry Richmond* escaped becoming a self-discrediting story.[14] He may have felt that Roy and his son ended by dividing between them the two halves of human nature and that the son, at least, could not therefore be fashioned into a rounded character. In his next novel, *Beauchamp's Career* (1875), he brought the two halves together. Nevil Beauchamp, the hero of the title, is romantic and rationalist, a man of passion and a man of ideas, a comic figure and a tragic one, a failure and a success. In the world of *Harry Richmond,* he would be both father and son.

Superficially, *Beauchamp's Career* is less autobiographical than *Harry Richmond*. It contains no elaborate father-fantasies, no disguised portraits of Janet Duff Gordon, no youths of dubious origin. Beneath the surface, however, are elements more intense and immediate—more pertinent to Meredith's maturity—than any that had yet appeared in his work. *Beauchamp's Career* carries in its very structure, as we shall see, a passionate assertion of the artist's right to deal as he chooses with his material. Since the material here consists of the consequences of a collision between an individual and society, the novel represents a conscious effort to make equally tangible the concrete conception, "an individual,"[15] and the abstraction, "society."

*Beauchamp,* often called a "political novel,"[16] fits this definition only in the profoundest sense. Its surface is misleading. Telling the story of Nevil Beauchamp, a young hero of the Crimean War who, despite his Tory background, becomes a follower of a pamphleteering champion of the "people," Dr. Shrapnel, as well as a Radical candidate for Parliament, the novel purports to concern itself with analytic definitions of Whigs, Tories, Liberals, and Radicals during the '60's.[17] Many critics have been beguiled by the brilliance and wit of these disquisitions into thinking that *Beauchamp's Career* is "about" party politics.[18] Still others have been led by the fact that the hero is a Radical candidate for office into believing that the novel is a brief for radicalism.[19] Indeed, Meredith himself was content to let certain people believe this. But the strength of *Beauchamp* derives from no such simple themes. It derives rather from Meredith's conviction that political principles designed to produce a rational society can be used as an excuse for disastrously irrational behavior.

Thus the theme of *Beauchamp* touches upon a certain ambiguity in the nature of political experience. But as we take note of this, an important fact claims our attention: many of Meredith's *Fortnightly* friends regarded any sort of ambiguity as a disreputable halfway house on the road to truth, and in adopting the point of view he did, Meredith set himself in opposition to these friends. It is my belief that he did so consciously and intentionally, and that he was contending against one member in particular of the *Fortnightly* group, John Morley.

Morley for a while had been Meredith's closest friend. He had been the man for whose good opinion Meredith had cared most and for whose bad ideas Meredith had had the least tolerance. But during the years of the writing of *Beauchamp*—1871 to 1874—a serious break, brought about by Morley, separated the two friends. It is my contention that Meredith was so hurt by the manner in which Morley instigated this break that he made *Beauchamp* a repudiation of many things for which Morley stood. The novel is of course much more than an instrument of personal attack, but the shape and function of such an instrument are embedded in its over-all design.

To see just how Morley's behavior influenced *Beauchamp*, we must first review the events leading up to the rupture, and the manner in which Morley brought it about; then we must relate certain aspects of the novel to these considerations. The best way to begin is to take note of a letter Meredith wrote to Morley in December 1870.*

---

* In the collected *Letters*, the letter is misdated December 1871. Whether the editor, who was Meredith's son William, deliberately changed the year in

Reporting an exchange he had had with Frederick Maxse, Meredith said in this letter:

He [Maxse] advises me in these serious times "to take to political writing." I reply that it takes special study. He insists that I have only to give my genuine convictions. . . . I am to be allowed to produce one vol. novels on Questions of the Day. *Morley is quoted as being utterly of his opinion* [italics mine]. I propose to him an Opera libretto to popularize the Democratic movement and bring our chief personages before the eyes of the nobility. O— in love with the Princess L— meditates the enlèvement of the lady that he may breed Radicals from Royalty: . . .

Fred savagely: "Good God! How can you spout buffoonery in times like these!"

Pathetic ballad by M. "In times like these."[20]

Meredith need only give his genuine convictions. How little, apparently, Maxse understood these. How little, too, the more formidable Morley had grasped, for he was quoted as being utterly of [Maxse's] opinion." Despite his bantering, is not Meredith, in repeating these words, reproving Morley for the latter's own lack of comprehension of what a novelist does? That, clearly, is the inference. And Morley must have detected the note of reproach, the superior tone, not only in this letter but in many of Meredith's dealings with him. Three months later, Morley suddenly—and savagely—precipitated the break in friendship.

The method Morley chose for doing this was to send Meredith a lacerating letter. Declaring that "for the past six months" Meredith's manner of speaking had clashed with his "opinions, ideas, and likings," Morley then announced that Meredith's society had become painful to him. And with what could only have been vindictive cruelty prompted by some unspecified resentment, he concluded by saying that Meredith was the only friend in whose company he did not feel he was deriving new strength.

To say that Meredith was wounded would be understatement. He was, in his own words, "shocked and grieved.[21] In his reply, he kept his dignity but made no effort to conceal his pain. After sorrowfully quoting Morley's most destructive attacks, he said:

---

order to obscure the breach between his father and Morley, or whether his error was an inadvertent one, we do not know. But it is important, for an understanding of how Morley relates to *Beauchamp,* that the correct date be stressed. We are indebted to Lionel Stevenson for having discovered and corrected the misleading date.

We will see one another as little as we can for two or three years, and by
and by may come together again naturally. . . . I suffer too much to-day
to desire that any explanation should restore us to our past footing . . .
as I am not a man to send such a letter as you have just written to me,
without deeply weighing every word in it and probable signification of its
burden to the reader . . . so I am not the man to receive one without
determining to abandon a position that has exposed me to be wounded.
What you have permitted yourself to write . . . cuts friendship to the
ground. That I should be the only one of your friends to have done you
harm, is not a nice distinction to reflect on. But I think I have said enough.[22]

Meredith proved prophetic. It was three years before they exchanged a word, and when they did finally come together again, they
did so "naturally." In the interval, common friends undoubtedly tried
to heal the breach, but if they did, their efforts were to no avail. Meredith felt his wound bitterly.* What began their reconciliation was a
business affair: in May 1874, Morley read the manuscript of Meredith's newest novel, submitted to him by Maxse and Frederick Greenwood, and accepted it for publication in *The Fortnightly,* thus making necessary correspondence with Meredith, in the course of which
friendship was restored. The novel that thus acted as peacemaker
was, of course, *Beauchamp's Career.*

These then are the events that make up the known history of how
the breach between Meredith and Morley came about, how long the
estrangement lasted, and how it was ended. What should be clear is
that *Beauchamp's Career* is woven into the fabric of the entire story.
Not only was it written during the years when his wound was relatively fresh and his feelings toward Morley were bitter, but Meredith
seems to have intended the novel, even at that period, for publication
in the periodical which Morley edited. Morley, in short, was very
much in his mind as Meredith wrote *Beauchamp,* and the result can
be seen in the theme and structure of the novel: they show the com-

* I say "bitterly" with considered intention. On January 1, 1873, at a time
when he was fully occupied with *Beauchamp,* Meredith referred, in a letter to
Greenwood, "to a famous case known to us" in which "a formal editorial letter"
had let him know he had given "offence." He continued: "All states of life have
their privileges, and mine is to be behind the scenes of many illustrious and ringing names, and to laugh. How truly wise is so and so! I hear, and I bow. The
aim of the pretenders must be to have this homage of the public, and who would
rob them of it because he happens to be behind them on the stage and peruses a
dead blank instead of the pretty picture confronting the praiser?" (*Letters,* I,
240.)

plicated influence of the blow Morley had dealt him. The fact that Meredith wished to see *Beauchamp* appear in *The Fortnightly* does not belie the significance I attach to the hurt he sustained. As we shall see, it merely emphasizes how complex the influence of that injury was.

If the importance of Morley's crushing letter of 1870 be granted, we must next try to understand a little better why Morley may have sent it, and what Meredith may have guessed concerning these reasons. The answer, I suggest, is that Meredith's ridicule of people who believed a novelist ought to write about "questions of the day" had probably been aimed at Morley more than once, and that Meredith knew how deeply Morley resented this repudiation of his "opinions, ideas, and likings" *concerning art,* the one area in which he no doubt felt unsure of himself vis-à-vis Meredith. Here, then, is the point. Meredith must have known that the question, *what is art?*—smudged over by Morley's fear and resentment—had played a leading role in bringing on the crisis. Now, during the very period when his own hurt and bitterness were deep and persistent, Meredith proceeded to answer the question in the best way possible: by creating a work of art. And, as we shall see, *Beauchamp* is a repudiation both of the faith in reason Morley adhered to and of the related, even more objectionable belief that art can or ought to be made to serve the ends of political propaganda.

However, this rejection of rationalist rigidity and theories of art is but one aspect of *Beauchamp* traceable to the break between Meredith and Morley. A wholly contrary aspect, the lively surface interest in contemporary politics, can also be partially connected with the breach in friendship. Even while telling Morley they had best not see each other for two or three years, Meredith had striven to convince him of his immutable affection. At one point in the letter in which he replied to Morley's attack he said, "When I last came over you I was bright with the happiness of being with you." At another he somewhat pathetically suggested an explanation for Morley's letter: "Possibly a nature I am proud to know never ceases in its growth, is passing now through some delicate stage which finds me importunate; or you feel you have outstripped me, and are tempted to rank me with the vulgar." And when declaring finally that they must sever their ties, he added: "By and by [we] may come together again naturally. And if not, you will know I am glad of the old time, am always proud of you, always heart in heart with you on all the great issues of our life, and in all that concerns your health and fortunes."²³ Taking all these expressions of affection together, and considering they were written while Meredith was virtually still bleeding, we should not be surprised to discover that in the very act designed to punish his friend, he strove anxiously to please him.

Just how desirous Meredith was to let *Beauchamp* be the instrument for assuring Morley of his admiration is made clear by his letters of 1874. After receiving the good news that Morley had accepted *Beauchamp*, Meredith wrote to thank him, thus ending the three years' silence between them. Meredith said: "Greenwood and Maxse told me that the work pleased you. I need scarcely assure you that I look upon your appreciation of my work as a good reward for it. I write for you and men like you." The irony of the last sentence will become apparent as we proceed. It need hardly be said, however, that in the pleased but awkward moment in which Meredith, eager for reconciliation, wrote it, he intended no irony. Meredith's avidity at the moment to please Morley made him even forget some of the facts about his own novel. Proposing to cut *Beauchamp* to a length more suitable to *The Fortnightly*, Meredith added:

It strikes me that the parts to lap will be the letters, a portion of the Visit to Normandy, the heavier of the electioneering passages, introductory paragraphs to chapters, and dialogues passim that may be considered not vital to the central idea. That, which may be stated to be the personal abnegation coming, in spite of errors here and there (and as it were in spite of the man himself), of a noble devotion to politics from the roots up, I think I can retain uninjured—possibly improved by the exclusion of a host of my own reflections.²⁴

Aside from his readiness to eliminate everything "not vital to the central idea," what we notice is that Meredith is at pains to assure Morley that the political part of the novel can easily be retained after he has made the cuts he speaks of. It turned out, however, that most of the political matter (of the kind likely to please Morley and men like him) was actually contained in the portions Meredith had volunteered to excise. More important, some of the material less likely to please Morley but quite vital to the central idea, was also in these. The result was that Meredith had laboriously and at length to rewrite *Beauchamp* for *The Fortnightly*.

In a subsequent letter, the first in which an affectionate close replaced a formal one, Meredith said, "I fancy the time is getting favorable for the political views and sayings that come incidentally throughout the story. All my excuses for troubling you, and I am your loving George Meredith."[25] Considered out of context, these words are innocuous enough. At the moment of writing them, Meredith was probably quite sincere about his "fancy"; he was probably unaware that a continuing need to elicit Morley's approval was behind what he had said. Nevertheless, we must conclude that the need existed and was manifesting itself in the words quoted. The reason we must so conclude is that the ending of *Beauchamp,* as we shall see, cancels all the "political views and sayings that come up incidentally." That Meredith, in spite of this, could intimate that these views and sayings might be potent with readers indicates that his "fancy" was preoccupied at the moment not with *Beauchamp* but with the man to whom he was writing the letter.

What he was doing, in effect, was calling Morley's attention to the surface of the novel. Had he been in better communion with himself when writing this letter, and the one preceding it, he would have been governed by the knowledge that he had not designed the heart of *Beauchamp* to please "a man like Morley." As for Morley himself, if he was too responsive to Meredith's appeals for approbation, he could only have missed the real meaning of *Beauchamp.*

Indeed, he would have had to miss an early warning of how the author was going to treat his subject. Near the outset of the work, Meredith said:

Following the counsel of a sage and seer, I must try to paint for you what is, not that which I imagine. This day, this hour, this life, and even politics, the centre and throbbing heart of it (enough, when unburlesqued, to blow the down off the gossamer-stump of fiction at a single breath, I have heard tell), must be treated of: men, and the ideas of men, which are—it is policy to be emphatic upon truisms—are actually the motives of men in a greater degree than their appetites: these are my theme; and may it be my fortune to keep them at blood heat, and myself calm as a statue of Memnon in prostrate Egypt!*

---

* Who was "the sage and seer"? Carlyle? Years earlier he had urged Meredith to write history rather than fiction. But *this* sage and seer had urged Meredith to write about immediate politics, not history. Was the reference, then, to Maxse? Perhaps, but to call this effusive, muddled activist "a sage and seer" would be to indulge in sarcasm, hardly something Meredith was wont to do in connection with "his beloved Maxse." Was it Morley who was alluded to? The

Two statements in this passage repudiate the interference of naïve rationalists ill-equipped to discuss literature: "I must try to paint for you what is, not that which I imagine" and "[my theme is] the ideas of men, which . . . are actually the motives of men in a greater degree than their appetites." Meredith is of course going to paint what he "imagines," because in a work of art the only way to get at what "is" is through the imagination. It is equally certain, though it will require a close reading to make this apparent, that the theme of *Beauchamp* is not at all "the ideas of men" but their passions—their "appetites," if Meredith meant this word to signify the same thing. Men and their ideas are shown, but the consequences of holding a particular set of ideas rather than any other are not. What Meredith does disclose are the consequences of acting out of passionate desire, envy, pride, or wrath.

All of Nevil Beauchamp's early actions are carried out passionately. When we first meet him, he is a very young midshipman attempting to challenge the colonels of the French Imperial Guard to a duel because French newspapers have printed attacks upon England. In the Crimean War, which soon follows, he distinguishes himself for gallantry and bravery far beyond the call of duty. In Venice, after the war, he falls in love with Renée de Croisnel, finds that she is already engaged to an aging marquis, and tries to move mountains to win her or at least prevent a marriage he considers execrable. He returns to England and, two hours after landing, meets Dr. Shrapnel, the Radical pamphleteer. He immediately becomes Dr. Shrapnel's avid disciple and, almost as quickly, the Radical candidate for Bevisham. These are the first key events in *Beauchamp's Career*; all involve commitments or decisions made on the impulse of the moment.

The second phase of Nevil's life is made up of the consequences

---

passage was undoubtedly written sometime during the year following receipt of the injurious letter. Morley, before the break, could have lectured Meredith for the flippant way in which he had burlesqued and reported Maxse's urging that he write about questions of the day (an urging with which Morley utterly agreed, we must remember). The tone of the passage is ironic, almost bitter and sneering. "It is policy to be emphatic upon truisms." Had Meredith, by insisting to Morley that something besides "ideas" motivates men, exposed himself to being irritably accused of not having the proper respect for the power of ideas? The hypothesis that the "sage and seer" was Morley must remain as conjectural as any other. But in the realm of conjecture it has an unmistakable attraction.

of these early impulsive commitments. He loses the election largely
because, having pledged himself to Renée for life, he obeys a cryptic
summons from her to rush to France at the height of the campaign.
He loses Cecilia Halkett, the wealthy heiress he wants next to marry,
because Renée later flees her desperate life in France and goes to give
herself to him. Though Nevil, faced with this ultimate test of his
loyalty, finds he cannot plunge himself into the consequences of running off with another man's wife—this is the turning point of the novel
—the scandal created by Renée's visit is enough to set in motion a
train of events leading to the engagement of Cecilia to Blackburn
Tuckham, an estimable young Tory.[26] The engagement is hurried
on by Cecilia's father, Colonel Halkett, as much to prevent his
daughter's marriage to Nevil as for any other reason.

The consequences of Nevil's embrace of Dr. Shrapnel's radicalism
also reinforce the theory that the actual theme of the novel is the
power of irrationality and passion to determine human destiny. It is
not so much Nevil's "ideas" that influence these consequences—the
falling out with his Uncle Everard Romfrey being the major one—as
it is his impetuosity and intensity. In themselves, Nevil's ideas amuse
rather than anger those who are close to him.[27]

Meredith's theme is also made manifest by the actions and destinies of the other characters. The central event of the second half of
the novel—the horsewhipping of Dr. Shrapnel by Everard Romfrey—
is directly traceable to a moment of impulsive jealousy on the part of
Rosamund Culling (Everard's confidential housekeeper and a woman
whose maternal love for Nevil is one of the more finely realized things
in the novel). Disturbed and made envious by Dr. Shrapnel's influence over Nevil, she permits Everard to imagine that Dr. Shrapnel has
insulted her. The fierce old lord, further incited by the scheming
Cecil Baskelett (Nevil's cousin and a rival for their uncle's interest),
then commits the violent act which leads to the first serious rupture
between him and Nevil. Everard's deed, too, is the result of the heat
of the moment. As he admits later, he should have stopped to look
into Cecil's story before he set off, horsewhip in hand, to call on
Dr. Shrapnel.

One more irrational deed, this one Nevil's, brings the novel to its
full complication. Against all advice, particularly against the advice
of Jenny Denham, Dr. Shrapnel's pretty, clear-eyed, level-headed
ward, Nevil insists on visiting a workman, dying of fever, who had

supported him during the election and had lost his job as a result. Catching the fever, Nevil lies for a long time at the edge of death. And as in *Richard Feverel* and *Harry Richmond,* Meredith makes the crisis of sickness the culminating point for all the errors of the past.

However, the pattern of *Beauchamp* does not duplicate that of *Feverel* or of *Harry Richmond.* Nevil, like Richard and Harry, recovers, but before he does Meredith gives the other characters an opportunity to free themselves from their earlier, passion-centered follies. In a sense they are allowed to purify themselves while the hero they have sinned against waits to be reborn. Under the persistent urging of Rosamund, whom he has married and who is pregnant (though she loves Nevil better than her unborn child), Lord Romfrey apologizes to Dr. Shrapnel.* When Nevil recovers and hears of this, his love for his uncle is again released. Renée, who comes once more to England, acting on the message that Nevil is near death, arrives in time to find him out of danger. But she has come this time to give him up, to inform us of a new selflessness she has achieved and of the resource she has found in her religion. As for Cecilia Halkett, she cannot move until Nevil, the man she really loves, is past the crisis. When he is, however, she unhesitatingly proceeds with her interrupted plan to marry Blackburn Tuckham. Indeed, she does this so effortlessly that we are almost persuaded that her passion for Nevil was but another instance of folly.[28]

The significance of these crisis and post-crisis developments cannot be overestimated. Their origin lies in the exact opposite of the irrationality and passion that caused all the difficulty in the first place. Their origin, in short, lies in "reason." And what happens to the secondary characters is but preparation for the most important event of all. Emerging from his fever, Nevil too embraces reason as the true faith.

The proof he has done so is that he proposes marriage to Jenny

---

* Rosamund's child, it should be added, is destined to die almost at birth. J. B. Priestley (p. 159) sees the whole episode concerning Everard, Rosamund, Nevil, and Dr. Shrapnel as an example of ironic reversal: "Romfrey determines to make Rosamund his wife and thus neatly revenge himself on Nevil. But just because of his coming heir, he is prepared to make his peace with Nevil and to apologize to Dr. Shrapnel. The child, when it comes, lives for one hour. Such ironic reversals are frequent in Meredith." In the language I am using, Priestley's "ironic reversals" are the consequences of deeds done at the promptings of ego, passion, or any desire that ignores "reason."

Denham. It might be argued that this move, too, is made impetuously, but such is not really the case. Nevil has known Jenny for many months. Unique among those close to Nevil, she always stressed moderation and spoke in praise of that marvelous faculty "reason," which everyone else, her guardian included, had often neglected.[29] It was she who carried the main burden of nursing Nevil through his sickness. And most important of all, Jenny, the third woman in Nevil's life, is more suited to a domestic existence than was either Renée or Cecilia; more suited, certainly, to be the wife of a Radical politician. Clearly, she is to Nevil what Janet Ilchester was to Harry Richmond, and Nevil's sudden proposal is better described as an inspiration of reason than as an impulsive act.

There is only one difficulty. Jenny, unlike Janet Ilchester, has not been harboring a secret passion. In fact, she is really not in love with Nevil at all. This certainly seems an insurmountable obstacle. But if we have been following the workings of Meredith's mind in these novels of the '70's, we will recognize that the difficulty has been created only by our romantic prejudice. Not only like Harry and Janet, but like the Princess Ottilia and her husband, like Blackburn Tuckham and Cecilia, Nevil and Jenny need but take the first mechanical step: reason's marvelous alchemy will do the rest, conferring the blessings which it alone has the power to bestow. And if there are any doubts that the proposed marriage of Nevil and Jenny will be so sanctified, Meredith takes care to dispel them. Jenny's beloved guardian, Dr. Shrapnel, desires more than anything else in the world to see the two united, and to please so good-natured and decent a soul is, in Meredith's scheme, to please reason. Also, Nevil, despite all his faults, is a hero and a man of noble virtues: it is *reasonable* to suppose he will make a good husband. Jenny marries him.

In the short space remaining in the novel, Meredith works hard to drive the moral to high and clear ground, though not, as we shall see in a moment, to give it ascendancy over the real theme of the story. The marriage of Nevil and Jenny, conceived rationally rather than romantically, is the begining of genuine happiness for them.* The

* The marriage begins with a compromise on Nevil's part, a church wedding. Meredith, it is my contention, means this as an indication that Beauchamp has learned to behave rationally, not to fight society where no evil (in Meredith's and Jenny's view) exists. The episode, of course, also has its comic overtones. Jack Lindsay, who takes note of the compromise (p. 220), does so while complaining that Nevil is not consistently "radical."

love of husband and wife grows after the wedding, thus demon-
strating a significant reversal of the romantic order. A son is born to
them. People remark that Jenny is a perfect wife, and that Nevil is
indeed a lucky fellow.

So far, there is a discernible parallel with *Harry Richmond*. But
Meredith had become a better novelist in the interval since he wrote
that work. He knew that in granting Nevil and Jenny the happiness
promised to Harry and Janet he had merely established more vividly
the moral of his earlier novel. But even in *Harry Richmond* he had
sensed the inadequacy of an ending which would have swept away
the wreckage and record of passional existence without acknowledging its permanent influence. He knew therefore how much less
adequate a simple affirmation that "Reason saves" would have been
as a conclusion to *Beauchamp's Career*, the real theme of which all
along had been that an underlying irrationality marks people fiercely
dedicated to "ideas," "common sense," and other idols of the mind.

Thus he made Nevil, who is both the father and son of *Harry
Richmond*, remain true to his demon, that fundamental part of his
character which Harry, similarly constituted, could exorcise by repudiating his father's leadership. He made the fate suffered by Richmond Roy, who leaves Harry free to browse for the rest of his life on
the plains of calm rationalism, the fate suffered here by the hero himself. Rowing in the harbor of Bevisham one day, overtired and in no
condition for additional strenuous effort, Nevil leaps into the water to
save two small boys whose boat has capsized. He does rescue one,
but when he dives in again for the second, he drowns.

And here, in a manner that could hardly have pleased Maxse, Morley, or any other member of "the party of humanity," Meredith confronts the confident Radical theory of progress with a question: how
measure the worth of an individual? As Lord Romfrey and Dr. Shrapnel stare at the little boy Nevil has saved, a boy whom Meredith un-
charitably but pointedly describes as an "insignificant bit of mudbank
life," they are united for the first time in a single thought: "This is
what we have in exchange for Beauchamp!" It is a savage thought,
and we can understand how it startled the humanitarians, the liberals,
all who believed they had been reading a novel in which radicalism,
as much as Nevil Beauchamp, was being held up for praise.

Meredith, in answer to protests, insisted that the logic of the novel, particularly of Beauchamp's characterization, required the hero's death.[30] As to why the boy saved should have had visited upon him such gratuitous contempt, Meredith gave no hint. But the answer should now be clear. The contempt for this representative of the "people"—actually for the people's future—is a direct reproach to all those, particularly Maxse and most particularly Morley, who demand that a novelist write about "questions of the day" and about "what is, not what he imagines." The irrational impulsiveness which is at once the source of Nevil's political idealism and the cause of his death is what Meredith wished to write about, and he merely used the questions of the day to give body to his theme. The poor boy is a surrogate. Meredith's contempt for this waif is his veiled contempt for those who would have him write otherwise. It should be added that Meredith's gesture of scorn is not, in context, a narrow, vindictive impulse, marring the structure of the novel. It fits perfectly, not only throwing into sharp relief the question hitherto noted—how value the worth of an individual?—but concluding the characterization of Dr. Shrapnel with a startling yet credible revelation.

One significant fact calls attention to itself as we observe that Meredith insists upon the autonomy of the artist: Nevil Beauchamp, in contrast, will admit no such freedom. In a revealing passage Nevil's position is made abundantly clear as he reflects on Cecilia Halkett and her magnificent yacht (I, 154–56):

As the yacht, so the mistress: things of wealth, owing their graces to wealth . . . splendid achievements of art both! . . .

Say that they were precious examples of an accomplished civilization; and perhaps they did offer a visible ideal of grace for the rough world to aim at. They might in the abstract address a bit of a monition [sic] to the uncultivated, and encourage the soul to strive toward perfection in beauty: and there is no contesting the value of beauty when the soul is taken into account. But were they not in too great a profusion in proportion to their utility? That was the question for Nevil Beauchamp. . . . And further, whether it was good for the country, the race, the species, that they should be so distinctly removed from the thousands who fought the grand, and the grisly, old battle with nature for the bread of life. . . .

He questioned his justification . . . for gratifying tastes in an ill-regulated world of wrong-doing, suffering, sin, and bounties unrighteously dispensed.

This passage strongly invites comparison with James's *The Prin-*

*cess Casamassima* (1886). To Hyacinth Robinson, the idea that beautiful objects, or accomplished women, could ever exist "in too great a profusion in proportion to their utility" would be absurd. He would deny that real beauty or grace can ever be other than rare. Nevil's assumption that the justification of art is social utility (though more in the sense of Ruskin's understanding of utility than of Mill's or Morley's)* would have been rejected out of hand by Hyacinth. Beauty, to Hyacinth, seemed tragically and inevitably dependent upon privilege and wealth; its moral strength lay not in its power to make all of society happy but in its visible power to redeem in part the otherwise meaningless history of human suffering.

But the most important difference between Nevil and Hyacinth lies in the consequences which follow when they think of "gratifying tastes in an ill-regulated world." For Hyacinth, this is not only one of the causes of his intolerable situation but a source of real guilt. Finding the problem insoluble, he commits suicide, thus affirming his loyalty to privileged beauty and at the same time acknowledging that this *is* an ill-regulated world. For Nevil, the problem proves ephemeral and, like the yacht, disappears over the horizon in a matter of hours. What is, in *The Princess Casamassima,* a central issue is, in *Beauchamp,* only an illustrative detail of the conflict between political and private life. Here the fundamental difference between James's novel and Meredith's becomes evident. In the first, political life requires dedication to destructive "action" for the sake of humanity while private life requires dissociation from mass values and concerns in order to experience the best that human existence has to offer. For Meredith, the "best" is not really very important in either the public or the private life. What matters in both is "people," and the conflict between the two lies in the different kinds of human relations they involve. Political life requires impersonality in one's dealings with other people, whereas "private" life implies the irra-

---

* This is not the first indication that Nevil has a certain enthusiasm for Ruskin. Early in the novel, soon after he had arrived in Venice and met Renée, they discussed *The Stones of Venice.* Renée doubted that the descendants of the people who produced the great architecture of the Middle Ages could have declined as sharply, in the Renaissance, as Ruskin would have it. Besides, she liked the work of the later period. Nevil tried hard to defend Ruskin against all her arguments.

tional passions, desires, "appetites" aroused by these dealings. Private life does not involve tastes, values, ideas that defy the expectations of society, as it does in James's story. These sensibilities are simply nonexistent in Meredith's world, and nothing makes the difference between James and Meredith clearer than the fact that for James "private" experience means heightened awareness while for Meredith it means the immoral indulgence of self in irrational "appetite."

Meredith's conception of "appetite" is connected with the single idea which can be said to operate as a human motive in the novel. This idea is that egoism has ever been the downfall of the class in power. Curiously, however, the better spokesmen on all sides in *Beauchamp* see egoism both as the outstanding fault of the opposition parties and as a danger besetting their own. Thus, the only "idea" in the novel that goes deeper than hortatory preaching is shared all around, and it provides no more opportunity for a dramatic conflict of thought than do the pseudo-ideas, "the political views and sayings."

The theme of egoism is a light glaze over *Beauchamp*'s developed subject, which is the power of the irrational to usurp control of lives presumably dominated by reason. Perception of egoism is at the heart of every effective observation, in the novel, to which Meredith himself would subscribe. Dr. Shrapnel, for example, is at his very best when he takes up the subject (II, 327–28):

Trace the course of Ego . . . . : first the king who conquers and can govern. In his egoism he dubs him holy; his family is of a selected blood; he makes the crown hereditary—Ego. Son by son the shame of egoism increases; valour abates; hereditary Crown, no hereditary qualities. The Barons rise. They in turn hold sway, and for their order—Ego. The traders overturn them; each class rides the classes under it can. . . . Now comes on the workman's era. Numbers win in the end: proof of small wisdom in the world. Anyhow . . . with numbers ego is inter-dependent and dispersed; it is universalized. Yet these may require correctives. If so, they will have it in a series of despots and revolutions that toss, mix, and bind the classes together: despots, revolutions; *panting alternations of the quickened heart of humanity.*

Elsewhere, Dr. Shrapnel not only elaborates his conception of egoism but makes a significant distinction between nature and society. Not surprisingly, it turns out to be Meredith's distinction between private and public experience (II, 481):

The world and nature, which are opposed in relation to our vital interests, each agrees to demand of us a perfect victory, on pain otherwise of proving it a stage performance; and the victory over the world, as over nature, is over self: and this victory lies in yielding perpetual service to the world, and none to nature: for the world has to be wrought out, nature to be subdued.

To these essentially disinterested observations we may add Nevil's comment on the egoism of the rich (II, 472): "The rich love the nation through their possessions . . . their hearts are eaten up by property."

In the other camp, the intellectual Tory, Seymour Austin, indicates a form of egoism afflicting his own party (I, 300): "The increasing wealth of the country is largely recruiting our ranks; and we shall be tempted to mistake numbers for strength, and perhaps again be reading Conservatism for a special thing of our own—a fortification. That would be a party sin." Further on, Austin describes Dr. Shrapnel in a manner that clearly reveals this dedicated Radical's egoism (II, 415–16):

He is the earnest man, and flies at politics as uneasy young brains fly to literature, fancying they can write because they can write with a pen. He perceives a bad adjustment of things: which is correct. He is honest, and takes his honesty for a virtue: and that entitles him to believe in himself: and that belief causes him to see in all opposition to him the wrong he has perceived in existing circumstances: and so in a dream of power he invokes the people: and as they do not stir, he takes to prophecy.

Blackburn Tuckham, the Tory who eventually marries Cecilia Halkett, points to another aspect of the Radicals' egoism, their readiness to use others for their own moral convenience (II, 549): "These men of their so-called progress are like the majority of religious minds: they can't believe without seeing and touching. . . . They don't believe in the abstract at all, but they go to work blindly by agitating . . . to get together a mass they can believe in." Stukely Culbrett, another of the intelligent Tories, criticizes the Radicals for egoistically appropriating the word "people," as if all nonmembers of the lower classes do not deserve to be designated by the term (II, 399–400). And Cecilia perceives the form of egoism of which she herself is guilty. She reflects (II, 547), "The aim of an ideal life closely approximates, or easily inclines, to self-worship."

Although the even distribution of these observations prevents their playing any part in the dramatic conflicts of the novel, taken together they weigh heavily among what may be called the elements of *Beauchamp's Career*. Then, too, this whole discussion of egoism invites an effort to place it in a tradition. Dr. Shrapnel's fear that the people, once they are in power, might fail to end the history of egoism was anticipated by Felix Holt, who said that "three-fourths of men see nothing in elections but self-interest, and nothing in self-interest but some form of greed."[31] A debate over "selfish" vs. "altruistic" self-interest, which stemmed from the problems raised by the Utilitarians, went on in all quarters during the Victorian period. *The Fortnightly* often carried contributions to this debate. Mark Pattison, for example, wrote: "[Civilization] implies that the sympathetic and affective nature is gaining ground in controlling the public conduct of nations and men, at the expense of the egotistic and selfish propensities. The solidarity of all the nations can only be founded on benevolence; interest is ever a dissociating and disorganising force."[32] George C. Broderick, discussing the question "What Are Liberal Principles?" proposed as one tenet "the deliberate preference of national interests over all minor interests, whether of classes, of sects, of professions, or of individuals."[33] Like the members of the *Fortnightly* group, Matthew Arnold confronted the problems posed by Mill and his followers. Starting boldly with a premise that Mill, in *Utilitarianism*, had labored cautiously to prove—the premise that the "self" has different qualitative potentials—Arnold went on to assert that the state (a necessary entity) will best be served by each class attempting to realize its "best self," instead of pushing the interests of its "ordinary self."[34] This view has the distinction of recognizing that the ego in some of its aspects ought to be affirmed, instead of being required to masquerade as a form of selflessness. It is a reason, perhaps, why Arnold speaks so directly to our own era. Yet Meredith's understanding of egoism, if less fashionable today than Arnold's, was not only "correct" during the '70's but contributed to the writing of his best works.

*Beauchamp's Career* is not the novel that gained most from Meredith's conception of egoism. This conception was rooted in a rationalist assumption—that human reason can choose between greed and altruism. When Dr. Shrapnel warns that the people, once in power, will have to choose altruism, he is implying they will have the ability to do so. Yet no such choice was made central to the novel. There was no conflict in *Beauchamp* between altruistic rationality (in the guise of a particular set of political ideas) and man's egoistic passions and appetites. Indeed, Meredith was never to write a novel in which this particular clash occurred. Instead, with *Beauchamp* behind him, he gave up the attempt to deal concretely with political life[35] and turned back to what in his novels had always been the central social theme: egoism and sex. And it was when he once again devoted himself to this theme that he achieved his most brilliant success in rendering into art his understanding of rationality.

Between the writing of *Harry Richmond* and *Beauchamp*, Meredith had learned that to write tragic novels was to acknowledge fully the power of the irrational. But learning this merely posed a dilemma. After all had been said and done, after he had revolted against the advice that he write about questions of the day, he felt the need to reassert the view of man and society which had led in the first place to his self-identification with "the party of humanity." Though his instincts as an artist cautioned him when he wrote, he had remained in love with the image of rational man. Aware that the irrational and the tragic could not be banished by fiat, he nevertheless knew that he could not continue to write about them without sacrificing his native subject and point of view. Good as *Beauchamp* was, it could not say what he wanted most to say. He did not, like George Eliot, write novels in order to share with readers a tragic vision of life. He wrote, before all other reasons, in order to show that ethical behavior is rational behavior. Clearly, however, it was difficult for him to translate this idea into narrative without becoming a superficial moralizer, and he had therefore to engage in a continuous search for the form which would allow him to say what he wished but would rigidly exclude enfeebling lapses. Wishing to attack irrationality and still create art, he had, in short, to be an experimenter.[36] As a consequence, his whole career points to the two works he produced during the last three years of the '70's: *The Essay on Comedy* (1877)[37] and *The Egoist* (1879).[38]

### THE MIND OF SOCIETY

The *Essay* tells us that man irrational, however inevitable he may seem when found in a tragedy, is not to be tolerated by society. He would subvert society if it took him at his own evaluation. Therefore, through its agent the comic spirit, society protects itself by subverting his self-image. And the artist who senses this will, if he has society's welfare at heart, become a devotee of the comic spirit, ridiculing rather than giving comfort to the would-be subversive.

The *Essay* also tells us, better than anything else Meredith wrote, how he looked at the world and how, as an artist, he viewed his own role in it. For these reasons, the *Essay* contains the clearest expression of his conception of society that he was ever to put into expository prose. Gone are the contradictions and the experimental identifications with points of view uncongenial and unconvincing to him. In their place are a clarity and steadiness of vision hitherto unattained.

It is important to note how Meredith achieved this clarification and firmness. He did so by blotting out of his field of attention those political and social class conflicts that he had never been able to manage for artistic purposes and therefore had never, as an artist, really believed in. This is not to say that Meredith lost awareness of class distinctions. On the contrary, his perceptions of them were never more acute. What happened was that he lost interest in the struggle for power *between* classes.

He announces unabashedly that his own interest as a comic artist is largely in the middle class (p. 13): "In all countries, the middle class presents the public which, fighting the world, and with a good footing in the fight, knows the world best. It may be the most selfish, but that is a question leading us into sophistries. Cultivated men and women, who do not skim the cream of life, and are attached to the duties, yet escape the harsher blows, make acute and balanced observers." Further on he says (p. 48) that those who perceive the comic, form the "unchallengeable upper class." If we put these two assertions together, we realize that Meredith is saying that the middle class best supplies the intelligent and perceptive individuals who form the true aristocracy. Moreover, we recognize that in thus designating the "unchallengeable upper class," he is pointing the way toward the discipline which is a mark of our own time and which is best described as cultural history. Though the modern cultural historian would attempt to use economic and political history, rather than ignore them as Meredith does, the understanding of the power of an artistic idea to transform or delineate a social class is an insight Meredith shares with us.

Present, too, in the *Essay*, are an emphasis upon the precariousness of civilization and a theory about what enables it to survive. Meredith tells us (p. 16) that civilization has been wrested from brutishness, with humanity engaged in a continuous struggle to keep its prize. Insofar as he has confidence that civilization will not slip back into barbarism, that confidence is grounded in his faith in "common sense." For Meredith, the term seemed to stand for the collective intelligence of society, which he felt resided in a relatively large body of men and women whom he designated as "cultivated" and who, we can again notice, represented the best of the middle class. The term "common sense" actually connotes a mystique of reason, a belief that the "mind" of society, so reminiscent of Rousseau's "general will," defends and promotes mankind's progress. We recognize in all this the wider nineteenth-century faith in science and reason, and indeed, the legacy of the Enlightenment. Meredith's peculiar contribution, however, lies in the next step he took: he created an ally of "common sense"—the comic spirit—and described it as the active opponent of those forces (irrationality being the chief) that would destroy society.[39]

At least one twentieth-century critic has bitterly condemned the *Essay* as an apology for the status quo.[40] And George Bernard Shaw, while assenting to the view that comedy explodes pretensions and hypocrisy, turned Meredith's analysis of comedy and common sense inside out. He said it was true that English society, as Meredith had observed, was founded on "common sense," but added that common sense to an Englishman meant praise of money and social standing. The last thing an Englishman's common sense would allow, said Shaw, would be the free play of the comic spirit, bound as it is to attack the very foundations of British society.[41]

Both criticisms contain some truth, but both miss the essential point of what Meredith was doing.* He was making common sense a function of cultivation, and, it must be repeated, making the middle

---

* As for Shaw's criticism, perhaps it would be just as well to assume that Shaw knew that he and Meredith were not really talking about the same thing. In all likelihood, he was only having his joke.

class the repository of both. What Meredith really meant by "common sense" was critical intelligence,[42] a virtue which humanistic moralists have always praised. And in looking to the middle class, he was merely responding to the fact that in the England of the 1870's it was the most energetic, the most powerful, and the most educable. He therefore expected it to produce the greater number of individuals possessing critical intelligence. Considering how completely this class has dominated the intellectual life of England in the twentieth century, supplying among others Meredith's keenest critics (quickest to detect his snobbery, sentimentalism, self-consciousness, and other middle-class vices), there hardly seems anything exceptionable in his having taken note of the prominent position in intellectual affairs it had already achieved in his own day. To put the matter briefly, it was the cultivated mind, not the class producing it, which Meredith equated with "society" and believed to be a stable and enduring human entity.

Not only does Meredith's conception of comedy not imply approval of the status quo, but there is a sense, albeit a problematic one, in which it seems to champion change and progress. E. A. Mooney has said that comedy for Meredith is an instrument of mind, and mind in the modern world is nature's chief instrument for furthering evolution. Comedy thus becomes an instrument of nature, employed to further nature's evolutionary purpose, which is presumably to make civilized man more civilized.[43] The note of necessitarianism that creeps into this argument does not help us to remember Meredith's real insight into the precariousness of all civilization, though it is true Meredith edged on the contradiction himself: he spoke of the comic spirit as an agent who brings man back to his "natural" self and who points him toward the ideal of a rational society, thus implying that the corrective process is also a progressive and teleological one.[44] Nevertheless, the drift of Meredith's reasoning is unmistakable. Not only is he a firm believer in free will and indeterminacy, but he minimizes discussion of the future, even saying of the comic spirit that "men's future on earth does not attract it; their honesty and shapeliness in the present does" (pp. 46–47). If we ask, then, what might have caused Mooney to see something evolutionary in the comic spirit, the answer, I suggest, is that he erroneously equated "improvement" with "evolution," and also that he may have been influenced by the fact that elsewhere, particularly in later works, Meredith does seem more responsive to evolutionary theory. In the *Essay*, however, and, as we shall see, in *The Egoist*, he is speaking not of the perfectibility of the human race but of the capacity of the individual to seek in the present what Matthew Arnold called "the best self."[45] In this sense, then, the comic spirit is an instrument of "progress," but the philosophy it represents could more readily be called existential than evolutionary.

SUBVERSION AND COMEDY

The obvious connection between the *Essay* and *The Egoist* has been cited often. The novel, appearing two years after Meredith had delivered his talk on comedy, "enabled the author to develop action out of motive, to probe subtleties of character, and to reveal the complex ironies in the interplay of personalities. His inquiry into the art of comedy as crystallized in his lecture, was applied to every scene in the book."[46] But there are two more connections, usually neglected, that deserve not only to be mentioned but to be emphasized. First, the narrative is a transformation into art of the view of society contained in the *Essay*. Second, it is the work in which Meredith, for the first time in his career, followed his own injunction, laid down in the *Essay*, that a writer—particularly a comic writer—should acknowledge his debt to the past. It is these two aspects, more than any others, that make the novel a brilliant fulfillment of the possibilities sketched in the *Essay*. *The Egoist* is the best of Meredith's novels, and the manner in which it converts the ideas of the *Essay* to its own uses is one of the main reasons for its unequaled success.

The principal character in *The Egoist* is the kind of man discussed in the *Essay*, the sort whom society in self-defense must subvert. His name is Sir Willoughby Patterne, and his special crime is that he has asked his betrothed, Clara Middleton, to substitute him for society as the outermost limit of her universe. Even before her troubles deepen, Clara opposes Willoughby on this score. She insists (I, 74–75) that people should be at home in the "world," i.e., society, and that there are two qualities, "generosity" and "heroism," which can make the world of men as beautiful as the world of nature. The desire of Sir Willoughby, then, is irrational, immoral, and repugnant: irrational, because what he asks, contrary to any "reasonable" mode of existence, would prove untenable; immoral, because Clara, were see C. Stephenson.

she to attempt to comply, would be injured before the inevitable failure of the arrangement occurred; repugnant, because a man's wish to have a woman take him for her sun and moon vilifies him in his capacity of lover. Thus, *The Egoist,* in expressing the Victorian contention that egoism is bad, plunges into the modern world and centers its argument on sex. Though the twentieth century, particularly as represented by D. H. Lawrence, might not agree with Meredith's theory that egoism is erotically loathsome, it recognizes that in this novel, at least, an egoist is convincingly portrayed as a sexually repulsive figure.[47]

The conception of Sir Willoughby and of Clara reveals how Meredith, in acknowledging his debt to the past (albeit with too much ambition aforethought), actually strengthened his hold upon the future. For it discloses that *The Egoist* is an attempt to improve upon Molière, who Meredith had said was perfect.[48] In fact he failed to improve upon him and succeeded instead in doing something much better: writing an original novel which, unlike anything he had written before, uses tradition in the service of originality. Sir Willoughby is Alceste,[49] but he is also the modern hero as spiritual exile, though seen through a comic glass. Clara Middleton is Célimène, but she is also the modern heroine who dares to feel sexually averse to a man of authentically "good character."

*The Egoist* is, moreover, the novel in which Meredith solved the problem of form and idea he had taken up and only partially solved in *Harry Richmond* and *Beauchamp's Career.* The defects of *Harry Richmond* are two. Although assuring us he was writing a novel of adventure, Meredith was incapable of creating movement. The result was the static jumbling of detail that caused more than one critic to cry chaos. The second defect was in the conclusion—notwithstanding its many merits. While credible, it depended too much upon the tragic death of Roy to give the nontragic destiny of Harry and Janet any depth. If the presence of irrationality in the neighborhood is necessary to touch the lives of two rationalists with emotion, the last word about the virtue inherent in rationalism and missing from irrationalism has not been said. In *Beauchamp,* Meredith moved forward. He gave up the attempt to create continuous, flowing narrative and frankly set about creating scenes. The result was the elimination of much of the debris and clutter that impeded the legitimate —that is, the psychological—movement of *Harry Richmond.* Moreover, Meredith put the irrationality, in the form of passion, into the rationalist hero himself; and if he thus lost the particular kind of pity and compassion he had won for Roy, he not only achieved the success of making his central character bear the central theme but he gave to Nevil's career a darker and more universal meaning.

Still, Meredith had not yet done what he wanted to do. He wanted to praise "mind." Ironically, the strength of *Beauchamp's Career* is a result partially of the fact that Meredith had temporarily lost interest in doing this. Returning now to the attempt, he faced the same problem all over again. He was too honest an artist to write a realistic novel in which mind would completely dominate the passional life. Realism in a novel seemed to call for the destructive triumph of the passions over reason. To write a realistic novel and force it to an opposite conclusion would be to sacrifice inwardness of characterization and run to heavy moralizing. Again, only the death of Roy prevents *Harry Richmond* from becoming a didactic tale. Yet Meredith wanted to be didactic and a true artist, all at once. In attempting to solve this contradiction he discovered, as the idea for *The Egoist* grew definite, the true form for his purpose—a comedy in narrative, a novel which would approximate the structure of a play.[50]

How, we may ask, does this narrative-dramatic structure relate to Meredith's preoccupation with "reason"? The answer is twofold. First and most simply, this structure is in itself a triumph of "mind." Second, its dramatic attributes enabled Meredith to create distance between himself and the reader, on the one hand, and the central character, Sir Willoughby, on the other. This distance in turn enabled him to demonstrate intellectually—i.e., comically as well as dramatically—that Willoughby's irrationalities are unacceptable. And what is most important, it enabled Meredith to do so without becoming pedantic, because the comic figure, whose cries of pain cannot be heard across the gap, seems deserving of whatever ridicule is heaped upon him. Such a figure, Meredith convinces us, ought to try to be more rational. Having prevented us from scrutinizing Sir Willoughby too closely, Meredith can deny with impunity that there is anything in that character's make-up or experience lending support to a thesis long entertained by writers of tragedy: that it is man's fate to be irrational.

Yet only insofar as *The Egoist* concerns Sir Willoughby does it
need to be (or is it) written from an external viewpoint. The effectiveness of Meredith's dramatic-narrative form becomes evident when
we realize that both the external and internal points of view are
essential to this story and are developed as it proceeds. The internal,
or analytic, one is necessary for the characterization of Clara Middleton, the unhappy girl betrothed to Sir Willoughby. The process
through which she comes to accept the full force of her feelings about
her intended husband demonstrates the necessity and propriety of
this interior viewpoint.[51] What the process consists of is a gradual
approach, through self-analysis, to horror at the thought of sexual
intimacy with Sir Willoughby. And it is a triumph of Meredith's
method that as Clara goes through the phases leading up to her confrontation of dread, the effect upon the reader, as upon her, is revelation rather than dissection; the force of what she feels is increased
rather than diminished by her attempt to understand.

The first sign of her awareness is given by Meredith rather than
by Clara herself. It is also presented lightly, as part of the comic
action of the novel. Nevertheless, it represents so positive an introduction of physicality into the list of matters troubling Clara, and,
though an external description, intimates so vividly what the girl
feels, that it links directly to the culminating self-discovery we have
been discussing.

This initial incident occurs after Clara's first attempt to get Sir
Willoughby to release her from their engagement. He refuses even
to acknowledge having understood what she has asked, and instead,
with his fatality for making wrong moves, tries unsuccessfully to
force his physical presence on her (I, 153): "The gulf of a caress
hove in view like an enormous billow hollowing under the curled
ridge. She stooped to a buttercup; the monster swept by."

Slight as this incident is, it leads directly, through a series of
transformations and disclosures, to the moment of full recognition
which decides Clara once and for all that she cannot go through with
the marriage (I, 239):

[Vernon]* had lived in this place, and so must she; and . . . he had not
failed of self-control, because he had a life within. She was almost imagin-

---

* Vernon Whitford: Willoughby's cousin and pensioner, and, in the sense
of worthiness, the hero of the novel.

ing she might imitate him, when the clash of a sharp physical thought: "The difference! the difference!" told her she was a woman and never could submit. . . . She tried to nestle deep away in herself: in some corner where the abstract view had comforted her, to flee from thinking as her feminine blood directed. It was a vain effort. The difference, the cruel fate, the defencelessness of women, pursued her, strung her to wild horses' backs, tossed her on savage wastes. In her case duty was shame: hence, it could not be broadly duty. That intolerable difference proscribed the word.

The word "duty" has here a double meaning. It refers not only to the conjugal duties she dreads but to the problem of obedience to her father, who wishes her to marry Sir Willoughby. Considering only the second of these meanings, we recognize how much more sophisticated Meredith's approach to this Victorian shibboleth, duty, has become since he created the Princess Ottilia. He does not disparage the concept; duty is, after all, as much a child of "reason" as is the comic spirit. But he does show that by merely attempting to be rational one does not, when in conflict, easily and automatically detect the "higher law" to follow. Meredith is not contradicting anything he said in *Harry Richmond*; he is only, in continuing to explore the ethical thesis first introduced in that novel, testing it in a richly complex situation and giving it in the process more depth and reality than it had before. Clara's instincts, not her father's wishes, are "in harmony with the laws of society" in *The Egoist*, for we recall that society, as defined in the *Essay*, has keen critical perception. "Society," in the world of this novel, decrees that sexual aversion cancels duty when there is a question as to whether or not a marriage should take place. Clara, significantly, is always the friend of society; like Célimène, she defends its values and usages when her betrothed speaks of withdrawing from it. She is a "rebel" only against father and fiancé, both of whom, it is equally significant to note, are basically unsocial in their habits and outlook. What is more natural therefore than that society, which is not so much an entity within the novel as it is an implicit viewpoint, should approve Clara's daring discovery that in some cases to be most reasonable may very well mean to be wholly instinctual?

Actually, she is assisted to her discovery, though the aid is rendered unintentionally, by Vernon Whitford. Vernon, like the comic

spirit, like Clara's instincts, and like Meredith himself, is the voice
of society in another guise. But he is, in addition, an adequately if
not superbly realized character. Technically, as we noted, he is the
novel's hero—it is he who eventually wins Clara—though his presence
on stage never creates the atmosphere of brilliance, dash, and activity
that Sir Willoughby's does. But what is most important is that Vernon, more than any other character we have met in Meredith's works,
is the hero as rational man.

Even the love that develops between Vernon and Clara has something highly rational about it, as a result largely of Vernon's character.
What distinguishes Vernon from Harry Richmond and Nevil Beauchamp is that it is not his vision of marriage, but his passion itself,
that is ruled by reason.[52] Meredith indicated the nature of this "right"
sort of love in the "Prelude," or first chapter, of *The Egoist*: "If . . .
she [the comic spirit] watches over sentimentalism with a birch-rod,
she is not opposed to romance. You may love, and warmly love, so
long as you are honest. Do not offend reason." Clara's respect and
eventual love for Vernon grow through the kind of dialogue that
occurs when he urges her to stay at Patterne Hall for the time being,
even though she is no longer willing to marry Sir Willoughby. To the
extent that Vernon is aware of his own motives, what he is urging her
to do is to consider Willoughby's just claims and also to follow the
path which will help her to discover what she really feels about the
situation, there being no certainty, at this point, that she will not,
after all, marry Willoughby. In the exchange which follows, Clara
speaks first ( I, 250–51):

"You expect me to be all reason!"
"Try to be. It's the way to learn whether you are really in earnest." . . .
". . . It has gone too far with me."
"Take the matter into the head: try the case there."
"Are you not counselling me as if I were a woman of intellect?" . . .
"You have intellect," he said.

We get another glimpse of how the passion of love works in Vernon when he finally realizes that Clara does not intend to marry
Willoughby and when he thus has to confront his own growing feeling for her. Meredith tells us that "he had not much vanity to trouble
him, and passion was quiet." Vernon "walks off" the vision of Clara,

who had looked at him as he slept under the symbolic double-blossom cherry tree. He walks, it may be specifically noted, "that his blood might be lively at the throne of understanding" (I, 136).

At an earlier point in the story Vernon had spoken of "the world" in a manner that had both exposed Willoughby and advanced his own cause (though he had not at the time intended this) with Clara. He said we have to treat the world with common sense, see it "muddy" here, "clear" there; "love it in the sense of serving it." Clara answered that Vernon's view commended itself to her reason (I, 85–86).

It is worth noting that Vernon was modeled on Leslie Stephen.[53] We now have other interpretations of Stephen—Mr. Ramsay in Virginia Woolf's *To the Lighthouse* and the portrait which emerges from Noel Annan's study, *Leslie Stephen*—and a comparison of Vernon with these two suggests that Meredith's impulse to transform his rationalist friend into the sort of hero he did must have been decidedly strong.

In *To the Lighthouse,* the figure we see is a pathetic egoist-rationalist, a man who is dependent on his wife rather than on his intellect, and whose preoccupation with self makes him an injurious father. When Mrs. Ramsay questions his dogmatic certainty in predicting bad weather, she raises a storm of anger and abuse. Mrs. Ramsay's response to her husband's raging represents Virginia Woolf's condemnation of Stephen's behavior: "To pursue truth with such astonishing lack of consideration for other people's feelings, to rend the thin veils of civilization so wantonly, so brutally, was to her so horrible an outrage of human decency that, without replying, dazed and blinded, she bent her head as if to let the pelt of jagged hail, the drench of dirty water, bespatter her unrebuked."[54] Ultimately we see that Virginia Woolf has been creating, in Mr. Ramsay, a character who compels our compassion as none other could. But by the time he is able to do so, his arrogant barbarism has been crumpled, along with the rest of him, in what is only the wreckage of his old self.

Noel Annan's portrait, while different—based on detached sympathy rather than compassion and rebuke—nevertheless makes clear the rigidities and intellectual limitations of this hobbled man. Placed next to either picture, Meredith's rendering of Stephen is startling. Vernon Whitford, in sharp contrast to Mr. Ramsay, is the incarnation of self-reliance. Not only is he an excellent scholar but he has about him an air of modest competence and confidence. Mr. Ramsay, we recall, was plagued by the anxious suspicion that his books were not really very good, while Noel Annan's Stephen, besides being judged an intellect of the second rank, often wrote from an aggressive and narrow point of view suggesting a lack of self-acceptance and repose. Vernon Whitford is a keen analyst of character, and except when love and modesty conspire to blind him, he is sensitively aware of other people's feelings. Mr. Ramsay, we have seen, is conspicuously deficient in this kind of sensibility, and so is the biographical Stephen.

It would not be too much to say that Meredith's Stephen was precisely what Richmond Roy was to the young Harry Richmond: an incarnation of glamor. As an artist, Meredith was trying to make his rationalist worthy of the love of a beautiful young girl, the prize romantic writers had reserved for more active and passionate types. Theoretically, there is no reason why Meredith should not have succeeded and why Vernon should not be as convincing a lover as Mr. Ramsay is a figure of insensitivity and pathos. In fact, however, he is not. Vernon Whitford, the avowed rationalist, is the weakest element in *The Egoist,* which is a triumph of rationalism in its structure and in the moral convincingly derived from Sir Willoughby's character and fate. Indeed, instead of consistently compelling belief in himself, Vernon sometimes arouses our suspicion that there was a popular and vulgar side to Meredith's admiration for professional rationalists, which he revealed when he failed to take precautions. It was a propensity to indulge in unsuccessful myth-making, to endow the trained intellect with every fair attribute of character that had traditionally belonged to the hero as man of action and noble soul.[55]

There is another reason why it is worth noticing that Vernon Whitford was modeled on Leslie Stephen. As we do, we suddenly realize that the heroes of two of the three novels Meredith wrote in the '70's were suggested by two of his three most intimate friends among the rationalists. We ask, therefore, where is Morley, more effective in politics than Maxse and at least as intellectually formidable in Meredith's eyes as Stephen?[56] The answer of course is that Meredith was never to create for the reading public a character patterned upon him.* The memory of the unexpected attack, keeping

* He *did* create such a character, but not for the public. See note 56.

Meredith unsure of what Morley would construe as the taking of liberties, his genuine deference to Morley in most intellectual matters, and perhaps some residual sense of hurt all combined to make it unlikely Meredith would ever feel comfortably in control of any character based on Morley.[57] There is only one important way[58] in which he appears in Meredith's works: he is the dark presence who hovers over *Beauchamp's Career* and who is banished startlingly and savagely in the novel's closing lines.

### THE PERSISTENCE OF THE HERO AS RATIONAL MAN

With *The Egoist* Meredith's ability to use his interest in rationalism for the purposes of his art achieved ripeness. Everything that was good and bad in that interest produced a corresponding effect in the novel. Happily, the preponderance of influence came from what was good, strengthening Meredith's sense of form and inspiring him to invent the comic spirit, really a point of view from which rationalist-moralist judgments could be made without depriving the judged—the actors—of roundness and depth. Enthusiasm for rationalism remained a current in Meredith's thought and a prompter of his imaginative powers till the end of his career,[59] but none of the works it helped produce after 1879 had anything like the magnificence of *The Egoist*. *The Tragic Comedians* (1880) is the story of a radical leader, Sigismund Alvan, who desires exceedingly to be the hero as rational man. But Alvan, whom Meredith based on Ferdinand Lassalle, fails to become credible: throughout the novel he remains only an idea for a character. Consequently, his aspirations are even less convincing than he is himself. Redworth, of *Diana of the Crossways* (1885), is another hero who is distinguished by his rationalist views. He is an improvement: we can believe in him as we cannot in Alvan. However, Redworth is not really the center of the novel, which is weighted and energized by the title heroine's impulsive and erratic approach to life. Besides, the novel itself—the medium through which we meet Redworth—is written in language so tortured (so irrational, as it were) and is so confused and jumbled in organization that it painfully suggests a decline in Meredith's ability to write in a style fitting his theme and to create a successful structure.* *Lord Ormont*

---

\* I am aware that *Diana* was the first of Meredith's novels to win genuine popularity and that it is still regarded highly.

*and His Aminta* (1894), in which Matey Weyburn is another hero meant to demonstrate the virtues of a rationalist view of life, is better, and achieves even some stylistic and intellectual advances of its own. But it does not have the perfect balance and lucid structure of *The Egoist*. *The Egoist* is indeed a unique triumph in Meredith's career as a novelist, and he must have had intimations of this. Perhaps that is why he allowed himself in the '80's to try, for the first time in more than twenty years, for success as a poet. Like Thomas Hardy, Meredith wanted above all to be remembered for his poetry,[60] but between *Modern Love* (1862) and *Poems and Lyrics of the Joy of Earth* (1883) he had refused to expose his feelings and to risk his reputation by publishing a volume of poems. It is a striking fact that Meredith did not return to poetry in a large way until after *The Egoist* had made its mark. But when he finally did, it was with an insistency that dramatically created a new phase in his career. Whereas he had not published any collection of poems during two previous decades, the '80's witnessed the appearance of no fewer than three such volumes: *Poems and Lyrics of the Joy of Earth, Ballads and Poems of Tragic Life* (1887), and *A Reading of Earth* (1888).*

Contained in the three is the greater part of Meredith's poetry. And as the titles of two of the volumes indicate, many of the most important poems give expression to his conception of nature, now developed in depth as the poems themselves are in style. Indeed, nature is the dominant theme of Meredith's poetry published in the '80's. It is not imposing an arbitrary pattern upon his career to say that from *Evan Harrington* to *The Egoist* Meredith developed his conception of society, moving from the idea that society is a battleground to the idea that it is a place where one must attempt to behave rationally; and that in the '80's he returned, through his poetry, to his earliest theme, nature. Of course his concern with nature was alive during the twenty-year period in which he was developing his vision of society; but when he again gave this interest first place, he offered to the world a substantial body of work, uneven in quality, but revelatory throughout of a mind eagerly seeking the magic that weds feeling to form and idea to music.

---

* A fourth volume, *Poems*, appeared relatively soon after these three. It was published in 1892. *A Reading of Life* (1901) can be regarded as his last book of poetry, if we except a posthumous collection of 1909.

# 4

# *Poetry and Beneficence*

## 1883–1909

### HIERARCHY AND EXCELLENCE

Meredith's later poetry exhibits a meaningful pattern of themes, but we cannot discover this pattern by reading the poems in strict chronological order. Rather, by viewing as a single body of contemporaneous work all the verse belonging to the last phase of his poetic career, we see a number of casually distributed themes that can be rearranged into an intelligible, hierarchical order.

However, when the ordering is complete, an anomaly discloses itself. There is no necessary correspondence between the level of any given theme and the relative merit of the poems expressing it. Superior poems or poetic passages represent lesser themes while not a single outstanding poem is devoted to the highest theme of all. This anomaly is ironic, but its irony will help us to determine just what aspects of Meredith's vision of nature really inspired his poetry.

The pattern revealed, when Meredith's poems have been approached in a manner that discloses it, is composed of these themes: the ideas following from his conception of egoism; the doctrine of work, itself a derivative of his attitude toward egoism; the idea of natural process, in many ways a parallel to the doctrine of work; the role of energy in this unfolding scheme; the role of "natural law"; and finally, the meaning, in Meredith's vision, of Earth the Mother and of God the Father. Certain long poems express a number of the aspects or parts of the pattern. Other poems, especially the shorter pieces, are best read as expressions of some one particular theme rather than of many.

EGOISM: THE SCALY DRAGON-FOWL

Logically, the first part of the pattern to consider is the one we have already discussed in connection with Meredith's novels: his conception of egoism. This theme has even greater overtones in his poetry, for here he links it with nature. Despite inklings he had that a distinction between "nature" and "society" might very well be a distinction between incommensurables, he always regarded nature as metaphysically closer to reality than society.

"The Woods of Westermain," which begins the volume titled *Poems and Lyrics of the Joy of Earth* (1883), contains the first extensive and important expression in Meredith's later poetry of the theme of egoism. In lines unfortunately marked by his worst characteristics—tortured syntax and warped imagery—an idea of fundamental importance for an understanding of Meredith appears (p. 196):[1]

> This is in the tune we play,
> Which no spring of strength would quell
> In subduing does not slay;
> Guides the channel, guards the well:
> Tempered holds the young blood-heat,
> Yet through measured grave accord
> Hears the heart of wildness beat
> Like a centaur's hoof on sward.
> Drink the sense the notes infuse,
> You a larger self will find:
> Sweetest fellowship ensues
> With the creatures of your kind.

Though it is difficult to visualize—or even hear—"the tune we play" as a phenomenon containing the indicated meanings, the meanings themselves are discernible. Though we balk at "drinking the sense the notes infuse,"[2] we understand that "the young blood-heat" is passionate egoism which can be "subdued" but not "slain."[3] Ego's pulse will always be heard through the "measured grave accord" of rational self-control. Nevertheless, self-restraint rather than the "centaur's hoof on sward" brings a reward. The reward will be a "larger self," that is, "fellowship . . . With the creatures of your kind."

We hear imperfect echoes here of the theme of *Beauchamp's Career*. With one foot in the eighteenth century and the other in the twentieth, Meredith has no doubt that "reason" can subdue and control the other components of human nature without causing any damage worth mentioning, but at the same time he is aware that "ego" exists and cannot be wished away. What becomes clear is that "ego" for Meredith means something very different from what it means today. As the novels suggest and as "The Woods of Westermain" makes explicit, egoism as he uses it is closer to what Freud designated by the term "id" than it is to what now goes by the name of egoism. Egoism for us has positive connotations. It connotes an awareness and affirmation of self that are all too difficult to achieve and all too rare in a world that makes personal identity a goal to be struggled for rather than a condition to begin with. Egoism, for us, suggests an essential component of personality whenever the latter is other than "negative" or "weak." As we shall see, Meredith, too, means "personality" when he speaks of egoism, but for him the mainspring of personality is not some form of necessary self-affirmation but is rather a greedy, libidinous, and usually destructive drive for self-aggrandizement at the expense of others. For Meredith, an economy of scarcity prevails in the emotional life: any attempt at enlargement of self through passional experience necessarily means, to him, the deprivation of other people.

In a world so constituted, restraints are obviously needed. These restraints are to take the form of ethical imperatives which mankind will more and more come to feel and be governed by. Moreover, these restraints, or ethical imperatives, will over a period of time cause substantive changes in the very nature of egoism, making it a force for good. Unfortunately, however, Meredith got the idea that organic changes are to be brought about through continuous repression: he is going to eliminate the tail of the rat not by cutting it off but by binding it at birth and continuing this Chinese torture through a number of generations. Thus, in a later passage of "The Woods of Westermain," in which the image for ego is "the scaly Dragon-fowl," we read (pp. 198–99):

> Muffled by his cavern-cowl
> Squats the scaly Dragon-fowl,
>
> . . . . . . .
>
> Oft has he been riven; slain
> Is no force in Westermain.
> Wait, and we shall forge him curbs,
> Put his fangs to uses, tame,
> Teach him, quick as cunning herbs,
> How to cure him sick and lame.

Him shall Change, transforming late,
Wonderously renovate.

. . . . . . .

Make of him who was all maw,
Inly only thrilling-shrewd,
Such a servant as none saw
Through his days of dragonhood.

This is not social Darwinism; it is social Lamarckism, Lamarck and not Darwin having argued the transmissibility of characteristics acquired through inculcation. This novel social-evolutionary theory arises out of the great fear Meredith has of those elemental forces in man's nature which, he rightly sees, cannot be extinguished by reason. Like most notions born in fear, it partakes of both the perceptive and the absurd, and amounts in the end to a form of intriguing confusion. Meredith, ahead of his time, has grasped the possibility of sublimation. But no sooner does he grasp it than he mixes it up with theories of organic evolution, so that finally we are not sure whether he believes that the need for repression will continue indefinitely or that some day egoism will actually be replaced at the root by a "tamed" version of itself. The latter seems to be implied, and if it is, Meredith has innocently and confidently stepped into theoretic quicksands.

Remarkably, however, he finally crosses to firm ground, successfully traversing, in his ignorance, bogs that would have swallowed a more wary and cautious thinker. Whatever confusion exists in his conception of ego is triumphed over by the simple act of changing ego from something approximating the "id" to a closer equivalent of what we now call "personality." Indeed, ego and personality become interchangeable terms for Meredith, and while both continue to imply the expression of irrationality, the introduction of the connotations present even in Meredith's day for the term "personality" makes clear that it is simply *individuation* that he wants to get rid of. By substituting personality for ego, he turns his "social Lamarckism" into a real historical possibility. For personality, with its more complex and subtle suggestions, is an historical phenomenon depending on specific social institutions and attitudes for its existence. Whatever may be true of "egoism" in Meredith's initial sense, whether it will always have to be repressed and sublimated or

whether it will wither away with disuse, "personality" can be extinguished either through social chaos leading to barbarism or through
the establishing of a conformist society that considers personality a
decadent concept. Meredith of course does not see the dangers—the
tragedy—inherent in an attack upon personality. To him it is simply
an attack upon selfishness and the social ills attendant upon self-
preoccupation. As always, he goes to nature for his model, and what
he finds there both inspires him and confirms him in his errors. Thus,
in "The Lark Ascending," another poem in the 1883 volume, he compares the song of the lark with the utterances of man. Meredith's
intention is heavily symbolic (p. 223):

> Was never voice of ours could say
> Our inmost in the sweetest way,
> Like yonder voice aloft, and link
> All hearers in the song they drink.
> Our wisdom speaks from failing blood,
> Our passion is too full in flood,
> We want the key of his wild note
> Of truthful in a tuneful throat,
> The song seraphically free
> Of taint of personality.

For Meredith, the lark's song is a symbol of the lack of egoism,
lack of self-awareness, lack of desire for individuality, that is the
mark of all creatures of nature except man. Presumably the lark is
content to be a minute particle of the organic entity that is nature
herself, and the lark has no need to be distinguished from other such
particles. Her song is a single note in a symphony of sound, and we
are to understand that the symphony, not the single note, is important. Significantly, though the song speaks of the lark's "inmost," its
function is not to give the lark "self-expression" but to "link all hearers
in the song they drink." Like the seraph, the lark is self-forgetful to
the utmost. But unlike the seraph, she occupies no special place in
the universe.

There is an interesting lesson here to be learned about the inherent
ambiguity—or infinite possibility—of any given symbol. Emerson
observes that Thoreau, in his intense individualism, preferred the
single voices of birds and other single sounds of nature to more complex patterns of sound. Far from being "free of taint of personality,"

the voice of a single lark was quite likely for Thoreau a glorious example of the singularity and completeness of every creature of nature—a melodious hint that personality is nature's highest achievement. He was probably not linked with all other hearers when he heard the lark; more probably he was confirmed in his belief in his own uniqueness and isolation.

Meredith, in his later poetry, saw nature not as a field full of folk but as a single living web in which it appeared only to the wrong kind of dreamers that the colorful nodules were individuated and independent parts. We must not quarrel with his vision, though we find it difficult to remain passively attentive when Meredith insists that after he has shifted his gaze from nature to society he continues to see the same structure and even some identical details. What we can do, however, is examine the relation between his anti-individualist view of both nature and society, and the didactic tone that pervades so much of his poetry. Surely this tone derives from the "moral" Meredith wishes to preach. Striving ever to make his hearers lose themselves in a sensation of partaking in a mass movement, of driving like a brave army into the penumbra of history beyond the known present, he exhorts as he rhapsodizes, urges and whips the laggards forward as he strives to convince them that what they are doing is fighting for the human race and that the fight is the very stuff of joy. It is of course for the "race," not for themselves or for any other individuals, that the march is to be made and the battle to be fought.

Meredith was both better and worse than the many other Victorians who were willing to dedicate themselves to the future of the human race. If these Victorians failed to see that a philosophy which requires an individual to think always of the future of life on earth is a philosophy which robs everybody of life (or at least of richness of experience) for generations on end, many of them implicitly believed that the New Jerusalem was not too far off, and that the need for self-denial would come to an historical end before the philosophy behind it became too absurd and contradictory. Not so Meredith. As we shall see, he wisely grasped the fact that man is in and of history and is not likely ever to escape. He envisioned no quietus, no stasis, as the ultimate reward and triumph for the race. His readiness to think of men as masses was not dependent on any faith in or desire for a distant rebirth of individualism. It was dependent, quite simply, on his belief that nature so regards them and that therefore men should look at themselves similarly. The rewards Meredith depicts as attendant on a willingness to "sink purely individual considerations in the general well-being of the race"[4] are ends in themselves. They are the rewards nature offers all her creatures: a sensation of being in harmony with the rest of existence; an absence of fear; and best of all, satisfaction derived from work—not from the products and fruits of labor but from the act itself. This leads us to the next aspect of Meredith's conception of nature.

THE DOCTRINE OF WORK

Once more we can see that Meredith is both like and unlike his important contemporaries. The doctrine of work was hardly original with him; yet, barring Carlyle, few Victorians were as willing as he to divorce the activity of labor from the goals of labor and to praise the former with so little reference to the latter. The reason Meredith was able so easily to affirm this essentially twentieth-century attitude is that he saw it as an antidote to the egoism he so vehemently denounced. But again we are confronted by irony: he affirmed it for reasons opposite to ours. Today we regard the activity of work as ideally an expression of personality; Meredith saw it as salvation from the larger context in which they occur. The possessive "their" of personality."

His view of work as the antidote to egoism is announced in a passage from "The Woods of Westermain" (p. 202):

> Life, the chisel, axe and sword,
> Wield who have her depths explored:
> Life, the dream, shall be their robe,
>
> .    .    .    .    .    .    .    .
>
> Life, the small self-dragon ramped,
> Thrill for service to be stamped.

It is most difficult to transpose the syntax of these lines into a more normative form. Their meaning, however, can be construed from the larger context in which they occur. The possessive "their" refers to men who have explored the depths of nature and have learned that nature "gives" men life for one purpose only: that they may "work" with chisel, axe, or sword. But before men can engage in work—their proper activity—"the small self-dragon" of egoism must be effectively repressed. Thus, work is both the antidote to egoism, which is bad on both moral and esthetic grounds, and the activity of a higher state of being than is possible while one is concerned with self.

One way we can better understand Meredith's ideas is to note the importance he attached to the conception "Earth." We shall have more to say about this conception, but we can mention here that when Meredith uses the term "Earth" he is striving to personify the fundamental reality which requires man to abjure his own desire for personality. Given the connotations the word had for him, Meredith, when he spoke of Earth, could repudiate the idea that nature (to some extent a word synonymous with Earth) is cruelly impersonal, an idea held by such of his contemporaries as Tennyson, Arnold, Mill, and Hardy. Earth, according to Meredith, both teaches the fundamental secret that work for its own sake is good and retains, in her wisdom, secrets about her own purposes. Man cannot know the latter, but he can extrapolate from what he does know of Earth to the confident conclusion that her purposes are beneficent. Thus he can and should come to the further conclusion that life is indeed a gift that Earth gives him in order that he may have the privilege of serving as her instrument. In this highly anthropomorphic scheme, work thus finally becomes something more than activity for its own sake, though it retains that meaning. It becomes a fulfillment of the obligation to Earth that man incurs simply by being born. "The Woods of Westermain" expresses this idea as explicitly as it does the others that align with it (p. 202):

> Till your little sun shall set;
> Leaving her the future task:
> Loving her too well to ask.
> Earth your haven, Earth your helm,
> You command a double realm;
> Labouring here to pay your debt,

We saw elsewhere that man is not to desire sensations of individuality; but the second line suggests that it is perfectly permissible for him to feel powerful. Serving Earth, he commands her as well as himself. In these lines a complexity of ideas is made compact in true poetic fashion, and here, at least, economy of expression is an instance

of poetic excellence rather than of obfuscation. We can note, too, another achievement in this passage. The first and most important stress
in the third, fifth, and sixth lines falls, respectively, on the words
"Labouring," "Leaving," and "Loving." The initial consonant, common to all, serves to bind together the three words and the lines in
which they occur. The meaning that is therefore reinforced—or
better, achieved—through the poetic device is that by "labouring"
we leave off doubt about Earth's purposes and that through this
twofold affirmation—"labouring," and "leaving" the future to her—we
are in fact "loving" Earth. The significance of the idea of love in this
connection is unmistakable. As powerful an idea as it is an experience, love here serves to emphasize the personal quality of Earth, the
quality which in the first place enables us to labor and leave off questioning.

That work, as an activity, may substitute for understanding (i.e.,
questioning) is made clear in a poem appearing in the 1888 volume,
*A Reading of Earth.* The poem is titled "Seed Time," and the main
speaker of the lines is Earth herself. When the poet, in a moment of
weakness during a chill autumn, cries for a day of long light, Earth
admonishingly answers him (p. 318):

> Master the blood, nor read by chills,
> . . . Hast thou ploughed,
> Sown, reaped, harvested grain for the mills,
> Thou hast the light over shadow of cloud.
> Steadily eying, before that wail,
> Animal-infant, thy mind began,
> Momently nearer me: should sight fail,
> Plod in the track of the husbandman.

Although plodding in the track of the husbandman is not precisely
equivalent to loving, we cannot help seeing that in Meredith's poetry
they bear a strong resemblance to each other. Both depend on not
questioning Earth's purposes or her sometimes perplexing mysteries.
Just as love is a substitute for understanding, so work is too. Moreover, what the quoted lines imply is that productive labor is equal in
moral value to intellectual grasp, rendered here by the word "sight."

The moral equivalence of productive labor and intellectual understanding is further emphasized in the poem titled "The Question
Whither." Again the plough, or the husbandman who wields it, is the

symbol for useful work, and again this useful labor is as eternal in meaning and value as the activity of mind, i.e., "reason" (p. 339):

> Enough if we have winked to sun,
> Have sped the plough a season;
> There is a soul for labour done,
> Endureth fixed as reason.

It is becoming clear that Meredith, though he believes that work is an end in itself, cannot rest content with the idea. While professing the greatest respect for Earth's reticence with regard to her purposes, he cannot resist prying and speculating. The very use of the plough as a symbol of work indicates hopefulness on Meredith's part that Earth's purposes are rational and have something to do with cultivation, growth, and renewal of life.

Three poems in particular help us to discover this metaphysic. They are "Earth and Man," "Men and Man," and "The Thrush in February." Taken together they tell us that human work has as its mission a transformation of Earth desired by herself. Man is an agent of her perpetual recreation and translation into new surface forms, and while Meredith does not attempt to envision any final stage of this process, it is clear that he believes Earth wishes to become a place of greater civilization, greater order, and greater cultivated— as against wild—beauty. In "Earth and Man," a poem in the 1883 volume, the poet says (p. 243):

> She hears him. Him she owes
> For half her loveliness a love well won
> By work that lights the shapeless and the dun,
> Their common foes.

Man does no less than impose significant form upon Earth. "The shapeless and the dun," her enemy as well as man's, is the colorless, orderless wilderness which characterized the early state of her existence. It is man who transforms her, through his art and industry, into her better self.*

It is noteworthy that although all men can or should labor in Earth's behalf, they are not of equal rank, for some are heroes—i.e.,

---

* There is an interesting comparison to be made here between Meredith and Wallace Stevens, particularly the Stevens who wrote "The Idea of Order at Key West." But for Stevens, Earth is not the enemy of chaos: she *is* chaos.

leaders—and some are followers. There is a distinction between "plodding in the track of the husbandman," the common order of work, and heroism, which is, in a Carlylean sense, a special kind of work. In "Men and Man," Meredith says, in seeming contradiction to his usual doctrine, that the angels do not admire men collectively; they admire only the individual hero. The latter the angels consider to be as worthy as themselves, and they assist him at his work. They help him to drain "a sluggish fen" and "quell a warring sea" (p. 302). Since there is no striking difference between these activities and the work of Everyman, the distinction between the two kinds of men seems finally much less dramatic than it does when first enunciated. It seems merely to be that the heroes take on the more difficult common tasks and also supply leadership in the war against "the shapeless and the dun," while ordinary men, laboring beside them, follow their directions.

Insofar as consistency is any virtue in a poet, it is just as well that Meredith did not make too much of heroism. As matters stand, we find it difficult enough to reconcile his insistence that work is the method for obliterating ego with his notion that a special personal quality distinguishes certain workers known as heroes. To get beyond this seeming contradiction we are obliged to understand that the heroes themselves are but servants who, though they may have genius, are content to regard themselves as instruments of Earth's purposes. This solution of the puzzle is plausible, but it relies on a repudiation of many connotations that Meredith elsewhere gave to the word "heroism." Since he does not bother to make this repudiation explicit, we are finally not certain just what he does mean by "hero."

However, some help in deciding Meredith's meaning is provided by "The Thrush in February," first published in *Macmillan's Magazine* in 1885 and reprinted in *A Reading of Earth* (1888). Referring to Earth, Meredith says (p. 330):

> Her double visage, double voice,
> In oneness rise to quench the doubt.
> This breath, her gift, has only choice
> Of service, breathe we in or out.
>
> Since Pain and Pleasure on each hand
> Led our wild steps from slimy rock
> To yonder sweeps of gardenland,
> We breathe but to be sword or block.

The revealing line is the last. We live only to be heroes (sword) or ordinary men (block) who are to be used by heroes in directed labor. Meredith's use of the sword as symbol for a heroic worker makes clear at least that whatever connotations of genius the word "heroism" may have for him, they are not artistic, or even creative in any subtle sense. Interpreting these two stanzas, G. M. Trevelyan has said: "[They] mean that Earth's double aspects of Pain and Pleasure, Life and Death, have but one aim: to make us active warriors of good —otherwise we can but serve as raw material for heroic life in others."[5] It is not clear to me that this is Meredith's meaning, but I agree that Meredith sees the heroes—the "swords"—hacking away at the rest of men—the "blocks"—presumably to shape them for their labor of love in Earth's behalf. What is most significant is that a sword does not impose its own image upon the material it strikes; it is an agent or instrument, which is precisely Meredith's conception, here at least, of the hero. We are, however, still far from any understanding of how Earth, the principal who wields the instrument—the "sword"—can be said to use it for creative purposes. The explanation, insofar as there is one, is that Meredith in this connection speaks like a thoroughgoing social Darwinist. The warlike connotations of the "sword" are meant merely to establish a connection between the fundamental character of evolution—struggle—and the condition of man. War is for Meredith at this point merely a convenient human activity for symbolizing the universal fact of unceasing struggle.

That it is really "struggle" and not war in particular that Meredith equates with work is made clear in "Earth and Man." Speaking of man, the poet says (p. 240):

> For he is in the lists
> Contentious with the elements, whose dower
> First sprang him; for swift vultures to devour
> If he desists.

Struggle is thus seen to be a form of "natural" work; indeed, it is a form of compulsory labor imposed upon man at the hour of his birth. Referring to these lines, Joseph Warren Beach observes: "Earth is here represented as having started man on his race and as now looking on to see how it will come out. . . . Man is inclined to quarrel with these hard conditions of his life, but in reality they are what have given him the strength he has, and have been the means of developing his faculties."[6]

Ceaseless struggle has an even more important effect than developing man's faculties. As Beach points out, Meredith believes it also enlarges man's vision of the ideal. Beach quotes the following lines from "The Test of Manhood" (p. 543), a poem which appears in the last volume of poetry Meredith was to publish, *A Reading of Life* (1901):

> This gift of penetration and embrace,
> His prize from tidal battles lost or won,
> Reveals the scheme to animate his race.

A significant aspect of Meredith's thought is that whenever the ideal is spoken of, as it is when "the scheme to animate [the] race" is alluded to, Meredith has in mind also the "real." As he insisted in a number of places, the "real" and the "ideal" must never be separated. Thus Beach is pertinent when he says at a later point in his discussion that Meredith believes "our work is a part of Reality." This triple identification of the ideal, the real, and man's work reveals the strong positivistic impulse which contends in Meredith for supremacy over his lyrical and spiritual aspirations. As Beach says: "Towards the ultimate philosophical questions (Whence and Whither) [Meredith] takes the same attitude as Swinburne in his 'Hymn of Man.' These problems are insoluble and they lead to the invention of legends that, as Swinburne says, 'give not aid.' Meredith . . . calls them 'the Questions that sow not nor spin.' The true answer to the questions is the work we do."[7] And Beach quotes from "The Question Whither" (p. 339):

> Our questions are of mortal brood,
> Our work is everlasting.

We have already noted that a belief in the doctrine of work was not peculiar to Meredith. We should add that neither was his embrace of the idea that universal struggle is the decree of Earth. During the Victorian period, both the doctrine of work and the Darwinian interpretation of struggle appealed to the poetic imagination not only because they seemed socially relevant but because they provided a replacement for the dramatic sense of life that Christianity had previously supplied. Instead of struggling against evil in a great cosmic drama, the one which had reached its triumphant literary expression in the works of Milton, the Victorians were engaged in a more humdrum but more bitter battle against nature and social greed. Population pressure against existing cultivated land, social injustice and degraded living conditions in the cities, but a pervasive feeling, nonetheless, that civilized life in general was an ideal—and a realizable one at that—all generated the moral passion and the poetic embrace of the future expressed in Meredith's work, as elsewhere.

Important in Meredith's use of the doctrine of work is an insistence, reminiscent of some of the Romantics, on harmonizing work with the activity of nature. Nowhere in Meredith's writing does man the laborer or man the artist or the hero struggle against nature. Drought, floods, devastating storms are either absent or, when they occur, actually celebrated. Thinking even of the poems we have already seen, we recognize a sharp contrast between Meredith's unqualified acceptance of nature and the more prevalent Victorian attitude, which for example finds significant expression in the poetry of Matthew Arnold. In the poem titled "In Harmony with Nature," Arnold says:

> 'In harmony with Nature?' Restless fool,
> Who with such heat dost preach what were to thee,
> When true, the last impossibility—
> To be like Nature strong, like Nature cool!
>
> Know, man hath all which Nature hath, but more,
> And in that *more* lie all his hopes of good.
> Nature is cruel; man is sick of blood;
> Nature is stubborn; man would fain adore;
>
> Nature is fickle; man hath need of rest;
> Nature forgives no debt, and fears no grave;
> Man would be mild, and with safe conscience blest.
>
> Man must begin, know this, where Nature ends;
> Nature and man can never be fast friends.
> Fool, if thou canst not pass her, rest her slave![8]

Arnold reiterates this position in "Religious Isolation" and in "Stagirius," and in the poem titled "Courage," which appears in the 1852 volume, *Empedocles on Etna*. Tennyson, too, sees the best part of man as alien to nature, as does John Stuart Mill in his essay "Nature." Though Arnold, Tennyson, and Mill do not deprecate nature for the reasons that many artists and thinkers do today, these three, more than Meredith, are in the line leading to the preoccupation with nonnatural form that characterizes our own era.

The explanation of the difference between their view and Meredith's takes us back to his conception of ego and personality. Meredith was probably unaware of just how fiercely opposed he was, in his poetry, to any philosophical position predicated upon individuality. Arnold and Tennyson, like most of the important Victorians, were concerned with the preservation of personality, in which they saw some shadow of religious meaning. For Meredith, personality was a querulous component of man that created false conflicts between him and the rest of nature's creatures. Thus, man does not work or struggle to subdue a contentious Earth or to realize his own individuality. He works to realize his identity with the flower, the tree, the rock, and the apparently destructive forces of storm and flood.

This conception of work, predicated as it is upon the eradication of personality and individuality, leads us to the third of the ideas that go to make up the "inscape" of Meredith's nature poetry. Work divorced from personality becomes, simply, another natural process, which—as a distinct aspect of the phenomena of nature—drew a deep response from Meredith.

### PROCESS, LYRICISM, AND ACCEPTANCE

In its simplest and most abstract form, process, to Meredith, means the fact of continuous change, which has as its corollary the permanent mutability of nature. Like repressed ego and like work, "change" is given spiritual meaning in "The Woods of Westermain," the poem which, unhappily uneven and largely a poetic failure, contains so many of the important aspects of Meredith's conception of nature. At one point in this long work, Meredith says (p. 199):

> Change, the strongest son of Life,
> Has the Spirit here to wife.

Meredith is saying that "change" is the dominant and highest attribute of life and that as such it merges with whatever in the universe transcends our worldly conception of life. Since "change," as we noted, is a form of process, the latter, by extension, also takes on a spiritual significance.

It is but one step from giving process this kind of meaning to establishing a moral attitude toward it. Meredith's view is that complaints about life's brevity are useless; that man should rather take joy in the processes which make up the sum of his existence. An entire poem, "The Day of the Daughter of Hades," is devoted to this theme. Skiágeneia, the daughter of Persephone and Hades, is permitted to spend one day in the light, and during that day finds love and takes delight in nature's processes. She does not waste her time lamenting the brevity of her twenty-four hours in the light. Meredith himself pointed to the meaning of the poem when in a letter to Richard Curle, dated January 3, 1905, he said, "The Daughter of Hades has intense enjoyment of her one day of light in life, and might read us a lesson. That was in my mind."[9]

This all-important idea, that man should take joy in the fundamental fact of natural process, is presented even more clearly in "Melampus," which, like "The Day of the Daughter of Hades," appears in the 1883 volume. Meredith speaks of the creatures of the woods (p. 227):

> Of earth and sun they are wise, they nourish their broods,
> Weave, build, hive, burrow and battle, take joy and pain
> Like swimmers varying billows: never in woods
> Runs white insanity fleeing itself: all sane
> The woods revolve: as the tree its shadowing limns
> To some resemblance in motion, the rooted life
> Restrains disorder: you hear the primitive hymns
> Of earth in woods issue wild of the web of strife.

There is no fear or denial of life—i.e., "white insanity fleeing itself" —among the creatures of the woods. The clear implication of this poem, which like so many of Meredith's nature poems is unfortunately didactic, is that man should learn from the creatures of the woods and should try to live his life as they live theirs. He should obliterate distinctions between the processes of his life and the processes of theirs. Once more we encounter the discomforting equation of human society with the ecology of nature, but these lines do not call down upon themselves quite the same philosophic objections as do other lines insisting upon the blurring of distinctions between man and the rest of nature. These lines succeed where, for example, parts of "The Woods of Westermain" fail, because Meredith in "Melampus," perhaps for the reason that he began with a Greek myth, seems more conscious that he is speaking symbolically rather than literally, and that what we "learn" from nature is not so much a way of doing things as an attitude toward ourselves. Accordingly, the philosophy of the poem, though still open to objections, is decidedly more viable.

Nevertheless, "Melampus" remains something less than a complete success, because of its didactic undertone. Meredith's first unqualifiedly successful poem inspired by his belief that the processes of man's life are equatable with the processes of nature in general was "Love in the Valley," which initially appeared in the 1851 volume, was rewritten and republished in 1878, and was included in its expanded form in *Poems and Lyrics of the Joy of Earth* (1883). It is the second version that makes the profound connections which concern us here.

"Love in the Valley" is a lyric, and as such it happily escapes Meredith's usual tendency to be didactic. It is far better poetry than any we have considered so far. Meredith, in this poem, describes a girl in terms of nature imagery and movement, and describes nature—particularly the qualities of the four seasons as they change—in terms of feminine beauty, using tones and images that connote tenderness, loveliness, and sensuality.

Here is the girl (p. 231):

> Shy as the squirrel and wayward as the swallow,
>    Swift as the swallow along the river's light
> Circleting the surface to meet his mirrored winglets,
>    Fleeter she seems in her stay than in her flight.
> Shy as the squirrel that leaps among the pine-tops,
>    Wayward as the swallow overhead at set of sun,
> She whom I love is hard to catch and conquer,
>    Hard, but O the glory of the winning were she won!

The images of the squirrel leaping among the pine-tops and of the swallow caught in a subdued light suggest all the energy and vitality that swiftness implies, and yet merge these qualities with a softness and gentleness that give poignancy to the poet's cry in the last line. The movement of the lines in this passage (as in the entire poem) is also appropriate to Meredith's purposes. The initial dactyls, running into anapests and other feet, some irregular, create a quick and skimming motion that has enough undulation and vitality to suggest lightness of being coupled with lively willfulness. This is indeed lyricism that conveys the intensity of the poet's feeling.

Here Meredith describes a wheat field at harvest time (p. 235):

O the golden sheaf, the rustling treasure-armful!
    O the nutbrown tresses nodding interlaced!
O the treasure-tresses one another over
    Nodding! O the girdle slack about the waist!
Slain are the poppies that shot their random scarlet
    Quick amid the wheatears: wound about the waist,
Gathered, see these brides of Earth one blush of ripeness!
    O the nutbrown tresses nodding interlaced!

Though the meter of this stanza is technically similar to the meter of the stanza previously discussed, the movement is clearly slower. The stresses are closer together, and the effect intended and achieved is the motion of sheaves of wheat being moved by the wind. That is to say, this is the effect created by the first four lines. But the last four quicken their pace and catch the movement of the observing eye as it rapidly takes in the poppies "That shot their random scarlet/ Quick among the wheatears."

The imagery is equally successful. The metaphoric description of stalks of wheat as nut-brown tresses is felicitous. It catches the silkiness of the wheat stalks and at the same time conveys Meredith's enraptured vision of Earth as a living creature of feminine beauty. Moreover, the wheat stalks are "brides of Earth" (that is, the brides produced by Earth, not married to Earth) and thus their "blush of ripeness" has the same suggestion of sensuality that the swallow and the squirrel had in the previous stanza.

Notably, Meredith in this poem has tempered his suspicion of "personality" and has created, ambivalently, both the individuality of the girl and her identity with Earth. His intention is most triumphantly realized by the juxtaposition of two stanzas near the end of the poem (pp. 235-36). In the first, "she" refers to the girl, and in the second, to Earth:

Hither she comes; she comes to me; she lingers,
    Deepens her brown eyebrows, while in new surprise
High rise the lashes in wonder of a stranger;
    Yet am I the light and living of her eyes.
Something friends have told her fills her heart to brimming,
    Nets her in her blushes, and wounds her, and tames.—
Sure of her haven, O like a dove alighting,
    Arms up, she dropped: our souls were in our names.

❖      ❖      ❖

Soon she will lie like a white-frost sunrise.
Yellow oats and brown wheat, barley pale as rye,
Long since your sheaves have yielded to the thresher,
Felt the girdle loosened, seen the tresses fly.
Soon will she lie like a blood-red sunset.
Swift with the to-morrow, green-winged Spring!
Sing from the South-West, bring her back the truants,
Nightingale and swallow, song and dipping wing.

The alternating hesitation and forward movement of the first of these two stanzas intensify the lyric delay and expectancy of the image. The second stanza moves in long, sweeping rhythms, suggesting the tender release following the union of the lovers in the last line of the previous stanza, while at the same time and more directly these rhythms evoke the swift approach of returning spring. As for imagery, the interchange between nature and human life is perfectly balanced. The girl, like a bird or wild animal, is "netted," "wounded," and "tamed." And in the next line she is precisely like "a dove alighting." In the following stanza, Earth's sheaves have "felt the girdle loosened, seen the tresses fly." Finally, the last three lines catch up again the image of birds in flight, particularly the swallow, which has already symbolized the girl and here figures the return of spring.

The largest effects of this interchange are twofold. The first can be stated simply. Not only are the graces and rhythms of nature lent convincingly to the girl, and vice versa, but because the equivalency is very real to Meredith he is able to describe the oneness he perceives in a manner so intense and vivid that we do not feel we are being overwhelmed in pathetic fallacies or grotesqueries. The second effect is philosophical. When we read these stanzas we recognize that Meredith has qualified his antagonism toward personality. True, human personality is not regarded here as a unique phenomenon: the girl lives as a creature of loveliness, but so does the face of Earth. Also, whether we credit his intention or not, we recognize that the heightened emotion Meredith feels when he contemplates Earth is meant to be equal in joy to the love, desire, tenderness, and excitement of expectancy aroused by the girl. We recognize that the effect intended for this equation is the union of the living girl with the living Earth, the transformation of both into spiritualized processes from which the "taint of personality" has been removed. Yet is this wholly the case? Though the girl has no name, though her face is never depicted in its entirety or with any play of emotion or expression, she exists in terms not only of lightness and sensuality but, as noted, of willfulness. Does not the latter suggest something ineluctably individual, or at least not merely to be assimilated with nature as Meredith sees it? Though the girl is not described through psychological motives, as she might have been were Browning writing the poem, her visible behavior suggests a complexity of feeling that really has no counterpart in the rest of nature. Ironically, though Meredith probably did not intend to convey this suggestion, it adds immeasurably to the beauty and richness of the poem. It exists without definition, never calling attention to itself sufficiently to destroy the equation between the girl and Earth, but always present to intimate that it is the personality of this particular girl—her willingness to give herself up to spontaneous, natural behavior—that makes the equation possible.

"Love in the Valley" is the best of Meredith's poems that transform into poetic activity the processes of nature. The transformation, in this case, is accomplished by his universalizing the lyric qualities of rhythmic, joyous movement found in nature—in the fields beneath the changing seasons and in a young girl whose emotions and moods are also subject to change, though their range in the poem is restricted to wild tenderness and sensuality.

Another good treatment of natural process, as well as the revelation of another aspect of this process, occurs in "Whimper of Sympathy." This poem expresses Meredith's acceptance of nature's grim ecology and reads like a comment upon Tennyson's lines,

> For nature is one with rapine, a harm no preacher can
> heal;
> The Mayfly is torn by the swallow, the sparrow spear'd
> by the shrike,
> And the whole little wood where I sit is a world of
> plunder and prey.[10]

Meredith's poem, given here in its entirety,[11] makes a striking contrast (p. 285):

> Hawk or shrike has done this deed
> Of downy feathers: rueful sight!
> Sweet sentimentalist, invite
> Your bosom's Power to intercede.

> So hard it seems that one must bleed
> Because another needs will bite!
> All round we find cold Nature slight
> The feelings of the totter-knee'd.
>
> O it were pleasant with you
> To fly from this tussle of foes,
> The shambles, the charnel, the wrinkle!
> To dwell in yon dribble of dew
> On the cheek of your sovereign rose,
> And live the young life of a twinkle.

This is not a great poem; its tone of biting scorn descending to sarcasm limits its power, but it is much better than most of Meredith's didactic verse. It has economy of expression. Also, in the first line, the four accents fall on "hawk," "shrike," "done," and "deed," all of which are emphatic monosyllables, the first two ending in the sharp "k" and the last two made heavy by the repetition of the initial "d." The effect is one of a heavy body striking downward. This contrasts expertly with the soft but precise image, "downy feathers," of the next line, and sets a spare, Spartan attitude that Meredith would have done well to maintain throughout the poem. Though he does not, and falls instead into the tone, as noted, of exaggerated scorn, he manages to keep his language clipped and economical while at the same time he avoids the syntactical involutions that mar so many of his longer poems—for example "The Woods of Westermain." Consequently the reader feels, as he reads "Whimper of Sympathy," the inevitability of nature's ways, i.e., of her processes, and accepts (while he reads the poem) the "anti-sentimental" attitude the poet insists upon.

Somewhat slighter than either "Love in the Valley" or "Whimper of Sympathy," but successful on its own poetic terms and also indicative of another aspect of Meredith's concern with natural process, is "Young Reynard" (p. 286):

### I

> Gracefullest leaper, the dappled fox-cub
> Curves over brambles with berries and buds,
> Light as a bubble that flies from the tub,
> Whisked by the laundry-wife out of her suds.
> Wavy he comes, woolly, all at his ease,
> Elegant, fashioned to foot with the deuce;
> Nature's own prince of the dance: then he sees
> Me, and retires as if making excuse.

## II

> Never closed minuet courtlier! Soon
> Cub-hunting troops were abroad, and a yelp
> Told of sure scent: ere the stroke upon noon
> Reynard the younger lay far beyond help.
> Wild, my poor friend, has the fate to be chased;
> Civil will conquer: were't other 'twere worse;
> Fair, by the flushed early morning embraced,
> Haply you live a day longer in verse.

The dactylic movement of this poem readily conveys the loping swiftness of the young fox, while Meredith's skillful use of enjambment creates pauses which turn the whole pattern of punctuated motion into a dance. The syntax is at ease, the imagery appropriate. The light, humorous tone, which seems odd because the poem is about death, is really not odd for two reasons. First, we already know how Meredith regards the death of the hunted in nature. "Accept!" is his only comment. Second, the poem has philosophical overtones which transform the fox into a symbol. He is the "wild"—i.e., the earth before the "civil," or civilization, appeared. Civilization, equally a part of nature according to Meredith, is bound to replace the wild. Far from being a cause for regret or sorrow, this is, for Meredith, an exhilarating glimpse of the teleology inherent in nature's processes.

But Meredith was not always so certain that he discerned a historic goal in nature's processes. Just as "work" in his poetry is sometimes labor in behalf of Earth's purposes and sometimes activity for its own sake, so "process" is sometimes a movement guided by those purposes and sometimes, as in "The Day of the Daughter of Hades," a complex of activity which is its own justification. What is most interesting is that both these conceptions of natural process influenced Meredith's attitude toward death.

"The Question Whither" expresses the first of these conceptions (p. 339):

> We children of Beneficence
> Are in its being sharers;
> And Whither vainer sounds than Whence,
> For word with such wayfarers.

This is positivism, both Comtian and post-Comtian. The poem is also existential in its import inasmuch as Meredith, though confident for his part that existence is meaningful, ironically registers the existentialist viewpoint that ultimate questions are "vain," i.e., absurd.

A similar attitude is voiced in the beautiful poem "In the Woods," which reads in part (p. 342):[12]

### I

Hill-sides are dark,
And hill-tops reach the star,
And down is the lark,
And I from my mark
Am far.

Unlighted I foot the ways.
I know that a dawn is before me,
And behind me many days;
Not what is o'er me.

### II

I am in deep woods,
Between the two twilights.

The lines "I am in deep woods / Between the two twilights" succinctly render Meredith's conviction that the "whence" and the "whither" of life are unknowable, and also touch the idea with tragedy, for man, in this image, is indeed in perilous danger of becoming lost. The poem brings to mind Robert Frost's "Stopping by Woods," and points, incidentally, to the subtle differences between Meredith and the most venerable of living nature poets writing in English. For Frost, the second twilight—"sleep"—is itself a goal, though he has many miles to go before he reaches it. Meredith's view, in the poem quoted above, is more austere. Man can do nothing *but* stop by woods; there is nowhere else to go.

Yet we know that Meredith does not believe life meaningless and that elsewhere he expresses his faith that "beneficence" exists. Actually, he succeeds in reconciling the grimness of "In the Woods" with his belief in life's larger purpose. He does so by explaining that death is indeed an obliteration for the individual but that individual death does not matter, so long as life itself continues. In the poem "Seed Time," this idea is clearly set forth (p. 318):

Verily now is our season of seed,
Now in our Autumn; and Earth discerns

Them that have served her in them that can read,
Glassing, where under the surface she burns,
Quick at her wheel, while the fuel, decay,
Brightens the fire of renewal: and we?
Death is the word of a bovine day,
Know you the breast of the springing To-be.

Any questions we ask about our particular fates get a summary answer. "Death," with its usual connotations, is repudiated. It is the "word of a bovine day." As conceived in this poem, death is rather the supplier of fuel for new life and is thus but a phase of a larger life cycle. This theme—the uses of death in the largest processes of nature—is the subject of one of the better poems in the group we are considering. The poem, called "Woodland Peace" (p. 338), is given below in its entirety:

Sweet as Eden is the air,
        And Eden-sweet the ray.
No Paradise is lost for them
Who foot by branching root and stem,
And lightly with the woodland share
        The change of night and day.

Here all say,
We serve her, even as I:
We brood, we strive to sky,
We gaze upon decay,
We wot of life through death,
How each feeds each we spy;
And is a tangle round,
Are patient; what is dumb
We question not, nor ask
The silent to give sound,
The hidden to unmask,
The distant to draw near.

And this the woodland saith:
I know not hope or fear;
I take what e'er may come;
I raise my head to aspects fair,
From foul I turn away.

Sweet as Eden is the air,
        And Eden-sweet the ray.

There is a gentleness about these lines that is much more effective
than the tone of strenuous exhortation that often accompanies Meredith's vision of life and death. This gentleness is the authentic note
of acceptance, which Meredith sounded in another poem, also a
good one, titled "Dirge in Woods." In it is heard, besides acceptance,
a tone that occurs only infrequently in Meredith's poetry: that of
sadness. It occurs when Meredith temporizes with the idea of tragedy
and allows it to rise near enough to the surface of his poetry to be
detected (pp. 341–42):

> A wind sways the pines,
> And below
> Not a breath of wild air;
> Still as the mosses that glow
> On the flooring and over the lines
> Of the roots here and there.
> The pine-tree drops its dead;
> They are quiet, as under the sea.
> Overhead, overhead
> Rushes life in a race,
> As the clouds the clouds chase;
> And we go,
> And we drop like the fruits of the tree,
> Even we,
> Even so.

Particularly effective is the way the quiet stillness of the early
lines changes easily to the rush of life—the word "rushes" dramatizing
life's brevity—and the way this pace gives way in turn and with equal
ease to the dirge-like movement of the closing lines. Also effective
is the use of rhyme. The line "And below," introducing the description of the still floor of earth, is linked by rhyme to the two lines
"And we go" and "Even so"; thus the idea that man's fate is the fate
of all nature is reinforced. In addition, the line "The pine-tree drops
its dead" is linked to "Overhead, overhead," which introduces the
description of intense life. The effect therefore is the linking of
death and life, which emphasizes that they are part of one larger
process. In both tone and structure this poem is expressive of its
own central idea, which is a way of saying that it is a very good
poem.

We have already seen Meredith "answering" Tennyson's pained
outcry in the face of nature's savagery. In the poem "In the Woods,"

Meredith sets himself against another of the attitudes comprising
Tennyson's sense of nature. In *In Memoriam,* Tennyson speaks of
nature as careless of the individual, and sees this fact as evidence of
nature's simple cruelty and indifference. Meredith's poem (p. 343)
is a reproving gloss upon Tennyson's words:

> With the butterfly roaming abroad
> On a sunny March day,
> The pine-cones opened and blew
> Winged seeds, and aloft they flew
> Butterfly-like in the ray,
> And hung to the breeze:
> Spinning they fell to the sod.
> Ask you my rhyme
> Which shall be trees?
> They have had their time.

The anti-Aristotelianism of this view is also, of course, a repudiation of the idea that nature is cruel and profligate. A seed that does
not come to fruition is not a tree that failed to become a tree. It is
a seed, an entity in its own right, that has "had its time." In short,
the phenomenon observed everywhere—in Tennyson's words, "of fifty
seeds / She often brings but one to bear"[13]—is merely for Meredith
another of nature's nontragic processes. And not only is it not meaningless, but it is, in his view, implicitly good. To have had one's
day, even as a seed, is to be indebted to "beneficence" for the gift of
life, however briefly held.

These observations lead us to still another aspect of Meredith's
conception of natural process. The greatest folly is to seek or desire
permanence, for impermanence of a state of being is the very mark
of process itself. In "A Faith on Trial," the long poem Meredith
wrote in 1885,* telling of his personal struggle to accept the ap-
proaching death of his second wife (who was soon to die of cancer),
he confronts himself and humanity (p. 355–56):

> Cry we for permanence fast,
> Permanence hangs by the grave;
> Sits on the grave green-grassed,
> On the roll of the heaved grave-mound.
> By Death, as by Life, are we fed:
> The two are one spring; our bond

---

\* It was not published until 1888, when Meredith included it in *A Reading
of Earth.*

With the numbers; with whom to unite
Here feathers wings for beyond:
Only they can waft us in flight.
For they are Reality's flower.

As poetry these lines are, unfortunately, bad. The tortured syntax that does not justify itself has reappeared, as it always does when Meredith attempts to use poetry as a medium for didactic moralizing. Similarly, the images are awkward and unnatural, and instead of capturing meaning seem to strain at it desperately. Nevertheless, these lines are significant for the thought they bear. They express the important doctrine that numbers, not individuals, are "reality's flower." The existence of numbers, the welfare of numbers, the abstract fact of numbers—these are real concerns and indestructible truths. We recognize here an echo of Swinburne, who wrote "Men perish, but man shall endure" and "All men born are mortal, but not man."[14] We see also that Meredith is contradicting the line of thought he expressed in "Men and Man," but more important, we recognize how many of Meredith's ideas previously considered lead into the one we are now confronting. If personality is undesirable, if work is its own reward or is service to nature, if man is not to ask where he is going, then truly numbers, not individuals, are what count.

Meredith's concern with numbers has many ramifications and deserves a discussion in itself, but to follow that discussion would be to digress from our main interest of the moment, which is still his understanding of nature as process. Like many other of Meredith's interests, this concern with process was part of a broad nineteenth-century movement. On one side it was a "reaction against the type of rationalism which tended to reduce man and the world to machines."[15] To conceive of nature as an organic process in which man was involved along with other creatures was a way of returning to man something of the dignity removed from him by a mechanistic view of the universe. Later in the century, a new source arose to swell the flow of interest in organicity and shortly to become its main current. This of course was Darwinism. As Beach and others have pointed out, biologists since Darwin have been inclined "to affirm the continuity of the life-process manifested throughout the vegetable and animal worlds, and—in spite of distinctions and degrees—to assume some sort of radical identity throughout."[16]

A literary result of the scientific emphasis on natural process has been noted by G. M. Young, who says: "From *In Memoriam* to *The Woods of Westermain*, from *The Woods of Westermain* to the choruses of *The Dynasts*, we can follow the secular intellect seeking its way to such an apprehension of Being as Process as might hereafter reconcile the spiritual demands of humanity with the rapt and cosmic indifference of Evolution."[17]

For Meredith, as we have seen, "reconciliation" meant acceptance —not exactly of the "cosmic indifference of Evolution" but of the impossibility and immorality of regarding any single life as the dramatic journey through time of a uniquely fated personality. Indeed, to speak of *In Memoriam* and "The Woods of Westermain" as forming part of the same tradition is to speak really of opposite responses to the same problem. Nor does *The Dynasts* actually contain the same accents as "The Woods of Westermain," or for that matter, as any other of Meredith's poems. For Hardy, the indifference of the cosmic process was, in fact, a central reality as well as a shocking one. He never quite got over his glimpse of what he took to be the truth, and his bitterness and melancholy mask a refusal to accept the attack upon personality that is inherent in nineteenth-century science. Meredith, on the other hand, saw no reason for despair in the idea that the individual is insignificant.[18] He could color the very concept "cosmic process" with grandeur and beneficence and proclaim it a concrete reality worthy of man's joyous acceptance.

It will be instructive at this point to compare Meredith with Wordsworth, who in so many ways is the point of departure for any study of English nineteenth-century nature poetry. Consider these lines from the ninth book of *The Excursion*:

> "To every Form of being is assigned,"
> Thus calmly spake the venerable Sage,
> "An *active* Principle:—howe'er removed
> From sense and observation, it subsists
> In all things, in all natures . . .
>
> .   .   .   .   .   .   .   .   .   .
>
> Whate'er exists hath properties that spread
> Beyond itself, communicating good,
> A simple blessing, or with evil mixed."[19]

Commenting on this passage, Beach has said: "Wordsworth is

endeavoring to express himself, so nearly as possible, in accurate philosophical language; that whether clear or confused, consistent or inconsistent, there is implied a notion of the fundamental character of the natural process which is more than poetical. Nature is here conceived of, not merely as the order of things, the norm of conduct . . . but more specifically as the animating or activating principle of all things in the universe—not merely of living things, but of all phenomena."[20]

True, and implicit both in Wordsworth's lines and in Beach's gloss is an idea that establishes a contrast with Meredith. For Wordsworth, the "animating principle" is *in* all things; the things themselves are real, not just a mask for the principle. For Meredith, as we shall see in a moment, "things" or "forms" are inconsequential. The underlying process is the only reality. Thus, as we have already observed, the abstract fact of numbers, rather than the individuals who make up *t*he numbers, is "reality's flower." There is something almost Oriental in Meredith's feeling, while Wordsworth's preserves the Christian and humanist emphasis on personality.

Meredith's thought about natural process has one rather curious side. Just because process is impersonal it is not, to his mind, therefore cold. Indeed, the impersonal processes of nature, we must always remember, constitute the activity of "beneficence," though "beneficence" is never to be interpreted as the granting of special favor or consideration.

What Meredith creates in effect is a strange picture of impersonal kindness or generosity, directed in a negligent way toward the recipient, yet presumably worthy of man's reverence and joyous praise. Thus, in the poem "Earth and a Wedded Woman" (pp. 335–37) a heavy rainstorm revives the dry spirit and failing loyalty of a soldier's wife who has not seen her husband in three years. We think not only of *Richard Feverel* and the significance of the rain there, but of Coleridge's "The Ancient Mariner" and the meaning of a similar natural process in that poem. The storm in Coleridge's work "strikes as a consequence of the Mariner's redemption and brings him the life-giving rain."[21] That is precisely the difference. In Coleridge's poem, the Mariner has sinned and the rain symbolizes a partial redemption. In Meredith's, the wedded woman is suffering through no fault of her own, and she is restored to faith in life almost accidentally, certainly through no intention on the part of Divine Power to give her special attention. The rain is life-giving, and symbolic of beneficence, but the whole process is carried on without any intimation that the thoughts or deeds of the woman are involved in the moral of the story. Had the rain not come and revived her spirit, she would have been obliged to bear the dull weight of her deadened hopes; since it did come, she is obliged to be thankful. No other meaning is to be read in the events. No other *could* be read, since personality or ego or individual soul (the origin, from different points of view, of volition and consequently of sin or crime) is to be suppressed in the interest of conjoining man and the rest of nature.

### THE PERMANENCE OF ENERGY

The use of a vigorous rainstorm as a symbol of the life-giving force of nature suggests a major aspect of Meredith's conception of natural process. The underlying physical basis, both in nature and in the responsive woman, has been an awakening and release of energy. Like Goethe, Meredith made a great deal of the mere energy of nature—the energy which underlies natural process. As early as 1851 he showed keen awareness of the possibilities poetry offered for expressing, through its very structure, the effects of energy. In a letter to Edmund Ollier, in which he defended the metrical system he had used in his early poem "South-West Wind in the Woodland," he wrote as follows:

What you say of my blank octo-syllabic may be true, and is quite just; but the "S. W. Wind in the Woodland," in which I used it, is a subject which, in my opinion, would have been marred by rhyme, nor could I find any better mode of giving my impression of the reckless rushing rapidity, and sweeping sound of the great wind among the foliage; which I felt impelled to do in such manner that the ear should only be conscious of swiftness, and not sweetness; and that there should be no direct pause throughout. This (in my mind) the hurrying measure of the four feet gives. The blank "stanzas" are more open to objection, I admit. Believe me, I venerate English poetry too much to make any variation on the old majestic metre of Epic, Pastoral, & Drama; I used it for a purpose; for such a purpose I would use it again, but only for such a purpose and under such a plea.[22]

Meredith's technique can readily be illustrated by quoting in part the last stanza of the poem (pp. 25–26):

The voice of nature is abroad
This night; she fills the air with balm;
Her mystery is o'er the land;
And who that hears her now and yields
His being to her yearning tones,
And seats his soul upon her wings,
And broadens o'er the wind-swept world
With her, will gather in the flight
More knowledge of her secret, more
Delight in her beneficence,
Than hours of musing, or the lore
That lives with men could ever give!
Nor will it pass away when morn
Shall look upon the lulling leaves,
And woodland sunshine, Eden-sweet,
Dreams o'er the paths of peaceful shade;—
For every elemental power
Is kindred to our hearts, and once
Acknowledged, wedded, once embraced,
Once taken to the unfettered sense,
Once claspt into the naked life,
The union is eternal.

Besides noting how the meter does convey the swift, rushing energy of nature, we note the obvious similarity here to Wordsworth's thought. But we see that in "South-West Wind in the Woodland" knowledge of nature has to be gathered by seating oneself upon nature's wings—must be gathered in "flight." The dynamic energetic motion that Meredith thus uses symbolically to represent the condition for receiving knowledge is in marked contrast to the sedate, reposeful state which Wordsworth makes a condition for knowing when he says,

One impulse from a vernal wood
May teach you more of man,
Of moral evil and of good,
Than all the sages can.[23]

The "impulse" comes from the vernal wood to man, who is presumably at rest. In Meredith's lines, the knowledge is actively gathered during the symbolic act of flight. Thus, what the comparison helps emphasize is that even in imagery Meredith evoked energetic motion to convey the effect of what nature is. Moreover, he did this even when he was most interested in the accessibility of nature's essence to man. The idea is remarkable, for it says in effect that nature can be known best when she is in the act of changing—change being one of the inevitable consequences of motion, the phenomenon symbolized by flight. Yet this is what Meredith believes, and the root reason for his belief is the feeling that the play of energy (the underlying reality beneath all change) can be apprehended by the senses. This "sense-knowledge" is, for Meredith, one of the profoundest forms of knowledge of nature.

As for the metrical technique Meredith employed in "The South-West Wind in the Woodland," we can say that notwithstanding his veneration for "the old majestic metre of Epic, Pastoral, & Drama," he was of course to use it very little. On the other hand, during his "second poetic period"—i.e., the late decades of his life—he again found occasion to use a fairly regular four-stress line to represent the swift energy of a day brought alive by the southwest wind. He did so in "The South-Wester" (p. 321), which appears in the 1888 volume, *A Reading of Earth*:

> Day of the cloud in fleets! O day
> Of wedded white and blue, that sail
> Immingled, with a footing ray
> In shadow-sandals down our vale!—
> And swift to ravish golden meads,
> Swift up the run of turf it speeds,
> Thy bright of head and dark of heel,
> To where the hilltop flings on sky,
> As hawk from wrist or dust from wheel,
> The tiptoe scalers tossed to fly:—
> Thee the last thunder's caverned peal
> Delivered from a wailful night.

Everything in these lines suggests bursting energy rushing dynamic natural processes through their paces. The day is "delivered from wailful night" by "the last thunder's caverned peal." The wind is "swift to ravish golden meads." Even the hill, usually thought of as the most inert of natural formations, is here activated and is engaged in the most energetic play, for it "flings on sky . . . The tiptoe scalers tossed to fly."

In "Hard Weather" (pp. 318–19), another poem in the 1888

volume, Meredith describes a storm. The delight he takes in the
sheer energy of the phenomenon, however destructive it may be, is
too obvious to require extensive comment.

> Bursts from a rending East in flaws
> The young green leaflet's harrier, sworn
> To strew the garden, strip the shaws,
> And show our Spring with banner torn.
> Was ever such virago morn?
> The wind has teeth, the wind has claws,
> All the wind's wolves through woods are loose,
> The wild wind's falconry aloft.
> Shrill underfoot the grassblade shrews,
> At gallop, clumped, and down the croft
> Bestrid by shadows, beaten, tossed;
> It seems a scythe, it seems a rod.
> The howl is up at the howl's accost;
> The shivers greet and the shivers nod.
>
> Is the land ship? we are rolled, we drive
> Tritonly, cleaving hiss and hum;
> Whirl with the dead, or mount or dive,
> Or down in dregs, or on in scum.
> And drums the distant, pipes the near,
> And vale and hill are grey in grey,
> As when the surge is crumbling sheer,
> And sea-mews wing the haze of spray.
> Clouds—are they bony witches?—swarms,
> Darting swift on the robber's flight,
> Hurry an infant sky in arms:
> It peeps, it becks; 'tis day, 'tis night.
> Black while over the loop of blue
> The swathe is closed, like shroud on corse.
> Lo, as if swift the Furies flew,
> The Fates at heel at a cry to horse!

Like so many other experiences registered in his poetry, the
pleasure Meredith takes in the energy of the storm is not only an
end in itself but a grounding—in feeling as it were—for a philosophic
attitude. We noted earlier that the impermanence of natural forms
was to Meredith no cause for sorrow and no proof of nature's hostility
to the "correct" aspirations of man. We can say now that it is the
profound response of his senses to nature's energy that enables him
to view the transformation and disappearance of forms with so little
concern.

Something of the connection is indicated in "A Faith on Trial."
In the following lines, Earth is speaking (p. 360):

> 'Let the types break,
> 'Men be grass, rocks rivers, all flow;
> 'All save the dream sink alike
> 'To the source of my vital in sap:
> 'Their battle, their loss, their ache,
> 'For my pledge of vitality know.'

What is noumenal and lasting is "the source of [Earth's] vital in
sap." Despite the awkwardness and vagueness of the line, it connotes
a source of energy. Meredith has caused Earth to utter the lesson of
his own experience. All forms pass away but something does remain.
That "something" is the surviving impress upon the senses of patterned energy. This impress, like Earth's "vital," must have a source,
one which Earth knows and can locate though he cannot.

The heroic tone of these lines is all the more striking in that
they are part of the poem Meredith wrote just after his wife's death.
The circumstances surrounding their composition help us to see
that though there is a forcing of issues in them, his determination
to accept the thought expressed is very real. And it is this determination that gives the lines their tone.

The tone makes for an interesting comparison with Tennyson's
response to the "breaking of types." "She," in the following lines,
as in Meredith's, is nature:

> 'So careful of the type?' but no.
> From scarped cliff and quarried stone
> She cries, 'A thousand types are gone;
> I care for nothing, all shall go.'[24]

This is better poetry than the passage just quoted from "A Faith
on Trial." There are no abstract, unclear images here, no unsuccessful
inversions of syntax as in Meredith's last two lines. Comparing
thought and attitude, however, calls for a different kind of observation. We note that insofar as nature herself is in charge of things,
nothing matters, according to Tennyson. No "pledge of vitality"—
i.e., of something more permanent than types—is given. Indeed, in
the context in which these lines appear, Tennyson is arraigning nature for her indifference to the desire for permanence which he, like
the rest of mankind, holds noble and precious. Her rebuff to mankind's yearnings has for Tennyson coldly tragic overtones, not to be

removed until an authentic religious affirmation becomes possible. Meredith, by contrast, takes nature's indifference to the permanence of types, as of individuals, as a sign of her gallant love for life: her "pledge of vitality." Her indifference to types is the corollary of her concern for something higher, the life force or energy which is real and permanent and does not betray the mind that seeks an anchor for faith. Again, there are resemblances here to mysticism and Eastern thought, as well, of course, as to German idealism and, by anticipation, to Bergson. This is ironic, for Meredith was anti-mystical as far as he knew himself. But these observations bring us back to the most important consideration of all. For Tennyson, as for most men in the Western tradition, the idea of love without permanence for the object of love is suspect; for Meredith it is the most reasonable idea in the world. Far from needing an abiding object, love itself is conceived by Meredith as an abstract force, similar in meaning sometimes to the very word "energy." This equation of meaning seems to have taken place in the following two lines, which occur in "The Woods of Westermain" (p. 197):

> Love, the great volcano, flings
> Fires of lower Earth to sky.

Commenting upon these lines and the context in which they appear (a discussion of "change"), Roppen has said: "Love is the 'nerve of change,' giving Earth features 'heavenly new'; it is the very 'clue' to her secret."[25] We can add that love is obviously in these lines the primal force or energy that has underlain all the transformations of evolution. Such love, by its very nature, is not interested in the permanence of objects or of types.

The close association in Meredith's mind between love and energy is indicated by a passage occurring in "The Thrush in February," though here energy, or vitality, is regarded as a quality of love rather than an equivalent (p.331):

> Love born of knowledge, love that gains
> Vitality as Earth it mates,
> The meaning of the Pleasures, Pains,
> The Life, the Death, illuminates.

"Love born of knowledge" gains vitality by becoming the love of things of Earth. But things of Earth are undergoing constant change, and thus the most authentic love is the kind that gains energy by "mating" with the impermanent, which is also, as we know, the vital.

The lines quoted, telling us that love thus brought to life "illuminates" the meaning of the experiences and processes that make up the existence of man, bring us to the final themes in the pattern we have watched emerge. The "illumination" is, by its very purpose and scope, religious, and thus Meredith's attempt to break away from a definition of love that depends on the existence of a fixed personality to be loved led him finally to the largest questions about the "spiritual." For us, in this discussion, his answers to these questions lie at the very heart of his conception of nature. Indeed, the other aspects of this conception—egoism, work, process, and energy—all lead us to the vital center these larger questions and their answers occupy.

EARTH, THE MOTHER

Before turning to the poetry expressing these central themes, let us take note of what others have said about the religious meaning of Meredith's conception of Earth. G. M. Trevelyan compares it with Wordsworth's:

Mr. Meredith's conception of life stands out in likeness and in contrast to that of Wordsworth. Each had a poetical philosophy claiming to interpret the face of nature, and each was certainly inspired to success in literature by perpetual and loving contact with Earth in all her moods. But Wordsworth was constrained by his beliefs to despise the breast upon which he fed his soul. In the *Ode on the Intimations of Immortality,* he gave the finest expression to the old orthodox view that we are children, not of Earth, but of Heaven. To Wordsworth, sojourn in this life here was an exile (. . . we come / From God, who is our home). Earth was not the mother, but only the foster-nurse . . .

Wordsworth supposed that his "high instincts," "the fountain-light of all his day," were not inherited from Earth, but implanted in him from Heaven above.

Not so Mr. Meredith. To him Earth is the Mother. . . .We are not dropped down from Heaven above. We are autochthonous. Earth, of which we are a part, is spirit as well as matter, flame as well as clod. What is spiritual comes out of Earth, as well as what is fleshly. . . . He uses Earth as the sanction for all his moral precepts, just as other poets and preachers have so used Heaven.[26]

Whether it is true or not that Wordsworth despised "the breast upon which he fed his soul," Trevelyan is dealing with a real difference between Wordsworth and Meredith. It is a difference bred not only by a half century of history but by temperament. The center

of Wordsworth's nature poetry—i.e., the dramatic actor in the poems—
is the thinking, feeling poet. At the center of Meredith's nature
poetry, in a post-Darwinian world in which Meredith himself, moreover, had never had any traditional beliefs to lose, is Earth herself.
Joseph Warren Beach has proffered an observation which throws
light on Meredith, though it does not concern him exclusively: "It is
not without significance that in nature-poetry the motherhood of
nature corresponds to the fatherhood of God in supernatural religion.
Essentially the same emotion reigns in naturalism as in traditional
religion. In the want of religion man rallies to nature in order not to
feel himself an orphan in the universe."[27]

Whether Meredith "rallied" to nature in order not to feel himself
an orphan in the universe is a question. As a young man, in order to
compensate for the fact that he was, actually, half-orphaned and
separated from his tailor father who still lived, he rallied to the
world of letters, where he found friends upon whom he became quite
dependent for awhile. Nevertheless, it is certainly true that the
"motherhood" of nature corresponds in Meredith's poetry to the *position* held by the fatherhood of God in traditional religion. It does
not, however, correspond to the *concept* of God, nor does it really
evoke the same emotion. Just how Meredith conceives of Mother
Earth is a matter that will require careful inquiry on our part. An
understanding of what kind of mother Earth, or nature, is to him is
essential for an understanding of the religious center of his conception
of nature.

As to what might be called the "character" of Mother Earth, a
comment by Trevelyan, though it will in part be disputed here, provides a clue. He says that in Meredith's poetry "God is identified, not
with all Nature, but with the good elements in her."[28] I question
the identification of "God" with "Nature" in Meredith's work and
shall show why. As a description of "Mother Earth," however, Trevelyan's statement would, it seems to me, be more just. Earth is, indeed, identified with the good elements in nature. And what this
tells us is that Meredith chose to idealize his Mother Earth, to insist
that her apparent cruelties and evils were merely chimeras seen only
by the coward or disobedient son (much the same thing) and that
her more admirable qualities were her real, "objective" ones. "The
Woods of Westermain" makes this clear.

However, Earth—and this is important—is not an overindulgent

mother anxious, long past their infancy, for the safety of her offspring. She is a mother who has read Darwin and has dedicated
her children to the historical drama he revealed to her (p. 330):

> She, judged of shrinking nerves, appears
> A Mother whom no cry can melt;
> But read her past desires and fears,
> The letters on her breast are spelt.
>
> A slayer, yea, as when she pressed
> Her savage to the slaughter-heaps,
> To sacrifice she prompts her best:
> She reaps them as the sower reaps.
>
> But read her thought to speed the race,
> And stars rush forth of blackest night:
> You chill not at a cold embrace
> To come, nor dread a dubious might.

Stern as Mother Earth is, however, she can be addressed. She
does offer, we recall, various kinds of "knowledge" to those of her
children whose inquiries are inspired by wisdom and courage. Indeed, she is a kind of schoolmistress, severe but responsive to the
pupil who is able to ask the relevant questions.

There is a rich field for speculation in the question, why did
Meredith, who hardly knew his own mother, turn Earth into a
tutorial preceptress rather than a gentler figure? Part of the answer
is that he had simply to deal with the facts of life: nature appeared
cruel to many of his contemporaries and he had taken it upon himself to defend her without indulging in "sentimentality." The preceptress figure seemed to him to rescue nature from indictments
such as Arnold's and Tennyson's without falsifying the record of her
conduct. In more personal terms, however, speculation must remain
meager and unsatisfying. Meredith's mother, who died when her son
was five, was undoubtedly a woman of strong character. If there is
any suggestion of her in Mrs. Mel, the mother of Evan Harrington,
she must indeed have been a forceful person. It seems hardly likely,
however, that the faint memories Meredith could have had of his
mother, whatever she was like, were neither softened nor prepared
to yield a tenderer figure. A better explanation of his conception
of Earth the Mother would seem to relate to a more general nineteenth-century desire to picture woman as a source of strength and

character and unsentimental wisdom. Meredith's Earth is not strikingly different from the best kind of Victorian mother: quiet but wise, devoted not to her children's whims but to their futures. But we are again touching upon a cultural fact rather than Meredith's particular experience. When we have said all there is to say, the irreducible personal element remains: the fantasized mother who is truly loved and revered but who has no gentle kindness or forgiving mercy. It is, to say the least, a strange fantasy.

To return, however, to the religious meaning of Earth, which must of course be discussed in itself and without dependent references to the psychological or even cultural meanings that coexist with it, we should note that Meredith also conceived of Earth as an intermediate entity between man and God. This very fact disallows Trevelyan's statement that in Meredith's poetry God is equated with certain elements of Earth. It is also worth noting that in representing God as being above nature, Meredith differs from Swinburne, with whose own conception of Earth Meredith's has regularly been compared.[29]

We have said that the position Meredith ascribes to Earth is all-important. For him Earth does indeed occupy the position that God the Father occupies in traditional religions. In "Earth and Man" Meredith makes this explicitly clear. "He" refers to man, and the feminine references are, of course, to Earth (p. 244):

### XXIX

If he aloft for aid
Imploring storms, her essence is the spur.
His cry to heaven is a cry to her
He would evade.

### XXX

Not elsewhere can he tend.
Those are her rules which bid him wash foul sins;
Those her revulsions from the skull that grins
To ape his end.

### XXXI

And her desires are those
For happiness, for lastingness, for light.
'Tis she who kindles in his haunting night
The hoped dawn-rose.

Regarding these lines, Beach has said:

However different his poetic idiom, Meredith is here taking sides with Swinburne and Goethe against the dualism of Tennyson and Browning. . . . Meredith is asserting here, as Swinburne asserted in "Hertha": out of Earth come "God and man." That is, our religious impulses, both those approved by nature, and those upon which she frowns, are an outgrowth of our natural instincts. There is nowhere any separate source of religious inspiration, transcending nature and giving the lie to her. There is not even in man a faculty for supplementing the teaching of nature which is not itself derived from nature.[30]

I do not see that these lines show Meredith agreeing with Swinburne that "out of Earth come 'God and Man.'" Elsewhere, moreover, Meredith gives definite if undetailed evidence that he conceives of God as "above" nature, not her invention. What these lines do indicate is that our religious impulses, according to Meredith, originate in Earth and must be directed back to Earth;* in Meredith's vision of the universe, Earth has the position but not the meaning that God has in other visions. We must ask aid of Earth, and we must behave religiously in accordance with her rules because the order of the universe requires us to. As for an ultimate origin of her power to make rules or grant certain requests (for knowledge), the poem says nothing, neither denying nor asserting the existence of such an origin.

It does seem to me, however, that Beach is correct in saying that according to Meredith "there is nowhere any separate source of religious inspiration, transcending nature and giving the lie to her." Earth in this poem is indeed the source of man's religious inspiration, whatever her own source may be. This creed was formulated early. In a letter to Maxse written in 1861 Meredith said: "Our great error has been (the error of all religion, as I fancy) to raise a spiritual system in antagonism to Nature."[31] Referring to this letter, Beach has observed: "He is obviously using the term 'spiritual system' for any system which professes to find the essential truth of life outside the frame of nature."[32]

---

* I see no reason to assume that Meredith equated the terms "God" and "religious impulses," as Swinburne certainly did. It does not follow that because Meredith regarded religious impulses as originating in Earth he must therefore have believed God had the same origin. In fact, the evidence points to the contrary.

Though once more there is nothing in Meredith's words that points to the denial of an ultimate concept beyond nature—i.e., to a denial of God—Beach's comment this time seems to me true. But what catches our attention is the word "system." It is not spiritual yearning or even the ordinary language in which religious experiences are reported that Meredith opposes but only religious *systems* raised in antagonism to nature. Meredith's language could even be construed as a desire for reconciliation between himself and theologians. Give Mother Earth her due, he seems to say, and I will respect your interest in what lies beyond nature.

Moreover, we would commit a great error if we loosely generalized Meredith's criticism of systems that create antagonism between "spirit" and nature into repudiation on his part of all systems. The truth is that Meredith's religious yearnings, sometimes seemingly mystical, were at bottom a striving to erect a substitute system of his own. Meredith never discovered or created this substitute, but the compass needle in his work keeps pointing toward one.

It is not his conception of Mother Earth that reveals the direction in which he was traveling; it is his insistence, over and over again, on the primacy of law. And an understanding of what he means by law, and of how this meaning is expressed as poetry, is necessary if we are to follow Meredith as he journeyed, making certain one foot or the other was always firmly planted on the ground, through what he took to be the realm of spirit.

### TRIUMPHANT AND IMMUTABLE LAW

His conception of law was not philosophically sophisticated. It had something to do with "natural law," but it would be difficult to relate his thinking in any specific way to the centuries-long debate over what natural law is. The law he bowed down to was the simple abstraction, "law." If he could not believe in the dogmas and doctrines of Christianity, he could not stop believing that the universe is governed by law, its workings and regularities discernible to the wise man. In some ways it would seem that Meredith had in mind the operational statements of the physicist, biologist, and psychologist, but he was never specific enough to enable us to go beyond mere speculation as to what it was he referred to.

What his work does reveal and allow us to note is that the

very existence of law in the universe was for him a fact of great spiritual significance. Actually, it was a fact that appealed to his senses rather than his intellect, just as his apprehension of natural process and of energy constituted a form of sensory experience for him. Nevertheless, his intellect did help his imagination create a vision of reality based on these experiences. Intellect enabled him to see reality as a universal process informed throughout by an energy he would readily have called divine and governed in its regular workings by "law."

In "The Last Contention" he says (p. 303):

> Admires thee Nature with much pride;
> She clasps thee for a gift of morn,
> Till thou art set against the tide,
> And then beware her scorn.

Nature's "tide" is nature's law, and he who opposes it will suffer— i.e., be the victim of nature's scorn, never a passive thing. To set oneself against her tide is to invite retribution as certain and specific as any conceived of within traditional religions.

Just how persistently Meredith's inchoate but undeniable system resembles arrangements more obviously religious in their inspiration is impressed upon us by the function Meredith assigns to love. Explaining again the relation between men and Earth, he says in "The Thrush in February" (p. 331):

> And why the sons of Strength have been
> Her cherished offspring ever; how
> The Spirit served by her is seen
> Through Law; perusing love will show.

The technical failures of these lines—the ineffectual effort at varied rhythm creating only the dying fall between the second and third lines; and the theatrical pause at the end of the third—should not prevent us from acknowledging their rightful place in the development of Meredith's thought. They tell us that our love of Earth will lead us to understand that the "Spirit" Earth serves, God, can be perceived only through grasp of the laws governing nature's processes. Here, as in so much traditional religious thought, love is the key to an understanding of God, though Meredith has added an idea that sounds as if it were inspired half by nineteenth-century science and half by Dante. "Perusing love" will enable man not only to comprehend the laws governing the universe but to see that those laws are of divine origin.

Thus the very idea of law is, in Meredith's philosophy, richly connotative of religious meaning. It is therefore not strange to find that laws are not only physical but moral in function. They are to be obeyed as well as understood. In "A Faith on Trial" they are presented as the decrees of Mother Earth, their ultimate source in "the Spirit she serves" being disregarded for the purposes of the poem. Yet these are the same laws that are so revelatory in "The Thrush in February." They have the same religious meaning. However, they are described now as instruments of reproof, which is what they become when man revolts against them, refusing to accept them. There is, incidentally, no contradiction in the fact that Meredith regards many of the practices encouraged by Christianity as just such a revolt against Earth and "the Spirit she serves."

Here are the lines that make clear the reproving function of natural laws, "she" again being Earth (p. 354):

> For the flesh in revolt at her laws,
> Neither song nor smile in ruth,
> Nor promise of things to reveal,
> Has she, nor a word she saith:
> We are asking her wheels to pause.
> Well knows she the cry of unfaith.
> If we strain to the farther shore,
> We are catching at comfort near.
> Assurances, symbols, saws,
> Revelations in legends, light
> To eyes rolling darkness, these
> Desired of the flesh in affright,
> For the which it will swear to adore,
> She yields not for prayers at her knees;
> The woolly beast bleating will shear.

In any contest to discover the worst line in English poetry, serious consideration would have to be given to "For the which it will swear to adore." What makes the matter even more uncomfortable is that the line is not improved when put back into context; it takes some time before we realize that the terrible "which" has as its antecedent "Assurances, symbols, saws,/ Revelations in legends, light." And realization, when it comes, brings no gratification.

Yet once more we are obliged to pluck meaning from briars and nettles that serve no discernible natural purpose. The meaning is that the cardinal sin in Meredith's theology is to ask the wrong questions, to pray for the wrong things, to petition, in short, for special, personal dispensation. We have touched again on Meredith's basic quarrel with Christianity: he abhors the implied uniqueness-of-being in the Christian concept, "soul," and like a good nineteenth-century scientist he swells with anger at any suggestion that "natural law," which he confidently assumes to be knowable and immutable, can be separated from any other system of law, such as "supernatural" law, for example.

One reason of course why Meredith feels no need to distinguish natural from supernatural law is that the former performs for him all the functions the Christian theologian usually ascribes to the latter. We recall that Meredith believes in the existence of "beneficence." It should not surprise us, therefore, to learn that natural law itself is a form of universal beneficence. In Meredith's exact words, Earth's law is "the one common weal." This provocative thought occurs in another passage of "A Faith on Trial." Again, "she" refers to Earth (pp. 354–55):

> Not she gives the tear for the tear:
> Harsh wisdom gives Earth, no more;
> In one the spur and the curb:
> And answer to thoughts or deeds;
> To the Legends an alien look;
> To the Questions a figure of clay.
> Yet we have but to see and hear,
> Crave we her medical herb,
> For the road to her soul is the Real:
> The root of the growth of man:
> And the senses must traverse it fresh
> With a love that no scourge shall abate,
> To reach the lone heights where we scan
> In the mind's rarer vision this flesh;
> In the charge of the Mother our fate;
> Her law as the one common weal.

For purposes of our discussion this passage is not only rich in perorations but begins a new excursion. The passage starts with an allusion to Mother Earth we find familiar: she is a mother who gives no comfort, only harsh wisdom. It goes on to say that she repudiates the doctrines (legends) of organized religions, and rejects also nonpositivistic questions, i.e., Whither and Whence. Yet if we love reality, Earth will cure our sick longings and ideas. We will, once cured, realize that she has charge of our fate and has provided us with a single boon: her law, the one immutable fact of existence.

That Meredith shared the characteristic nineteenth-century belief that natural law—or man's reading of it—could be "immutable," is made even clearer somewhat further on in "A Faith on Trial" when the poet says (p. 358) that man's task with respect to Earth is

> To know her a thing alive,
> Whose aspects mutably swerve.
> Whose laws immutably reign.

Here is a new absolutism, the one accent needed to complete Meredith's eclectic but fairly coherent theology. In a world in which the very fact of change—decay, mutability of forms, disappearance of loved ones—is to be accepted without grief or protest, something (Meredith apparently feels) has to hold still if man's faith is to be justified. That something is law, so abstract and indeterminate in Meredith's use of the concept that it is indeed safe: safe from the undermining probes that closer inspection would permit. Ironically, the only way to discuss Meredith's belief in the immutability of law, a phrase which in his usage has indistinct scientific connotations, is to describe this belief as an article of faith holding together his vision of the universe.

But there is something more important about this unreasoned belief than the fact that it is ironic. "A Faith on Trial" is not very good poetry. It is not a successful employment for poetic purposes of Meredith's reverence for law. Yet happily this reverence, or faith, did inspire one of his best poems, "Lucifer in Starlight," a sonnet included in the 1883 volume, *Poems and Lyrics of the Joy of Earth.* Here is "Lucifer" (pp. 181–82):

> On a starred night Prince Lucifer uprose.
> Tired of his dark dominion swung the fiend
> Above the rolling ball in cloud part screened,
> Where sinners hugged their spectre of repose.
> Poor prey to his hot fit of pride were those.
> And now upon his western wing he leaned,

Now his huge bulk o'er Afric's sands careened,
Now the black planet shadowed Arctic snows.
Soaring through wider zones that pricked his scars
With memory of the old revolt from Awe,
He reached a middle height, and at the stars,
Which are the brain of heaven, he looked, and sank.
Around the ancient track marched, rank on rank,
The army of unalterable law.

This poem has received considerable attention from critics of
our own day who normally find Meredith's poetry unworthy of their
concern. Brooks and Warren, for example, subject it to close scrutiny
in their influential *Understanding Poetry*. They begin by classifying
"Lucifer" as an example of how a poet treats "theme," rather than
metrics, tone, attitude, or imagery—their other analytic categories.
They get around to these other aspects of the poem, but they clearly
feel that Meredith's immediate appeal to the reader has something to
do with this theme, or in other words, his ideas. They see his theme
as the conflict in the universe between the principle of anarchy and
the principle of order. They call attention to the way Meredith has
absorbed science without changing the enduring meaning of the
Lucifer myth:

Meredith attempts to give as vivid a picture as possible of the enormous
bulk of the Fiend, like a planet, flying so near the "rolling ball" of the
earth that he shadows it, presumably, from the moon. One may notice
that in giving this picture Meredith casts the mythical figure of the Fiend
into the universe as we now conceive it, describing the Earth revolving in
its orbit, and does not use the fixed, central earth of the Ptolemaic conception, which Milton, for instance, used. This detail, though small in itself,
gives a certain novelty to Meredith's treatment. It seems to imply, perhaps as a kind of undertone to the poem, that the old force of anarchy is
still operating, despite changes in human conceptions, and trying to reach
out, even beyond human affairs, to the very center of the universe.[33]

It will be noticed that despite their desire to reconcile Meredith's
with a traditional point of view, Brooks and Warren do see a "novelty" in the shift from a Ptolemaic universe. We can only be puzzled
as to why, since they began by citing "Lucifer" as an example of
"thematic" poetry, they make so little of what was, after all, a religious and philosophical shift. However, they make amends a moment
later: curiously ignoring the laconic and deprecating implications of

their use of the word "novelty," they decide that the reason given
by Meredith for Lucifer's failure to proceed with his present rebellion
is significantly new.

[Lucifer] does not sink again because he encounters the divine force that
once hurled him down. . . . The stars, the poet says, are "the brain of
heaven." Apparently, the recognition of this fact is what conquers the impulse of the Fiend. The order of the stars demonstrates the reasonable
nature of the universe, against which it is useless to rebel. One need
not call on an exhibition of divine powers, the poet is saying, to conquer
the impulse of anarchy and rebellion; the slightest understanding of the
construction of the universe is enough.

As for the way the metric pattern contributes to the expression
of Meredith's meaning, Brooks and Warren have the following to say:

One can observe that the relatively regular and heavy beat of the verse,
the preponderance of monosyllables and hovering accents making for a
retarded movement, and the many end-stop lines with light caesura, help
give the impression of ponderous, sullen majesty which the image of Lucifer
inspires. But there are some more special details that are worthy of notice.
The relative absence of heavy internal pauses in the lines makes such
pauses come, by contrast, with a special emphasis. The first one appears in
line 11 to give an emphatic preparation for the "stars," the word that
raises the fundamental idea of the poem. In line 12 the pauses set off
"he looked," and "and sank" so that the pauses contribute to the impression
of Lucifer's taking a long and thoughtful inspection of the firmament and
then slowly descending. In line 13 the fourth foot of the line is composed
of the words *marched, rank,* but the foot gives a spondaic effect, because
of the hovering accent, which occurs elsewhere as in the second foot,
*black plan*—of line 8. This fact, and the preparatory pause before *rank*
give a powerful emphasis. In line 14 the most important idea, in fact the
most important idea of the poem, is contained in the word *unalterable.*
This word is composed of five syllables. It is two syllables longer than
any other in the poem, standing in contrast to the prevailing use of monosyllables. It is divided *un-al-ter-a-ble.* The accent falls on the second
syllable, *al,* and the last three syllables tend to be slurred together. But in
the iambic pentameter line in which the word appears in the poem, two
of the regular metrical beats fall on syllables of the word: *un-ál-ter-á-ble.*
This means that the entire word is given more force than is usual; and this
is effective, because of the importance of the word in relation to the subject of the poem.

The exhaustive and exhausting thoroughness of this metrical analysis discourages any desire I might have had to present one myself,
particularly since I see nothing to disagree with in the passage quoted.

Rather, I would call attention to the fact that Brooks and Warren, who presumably approached the poem without any special interest in the theme of immutable law in Meredith's work and thought as a whole, have found the conception and the words that express it so poetically powerful in "Lucifer." The proportion of their analysis that is devoted to showing the effectiveness of this one idea[34] bears out, I feel, my own assertion that "Lucifer" is the best of Meredith's poems to have been inspired by his faith in immutable natural law.

Ironically, "Lucifer" is better than Meredith's other poems whose theme is "law" because, unlike them, it is governed by law. "Lucifer" is an Italian sonnet and, except for the rhyme scheme of the sestet, involves no attempt at experiment. Can it be that Meredith was not destined to be a successful experimenter in verse, that he would have done better to avoid extravagant inversions, strained abstract images, stanzas running to hundreds of lines?

The answer of course depends upon a choice of values. It is too early to assess Meredith's contribution to the history of poetic form, though there is not too much to expect because no major poet in the past fifty years of intense experimentation in verse has acknowledged any large debt to Meredith.[35] Perhaps he will always be eclipsed by Browning, a much more successful experimenter. Yet it seems unspeakably narrow, as an attitude toward literary history, to wish that a failure who was bold had been less bold, even though he demonstrated how much better he could be when he submitted to tradition. All we can properly do is note that on one of the few occasions on which Meredith accepted some poetic "law" he gave supremely good poetic expression to one of his most firmly held convictions, which is none other than that man should and must comply with law.

We turn now to the theme, already noted in part, which is the logical culmination of Meredith's religious understanding, and which, though it did not inspire the kind of poetry we have just observed, is as essential to a full rendering of his religious vision as Dante's *Paradise* was to his own poetic purpose. I speak, of course, of Meredith's conception of God.

## THE GOD OF EARTH AND MAN

As we observed, it is often assumed that Meredith worked hard to avoid acknowledging the validity of any such conception; that, like Swinburne, he quite literally substituted Mother Earth for God.

However, we have already noted allusions in Meredith's poetry that refute this loose identification of his point of view with Swinburne's. We can now take cognizance of other references which show that Meredith, however much—given certain of his ideas—he ought to have been as antitheistic as Swinburne, actually took pains to announce he was not.

In "Earth and Man" Meredith refers to Earth's "just Lord," and it would be as wrong to say that this reference represents an intellectual lapse on Meredith's part as it would, probably, to say that it represents a momentary upsurge of traditional belief. However, no twisting and turning of the meaning, whatever the state of his mind and feelings when he wrote the words, can change the fact that Meredith makes an explicit reference to God. In the following lines, "she" refers to Earth and "he" to man. Meredith says (p. 245):

> She her just Lord may view,
> Not he, her creature, till his soul has yearned
> With all her gifts to reach the light discerned
> Her spirit through.

Earth, in other words, is but a representative—or a representation—after all, albeit one more readily apprehended by man than is God directly. In "A Faith on Trial," Earth envisions herself in precisely such terms when she describes herself as "The flag of the Master I serve" (p. 361). In the lines quoted from "Earth and Man" there may be a historical suggestion, i.e., that man is not yet ready to see God directly and will not be until he has learned to use the gifts nature has given him "to reach the light." We are being conjectural, but if Meredith means anything at all he has obviously involved himself deeply in speculative theology. The use of the "light" symbol is of course reminiscent of Dante's vision and of other religious poetry.

In a later poem, "The Test of Manhood," we get references to God that are both affirmative and evasive. The poet says (pp. 541–42):

> In fellowship religion has its founts:
> The solitary his own God reveres:
> Ascend no sacred Mounts
> Our hungers or our fears.
> As only for the numbers Nature's care
> Is shown, and she the personal nothing heeds,
> So to Divinity the spring of prayer
> From brotherhood the one way upward leads.

Brotherhood may be the condition for effective prayer, but the prayer is nevertheless directed to "Divinity," a fact which raises a slight contradiction with respect to Meredith's earlier assertions that man must pray to Earth. Further on in the poem Meredith adds to this newer conception by referring to "the Master mind discerned,/ The Great Unseen, nowise the Dark Unknown." In short, God, though unseen, is knowable. We may presume, however, that the knowledge is to be gained through knowledge of Earth, so the contradiction of earlier poems is somewhat mitigated.

Yet when we look once more at the way God has been added to the vision of reality, and reflect on how a full understanding of the role of Mother Earth has had to await this addition of God, we come to a wry conclusion. The poet who insisted in "A Faith on Trial" that a cry to God for personal salvation is an evasion of acknowledging the role Mother Earth plays in the scheme of the universe has intermittently but persistently suggested that beyond Earth is a Master, a Lord, a Great-Unseen-but-Nowise-Unknowable. What happens, then, in retrospect, to Meredith's conception of Mother Earth? It becomes, indeed, a kind of pagan substitute for the veneration of Mary, though as our previous description makes clear, Meredith's stern Mother Earth is markedly different from the traditional Catholic image of Mary as the fount of mercy and the compassionate interceder between man and God. A further conclusion, equally wry, follows this one: though Meredith could find no rest or satisfaction or possibility of belief in the doctrines of Christianity—the "legends" he spurns more than once—his efforts to give structure to the universe suggest a mind busily engaged in making up its own legends.

IGNORANCE AS GRACE

What then, by way of a final, general conclusion, shall we say of the poetry that expresses these legends? Though the idea of grace, in any of its Christian meanings, could not have been very congenial to Meredith, it is a temptation to say that he was denied grace when he essayed poems about his "Mother Earth" and was granted it when he stayed within the limits of his nineteenth-century rational understanding and asserted the immutability of "law"; or, on the other hand, when he played the pagan metaphysician, celebrating nature's processes and energy for their own sake. We would also have to say, if we speak in this manner, that he was denied grace when he made poetic references to God. Clearly the lines referring to God are not authentically devotional or even perfervid: Meredith was not Gerard Manley Hopkins, not part of the Christian revival. In a world in which a juggler's gifts are supremely acceptable, however, it is not surprising that Meredith's best offerings, though he did not realize it, were made when he was least theological, least intellectual, or least contentious and experimental—when he worked within his own limits. These limits were rather narrow, and it is therefore doubtful that he will ever have the poetic reputation he desired. Yet even here a conserving word is in order. When he trespassed beyond his limits, he did not fall into the void. He presented us with the mind of nineteenth-century man searching for something to believe, pretending to believe, yet saved, by ignorance of its own contradictions and by lack of insight, from enervating anxiety, and thus able to go on and work. Perhaps, then, Meredith's confident ignorance of his own failures as a poet and as a spiritual thinker may be viewed as a form of saving grace. It enabled him to write the handful of good poems that accrue to his credit, and it enabled him to affirm the purposefulness of his own activity, surely proof of election or reward, as the case may be.

# 5

## The Final Vision

### THE 1890's

If old age is a period of summation and recapitulation, of self-removal from whatever is new and disordering, then Meredith, as a writer, never had an old age. He had no time to be old, for as he entered his last years the major issues of his life's work remained unresolved. He had insisted that nature's laws and society's ideal rules are identical, yet his novelistic instincts had often, as in *Harry Richmond* and *Beauchamp's Career*, repudiated the identity. His poetic instincts had avoided the problem altogether, for in his best poems nature and the *spiritus mundi* are joined in a vision that takes hardly any account at all of society. Thus the problem remained: how to reconcile firmly nature and society. Characteristically, Meredith, having shown the obstacles to the union, was only the more determined to remove them.

Our view of the works produced by this final effort is enriched and complicated by the fact that they appeared during the decade of restless engagements and eager disengagements with which the century ended. In the 1890's, when Meredith, past sixty, wrote his last important works, W. E. Henley stood high in influence as editor and critic, the young Yeats arrived on the literary scene, Shaw emerged as a new shaper of drama, Hardy published his own last and best novels, Henry James wrote some and projected others of his final great works, Oscar Wilde produced the excitement of the decadence, and George Gissing, Meredith's own disciple, struggled briefly for success. Politically and socially, the '90's were "the hey-day of British

imperialism," the period in which "the proletariat 'found itself,' " **the**
era marked by "the revulsion from puritanism" and the vulgarization
of taste, and the one which witnessed "the dawning-hour of a new
popular enlightenment."[1]

Differing and even conflicting with each other, these men and
movements nevertheless share one central concern: the idea of freedom. Richard Le Gallienne, arguing that "those last ten years of the
nineteenth century properly belong to the twentieth century," says
that they "were years of an immense and multifarious renaissance,"
in which all our new freedoms began.[2] We can compensate for Le
Gallienne's uncritical fervor by noting that for some political figures
of the decade, freedom was a specious concept—an ideological
weapon employed in a struggle for power—and that for some writers
and painters freedom meant a refusal to accept social responsibility
in an age when "former clear objectives were gone, and as yet nothing
took their place."[3] But it remains true that for the best minds, freedom was an idea that required redefinition, serious exploration, and
fresh realization as social and cultural experience. Hardly a new concept, it needed, they saw, a new birth in fact and form.

It is at this very center, which unites them all, that Meredith
relates to his younger contemporaries. Striving to reconcile nature
and society, he arrived at a full confrontation of the problem of freedom. We glimpse suddenly a remarkable fact: because of his need
to resolve a personal dilemma, Meredith, an old man by the standards
of his generation, shared in the making of a new era.

He made his contribution in three novels, *One of Our Conquerors*
(1891), *Lord Ormont and His Aminta* (1894), and *The Amazing
Marriage* (1895); and in a unified series of poems titled *Odes in Contribution to the Song of French History* (1898). In all these works,
the attempt to reconcile nature and society is carried on with a vigor
and deliberateness of intention hardly matched before. The attempt,
through a logic at once simple and devious, leads Meredith to a re-
examination of freedom. It leads him to remove the emphasis that
characterized his poetry of the '80's. Particularly in the novels, he
no longer condemns egoism. He transmutes it into an authentic individualism, for his instinct told him that it was on this latter concept,
not on the view of mankind as an undifferentiated mass, that his final
endeavor to harmonize nature and society would have to rely.

Actually, Meredith's shift from egoism to individualism as a central concern begins with *Diana of the Crossways* (1885). But Diana is truly a transitional figure. Her independence of mind and her defiance of society (as far as they go) are exciting and admirable, but curiously only a few accentuating touches seem needed to reveal her as sister to Sir Willoughby Patterne, the archetypal egoist. A few dabs of the brush; and her spendthrift habits, her exaggerated concern with wit, her sale of the political secrets of Percy Dacier, her lover, would no longer appear plausible and excusable—the consequences of her brilliance, impulsiveness, and need. They would seem absurd or grimly comic, the result of a diminished character having artificially and unstably enlarged itself. The moral meaning of the novel, when so little is needed to transform it, thus remains as consonant with the theme of Meredith's poetry of the '80's as it is anticipatory of the new emphasis marking the novels of the '90's.

### A CANCELLATION OF ERRORS

*One of Our Conquerors*, the first of these, recalls *The Egoist* in its close organization. The story begins in the month of April and reaches its tragic resolution as April, one year later, signifies the return of spring. Often in his poetry Meredith had celebrated spring as the beginning of rebirth and renewal, but his deliberate ironic use of the season, in this novel, as a time of waste and destruction is new and puts us in mind of more recent writers like D. H. Lawrence, Virginia Woolf, and T. S. Eliot. It indicates a less lyrical and more ambiguous sense of nature as a literary resource than Meredith had previously revealed. It indicates, too, a new use in the novel of time as an organizing principle—a richly meaningful use—suggesting the ultimate restriction which a young reader of Meredith was to make, some years later, when he compressed a universe and its drama into the twenty-four hours of Bloomsday.

Another aspect of *One of Our Conquerors* which recalls Meredith in the '70's, the period of his intense commitment to the art of the novel, is the pace at which the story moves. It is a slow pace, and Meredith defends it at the outset by telling us that though unfashionable it is necessary for presenting the mind of a character. He chastises the popular "tale," which, he maintains, is all motion without action. For action, we read, of course, psychological development.

In style, *One of Our Conquerors* is Meredith at his most experimental and defiant. J. B. Priestley informs us that Meredith, just before beginning the novel, inherited a small sum of money and was feeling quite independent of reviewers and the public when he started to write. Thus, says Priestley, quoting Meredith, he was intent on giving the world "a strong dose of my most indigestible production."[4] Siegfried Sassoon, on the other hand, quotes Desmond MacCarthy to the effect that the style of the novel represents an organic stage of development in Meredith's history as an artist. MacCarthy says that "the fact that he had been engaged during six years principally in writing verse accounts for the style of *One of Our Conquerors*," a mode of expression which "is full of originality, picturesqueness, and vigour, but all cased and slated over in metaphor and trope. It is distracted into tortuiosities, dislocations, crochets, cramped terms, and quaintness."[5]

However just his description, MacCarthy has sensed, as have many others, the vigorous note of independence and self-assertion that characterizes the language of the novel. It is interesting to note, as we approach *One of Our Conquerors* and Meredith's other novels of the '90's, what F. W. Dupee has said of Henry James and the works he wrote during the latter part of the decade: "Of all his various 'periods,' that of the years 1896–1900 is the least readily summarized and appraised. . . . Having ceased to expect a wide acclaim, he was frankly trying his hand; 'difficulty' alone interested him now." The difficulty that "he courted," Dupee tells us, was not only the attempt to impose "a stricter form on fiction" but "the task of making sense, of wresting a meaning from modern life."[6]

How remarkably this account brings Meredith to mind, not only because he too courted difficulty, as Priestley and MacCarthy observe, but because of his response to the critical reception of *One of Our Conquerors*. On June 16, 1891, just about two months after the story appeared in volume form,[7] Meredith wrote to George Stevenson: "The Novel has been kicked about by reviewers, as I expected. And clearly there is no further chance of peace between us. What they call digressions, is a presentation of the atmosphere of the present time, of which the story issues!"[8] It would be wrong to carry the parallel any further, to suggest that Meredith's rendering of "the present time" resembles closely James's portrayal of "modern life"; yet different as they are, they touch, if only as contrasting views, upon the same questions concerning the meaning of experience in the world contemporary to both authors.

*One of Our Conquerors* is the story of Victor Radnor, an ambitious and successful man, and of Nataly, the woman with whom he has lived for many years and who would be his wife were it not that Mrs. Burman, an aged lady whom Victor married in a season of youthful error and then in desperation deserted, inconsiderately hangs on to life. It is the story also of Nesta, who is the daughter of Victor and Nataly and whose fate forces the moral crises and disclosures of the novel to occur.

In both its superficial and its deeper aspects, *One of Our Conquerors* is a novel of the '90's. For the first time in a story of Meredith's, London and London experience play a central role. Victor Radnor is a City man, a business giant and shrewd financial speculator, and a would-be public benefactor who uses the power he gains in commerce to open a way for himself in politics. As Jack Lindsay points out, he reminds us of Joseph Chamberlain, though it remains true that London, not any individual model, defines Victor. The opening pages, in which we encounter Victor crossing London Bridge and then are given a prose-song of the City, contrasting glory and sordidness, not only place Victor in his element but recall Le Gallienne's observation that there occurred in the '90's a revival of interest "in town and urban things" and that several writers of the decade "seem to have awakened simultaneously to the poetry of London," so that "in prose as well as verse there was, for a time, quite a cult of London and its varied life, from costers to courtesans."[9]

Even more clearly, the central situation—the illegal union of Victor and Nataly—makes *One of Our Conquerors* a novel of the '90's. We need only remember that Diana of the Crossways, who suffers as much with her husband as Victor does with Mrs. Burman, chooses, at the last moment, to endure her situation rather than to run off with Percy Dacier, who seems to have all the *desiderata* of a knightly savior. That her decision proves right is beside the point. In the '80's, neither the temper of the times nor Meredith's own conception of life permitted Diana to reject suffering and still remain a heroine.*
In the '90's, both the prevailing attitudes and the stage of develop-

---

* She is permitted, it is true, to live apart from her husband, Mr. Warwick, but her separate existence, full of temptations, trials, and restrictions, is hardly one of freedom—hardly a real escape from suffering.

ment Meredith had reached as a moralist required Victor to repudiate the intolerable marriage he had contracted, in his youth, with a middle-aged widow.

The suggestion is that Meredith, in quest of a new definition of freedom and individualism, chose marriage as the area for his explorations. His choice was in many ways inevitable. His own tragic first marriage had ended in a manner that could hardly be called resolution—with cruelty on both sides, with the death of Mary Peacock Meredith, with the death, finally, of their son, Arthur, on September 3, 1890, after a long and gradual estrangement between father and son. Certainly this death, at the beginning of the '90's, heightened Meredith's ready inclination to confront, in his art, the consequences of a bad marriage. It is interesting that a number of Meredith's notebooks, as well as collections of loose manuscript sheets, contain sketches and ideas for stories based on tragic marriage situations.[10] And before the '90's, the theme had already been made paramount in *Richard Feverel*, *Modern Love*, and *Diana of the Crossways*. But in the works of this decade, the marriage situation becomes, for the first time, a combined inferno and purgatory, in which the soul does not simply burn for the sake of burning but is reduced to its essence and begins, slowly and painfully, to emerge into knowledge of freedom. Not only in *One of Our Conquerors*, but in *Lord Ormont* and in *The Amazing Marriage* this transformation takes place.

Yet it would be wrong to assume that freedom, for Meredith, is a simple virtue or a concept easily grasped. Its affirmation, in these works of the '90's, leads to paradox, irony, and ultimately to a sense of freedom's limits. In *One of Our Conquerors*, Nataly and Victor, for whom individualism and commitment to freedom are particularizing characteristics, are not completely delineated until the strictures their actions caused have worked upon them.

Victor—as one of his friends, the Reverend Septimus Barmby, declares (p. 87)—is a leader of men. Meredith's admiration for Victor's ability in business matters—in financial speculation—is genuine and without any suggestion that City manipulations are in themselves corrupting.[11] By the '90's, Meredith had begun to invest his own modest capital in securities, and it is all the more likely that Victor, in part, represents Meredith's admiration for the man of action, lately revealed to him in the guise of speculator. Victor is compared advantageously to his timid partner, unsubtly named Mr. Inchling, who is the sort of old-fashioned British businessman who Meredith apparently believed was responsible for the fact that English commerce, in the '90's, was losing ground to the Germans and Americans. Victor is also a would-be philanthropist, with a plan for improving London (parks and refreshment booths for honest workingmen) and with a desire to present gifts of art to the nation. Clearly he is the right kind of modern conqueror: the aggressive entrepreneur turned civic benefactor.

But admirable as are the qualities which mark Victor as such, they are peripheral in the pattern of his character. At the center is Victor's Idea, and as he reaches and fumbles for this lamp—his grasp of it is very uncertain—the intricacies of his motives and the fullness of his personality emerge with brilliant clarity.[12]

Victor has an Idea, and he also has Projects; somehow they are related. His projects are many, but the major ones are three. He is determined to establish Nataly and himself in Lakelands, a magnificent country estate that is to be both a plea for social acceptance of their unorthodox union and a defiance of the social judgment that says they ought to seek obscurity. He wants to marry Nesta to Dudley Sowerby, heir to a title and thus protection for Nesta if the world should learn that her parents are unmarried. Finally, he seeks to enter Parliament and to use politics as a new outlet for his restless drive. And as he bustles energetically in pursuit of his principal goals, and of many minor ones too, his Idea, like the ghost of Hamlet's father, alternately approaches and recedes before his eyes.

What is Victor's Idea? It is never presented explicitly (how could it be, since Victor himself only feebly discerns it?) but is hinted at, darted at, obliquely glanced at with all the electric, apparent negligence that exasperates the unsympathetic reader of Meredith but that is made, in this novel at least, to produce a controlled effect. At one point (p. 435), as Victor thinks happily about Nesta's purity, his Idea seems to have to do with "a Goddess Nature" in a "chastened nature." At another (p. 493), it seems to mean the "right use of riches" and the need for England's wealthy to "live for the promotion of brotherhood" (p. 485). Then, as Victor tries to throw off the guilt—or the moral discomfort—that wealth seems to lay upon his shoulders, his Idea takes a contradictory turn (p. 498): "Dispersion of wealth, is

the secret," he says, for the preservation of the "*true* aristocracy amid
a positively democratic flood of riches." Later, shifting its form once
more, Victor's spectral visitor becomes paternal and insular. The
English, Victor tells Nesta (p. 504), have "power to rise to spiritual
ascendancy, and be once more the Islanders heading the world of
a new epoch abjuring materialism."

Scattered and inconclusive as these oblique references are, they
have one solid characteristic in common: they all reveal that Victor's
Idea, whatever it is, is concerned with the welfare of humanity, or
at least of England, and not with his own; not, that is, with a solution
to his pressing and disturbing personal problems. Holding this irony
steadily in view, Meredith makes contradiction serve richly the purposes of characterization. Victor's actions, in contrast to his Idea,
are concerned only with his personal problems. He is a man at bay,
pained for Nataly's and Nesta's sake, but not at rest either in his own
relation to society. He must have the largest house in his part of
England; he must be the most aggressive speculator in the City; he
must, ultimately, run for Parliament. The compulsion is the penalty
he pays for the "crime" he will not consciously admit. The "aristocracy of self-denying discipline" (p. 479) at the heart of his Idea
is a reflex of his shadowy fear that in deserting Mrs. Burman he had
confessed himself incapable of self-denying discipline. His Idea is
a self-image without a face, since his best qualities, those that would
have helped delineate the features, have been puffed away into ab-
stractions. He cannot believe that, did it have a face, his self-image
would be anything but frightening because he cannot believe that
any of his own qualities are really good.

But however pathetic this may be, it is a form of falseness, and in
Meredith's astringent view need not be described too gently. Victor
is a "histrionic self-deceiver" who enjoys "the coveted reality through
the partial simulation of possessing it" (p. 55). His Idea is an index
of his self-alienation, which is cause and consequence of his self-
removal from reality.* W. F. Wright justly answers the question,
"What is Victor's Idea?" when he says: "[Victor] must build up an

---

* Meredith was keenly aware that this sort of removal was a general phenomenon, much in need of change. In 1901, he wrote to Lady Ulrica Duncombe:
"We have to know that we know ourselves. Those who tell us we do not know,
cannot have meditated the word Conscience. In truth, so well do we know our-

image of himself in relation to other people which has no taint of
guilt and none of failure, and yet he finds that this is not his true
identity. The certainty that it is not determines him only to continue
modifying the illusion to evade seeing the reality."[13] Actually, Wright
has analyzed Victor's behavior rather than his Idea, but the substitu-
tion is correct. Victor's immediate need in terms of action—to win
approval and to avoid the face of reality—generates his benevolent
vision, i.e., his Idea.

To what extent then is Victor to be regarded as free and individualistic? He is to the extent that his contradictions and fears do
not seriously impair our sympathy for him, and his is, for the most
part, a sympathetic characterization. However much guilt Victor
feels, Meredith makes it clear that he had to separate from Mrs.
Burman to save his life. Moreover, though he may be enslaved by
ambition, he is not ambitious for power in any vulgar sense. He
wants people freely to admire, love, and excuse him. He does not
wish to dominate them or force them, against their will, to accept
him. Most important, he is, like other figures in Meredith's novels
of the '90's, a person who, though he defies society, is not lawless:
"Although this man was a presentation to mankind of the force in
Nature which drives to unresting speed . . . he knew himself for
the reverse of lawless; he inclined altogether to good citizenship"
(pp. 136–37).

Here, for the time being, is the very essence of freedom for
Meredith. A specific social convention (e.g., the legal marriage
bond) may be dispensed with, but "good citizenship" must ever
remain the general ideal of conduct. Meredith is thus participating
in the fragmentation of Victorian morality that marked the '90's,
holding on to the parts that had become part of his own nature,
scorning the others. Victor would have disdained the decadents,
the search for experience for its own sake, even the Wildean paro-
dies of middle-class morality. In all his ways, after he leaves Mrs.

---

selves, that there is a general resolve to know someone else instead. We set up an
ideal of the cherished object; we try our friends and the world by the standard we
have raised within, supported by pride, obscured by the passions. . . . I preach
for the mind's acceptance of Reality in all its forms." (*Letters*, II, 518.) But
Victor cannot accept reality in one of its most basic forms for him: the fact that
his desertion of Mrs. Burman was both right and wrong.

Burman, he is truly "a foremost pillar of society."[14] He seems even
to repudiate the spirit of the '90's when he speaks approvingly of a
"Dr. Schlesien," another of Meredith's wise but somehow unattrac-
tive German critics of England, who says (p. 22) that the British
"individualismus" is "another name for selfishness" and shows "the
usual deficiency of external features." But in these words we see
what Meredith is after—a definition of individualism that would reveal it as something better than the kind he saw, or believed he saw,
around him. Victor is an attempt by Meredith to return to the old
view that the heroic is the truly individualistic. As the ambiguous
title of the novel indicates, Victor wishes to be, and to some extent
is, an authentic leader. But he has to lead at a time when Victorian
society and its code are dissolving. Victor, in his role as leader, is
not destroying the old. It has already disintegrated and must be sal-
vaged critically and selectively piece by piece: only the essential
parts are to be preserved. The task is not simple, for the rejected
elements have a way of asserting their vitality long after they have
been decreed dead or useless. Thus Victor is a man trying to build
the present and future while the ruins of the past, clearly symbolized
by Mrs. Burman, entangle him and hobble his step.

The role of Mrs. Burman embodies an ambiguity that gives the
novel its life. She is the source of Victor's guilt and self-evasiveness,
and as such a measure of his weakness; and she is an unjustified con-
straint that, forcing him to act determinedly within imposed limits,
adds to his stature. The ethical paradox that she thus creates in Victor's life is never resolved. All his actions have a double meaning:
they declare him coward and leader, slave and individual.

Meaningful as the characterization of Victor is, the problem of
freedom—its definition, its penalties, and its contradictions—is even
more clearly seen in Meredith's conception of Nataly. "Of all the
later heroines, easily the finest . . . is Nataly. . . . She is a mature
woman, the mother of a grown-up daughter, and is presented convincingly as such, and yet there blooms in her all the glamorous girl-
hood of the younger heroines. Her situation, as unmarried wife and
mother, attached to a man who invites the stabs of public opinion,
is the cruellest in which any Meredith woman finds herself, just as she
herself is the noblest of them."[15]

The "cruelty" of her situation is the necessary condition for Meredith's purposes. It tightens the moral tensions and clarifies the moral issues. Only if matters are carried to extremes, as they are in Nataly's heart, can the evasion of reality practiced by Victor be finally thwarted and replaced by confrontation.

Forced by her feminine sense of their social situation to see more deeply than Victor, Nataly, early in the novel, is actually stronger, more authentically independent, than Victor. Meredith says (p. 120): "Now, as long as they did no palpable wrong about them, Nataly could argue her case in her conscience—deep down and out of hearing, where women under scourge of the laws they have not helped decree may and do deliver their minds. She stood in that subterranean recess for Nature against the Institutions of Man."

Nataly supplies the way out of the dilemma of how to violate the marriage laws and yet remain a good citizen. Clearly the implication is that by championing nature we unerringly defy only those institutions of man which have nothing to do with "good citizenship." To put it more strongly, "good citizenship" can be defined as allegiance to nature in the faith that this adherence best prepares us for life in society. Like all faith, it is nonrational, and like Meredith's earlier efforts to reconcile nature and society, it is reminiscent of Rousseau and of much of the Romantic tradition. What is new for Meredith is the close exploration, in the wake of this tradition, of an embattled individual, one who is intensely conscious of her situation. In *The Egoist*, Clara Middleton is not so much a conscious individual—she never thinks of herself as a rebel—as an inadvertent representative of society's best thought. The Princess Ottilia of *Harry Richmond* deliberately looks to society to tell her what her heart—that is, her "nature"—should feel. And Diana of the Crossways, though endowed with many of the instincts that point forward to the heroines of the novels of the '90's, is erratic and confused, and never looks deeply enough into herself to gain the larger sensibility to moral issues that clarifies what pain obscures; she does not really see the relation between nature and society, though she tries fumblingly to act on that relation. Nataly is the first of Meredith's women who, in order to follow nature, is forced to be an individual and defy a social code. And freedom, in her case, means not only this defiance but also suffering for the sake of a purer law than the one she breaks.

Ultimately, however, Nataly, though she has more insight, becomes as much a victim of fear as is Victor, though her fear is different. It is not a trembling before the prospect of self-knowledge; it is a trembling before the unknown future of Nesta. In her anxiety to see Nesta protected—married to Dudley Sowerby—she commits violence against the ethical rules revealed to her by nature. She rebukes Nesta for showing charity to a woman with a bad reputation; she blinds herself to the fact that Dudley is weak and selfish.

When, finally, Victor is about to make his first political speech, to begin a new career that will expose her and Nesta to even more danger than heretofore, Nataly confronts the ultimate truth about herself—the truth beyond the verity that nature approves of her. She faces the fact that she can no longer endure the consequences of the freedom she originally chose in good conscience. She dies, thus escaping past and present both.

The shock is too much for Victor, the self-alienated apostle of freedom, and he suffers a complete breakdown. It is as if Meredith, when he wrote *One of Our Conquerors*, regarded love of freedom as an inherently tragic virtue. Neither Victor nor Nataly is blamed. Rather, at the novel's end we are told that Colney Durance, one of their friends, discerns, "when looking on their child"—the pure, courageous Nesta who is destined to be happy—"that for a cancelling of the errors chargeable to them, the father and mother had kept faith with Nature."

The tragedy of freedom is a curious one. Victor and Nataly are not justified by the manner of their deaths, as would be the case in either classical or Christian tragedy, but by their principal deeds. The manner of their deaths may in fact be regarded as one of the errors chargeable to them—though canceled by the retrospective view of their lives. The affirmation in their tragedy is not that they achieve nobility or enduring life in heaven or memory by the manner of their deaths, but that, obliterated as they surely are from the world of men, they live on in this perfected child, who is destined to be greater and better than either of them. We see here the morality, and religion, of nature; what we see ultimately about Nataly is that her life is not justified by any internal principle of strength or honesty placing her eternally above her fellows, but by her early grasp of a precept of nature. For this she is rewarded with a superior child. But as the child grows stronger, Nataly grows weaker, a phenomenon which, though not decreed by nature in the moral sphere, is nevertheless understandable without violation of the probabilities of fate and character.

It is interesting to compare Nataly with the great women who appear in Henry James's novels of the '90's and after. Speaking of Mrs. Brookenham, of *The Awkward Age* (1899), F. W. Dupee has said: "Living in society necessarily involves one in false positions; its values collide with those of personal honor . . . such a career is half a splendid art, half a sordid and exhausting business. This is the tragi-comic fact which Mrs. Brook alone faces fully and which she tries to make endurable by her policy of honesty among friends."[16]

Besides having marriageable daughters, Nataly and Mrs. Brookenham are similar in being closely connected to a circle of intimates. But in this similarity lies the difference in characterization. Mrs. Brookenham's friends are a constant test of her social genius; the untrammeled employ of that genius, which she achieves despite difficulties, would be her own definition of freedom. The Radnor circle is composed, with a few exceptions, of harmless eccentrics. They require nothing of Nataly, and she presides competently and good-humoredly over their contentions. "They are dears," she says (p. 75); and Meredith adds, "They were the dearer for their fads and foibles." In contrast to Mrs. Brookenham's friends, Nataly's are a temporary protection against the real test of her ability to be individual and free. The contrast is a measure of the difference between Meredith's and James's intentions in creating these two women. Nataly's is a derived strength, based on her knowledge that she is true to nature. It proves insufficient to sustain her when she must cope in a detailed and varied way with the problems posed by society. Mrs. Brookenham's strength, on the other hand, is an inward principle and equips her for meeting precisely those difficulties that derive from the intricate structure and behavior of society. It is her superior knowledge of society that enhances her strength and encourages her honesty. Nataly, with knowledge primarily of nature, finds both her strength and honesty unequal to the challenge of society.

A similar comparison might be made between Nataly and Mme.

de Vionnet, of *The Ambassadors* (1903). Again there are similarities
of external situation. Both women have marriageable daughters and
both have to keep secret the circumstances of their love for a man.
But Mme. de Vionnet is aided not only by her social capability, as
is Mrs. Brookenham in a different situation, but by tradition, which
functions for her much as does nature for Nataly. Mme. de Vionnet,
in the knowledge which tradition gives her of what is possible in
society, and of the prices and penalties for all things, is at least supported in her social individualism. Nataly, in her knowledge of nature only, finds her individualism inadequate when society creates
complexities not dealt with by that knowledge.

One of the women of Thomas Hardy's novels also comes to mind
when we think of Nataly. Sue Bridehead, of *Jude the Obscure*
(1895), begins, like Nataly, as an individualist, and, like James's
women, as one who looks within herself for a principle of strength.
But for Hardy, James's conception of character is merely the beginning of irony, and thus, though the differences between Hardy's
world and Meredith's are enormous, Sue Bridehead and Nataly follow
oddly similar paths. As *One of Our Conquerors* nears its climax,
Victor confesses himself disappointed by Nataly's growing timidity.
Similarly (when Sue, after the scandal of her staying away overnight
from the teachers' training school, marries Mr. Phillotson) Jude
Fawley observes gloomily that perhaps under her affectation of independent views she is as "enslaved to the social code" as any woman
he knows. Much later in the novel, after Jude and Sue have lived
a number of years in exquisite misery, Sue, even more violently than
Nataly, reacts against the form, substance, and ethics of the "freedom" she originally inspired her partner to believe in.

Even closer to Meredith than James or Hardy is George Gissing.
*Denzil Quarrier* (1892) was, as Jack Lindsay has pointed out,
strongly influenced by *One of Our Conquerors*. Gissing's novel also
concerns an illegal union in which the husband is a successful businessman with political ambitions. Again it is the woman who is weak
and finally breaks under pressures that are connected with her lover's
political campaigning. But Gissing never shared Meredith's faith in
nature, and so he brings his novel to a very different conclusion.
When Denzil Quarrier, whose role parallels Victor's, learns that the
death of Lillian Allen, the woman he has loved and lived with ille-

gally, has been caused partly by the duplicity of a supposed friend, he remarks ruefully, "Now I understand the necessity of social law!" and with this line the novel ends. The conclusion reads more as if Gissing had been impressed by some of Meredith's didactic remarks on "good citizenship" than as if he had read *One of Our Conquerors* carefully. Or perhaps he was deliberately repudiating Meredith's novel and its nature creed, much as he admired Meredith. In any event, Gissing's point seems to be that social law is needed, not because, as in *One of Our Conquerors*, it mirrors at its best the law of nature but because human motives, even in ostensibly decent people, are so destructive that only "social law" provides protection against them.

How different Meredith is from all three—James, Hardy, and Gissing. He does not have James's vivid social imagination, making society the arena for the ultimate and rich rewards of the intensely lived inner life. He does not have Hardy's almost pathological genius for turning society into a cruelly contrived labyrinth, in which the individual is forced, from turn to turn, to the ultimate horror mirror casting back the image of a puny victim in his last degradation. Nor does he have Gissing's almost carelessly modern ability to dissociate psychology from morality, and to make the latter a merely pragmatic defense against the inherent danger of the former. What he has is an energetic, confident, romantic myth-making propensity. Only Meredith, among those noted here, would undertake to create two sympathetic characters; assure us that they do no wrong since they follow nature; then, without the least suggestion of irony, destroy these sympathetic characters, Nataly and Victor; and end on a note of triumph and victory, as he does when he brings Nesta to the center of the stage.

But Meredith, who courts the label of naïve as James, Hardy, and Gissing—whatever their own limits of understanding—do not, is as convincing in his own way as James and Hardy are in theirs, and more so than Gissing. As we look at Nesta, at the end of the novel, our perplexity over the ethical meaning of the fate of Victor and Nataly is mitigated. In the characterization of Nesta, all doubts are resolved. All the virtues that in her parents were imperfect are in her perfected. Besides following nature, she has courage, abundant self-knowledge, and the ability to rebel against the social code with-

out feeling guilty. She promises, in short, to be a supremely successful individualist, a discriminating rebel who in every detail of conduct
will be Meredith's "good citizen."

In her, nature and society are reconciled. Indeed, when she marries the manly, generous Captain Dartrey Fenellan, we realize that
"society," in this novel, is, at worst, passive before triumphant nature,
for social judgment will have no power to touch Dartrey and Nesta,
despite Nesta's birth. In retrospect, we realize that the only puissant
enemy of Victor and Nataly was their own frailty—certainly not "society," which presumably would have deferred to them as readily, had
they been stronger, as it does to Nesta and Dartrey.

But the ending of *One of Our Conquerors*, however right and however much it answers the questions posed within the special limits of
the situation set forth in the novel, leaves many aspects of the idea of
freedom unexplored. The strength of Nesta and her manly, generous
husband will never be seriously tested; thus the reconciliation of nature and society in Nesta, credible as it is, will never be seriously
examined for flaws and contradictions. What, however, of less convenient arrangements of character and circumstance? What of individuals who have to achieve through *will* the freedom Nesta is given
by life: freedom which in her case is created by early innocence, un-
compromising personal relations, and the immediate assistance of
Dartrey when she is on her own? This is the problem of Meredith's
next novel, *Lord Ormont and His Aminta* (1894).

Matey Weyburn and Aminta Farrell (later Lady Ormont) are
the characters faced with the problem. Matey, the son of a brave
soldier, is the natural leader of the boys at Cuper's School, where he
gets his early education. Aminta Farrell is enrolled at the neighbor-
ing Miss Vincent's, and she and Matey become childhood sweethearts.
When we next meet Matey he is grown, has lost touch with Aminta,
and has acquired the unlikely ambition of founding a school of his
own. While getting ready for his career, he takes employment as
secretary to his boyhood hero, Lord Ormont, who has been the victim of official reproof for having violated, in India, the orders of a
civilian placed over him. Lord Ormont is a famous cavalry general.[17]
Unknown to Matey, Aminta has married the great Lord Ormont,
whom Matey had rhapsodically described to her during their school

days. When Matey becomes Lord Ormont's secretary, he and Aminta, not having seen each other for years, are brought together under the same roof.

The past love of the secretary and the wife is a powder train. It is not, however, liable to spontaneous combustion. Matey and Aminta are too strong and noble ever to rekindle intentionally a relationship that began and ended during their juvenile years. Besides, Aminta loves her husband. The necessary spark is supplied by Lord Ormont himself. Chagrined by his countrymen's treatment of him (the newspapers were not sympathetic to him during his quarrel with Authority), he refuses to acknowledge his young wife to British society. Thus, he believes, he is showing contempt for the world that has hurt him. In his pride and anger, he does not see that he is also putting an intolerable burden upon Aminta.

Because Lord Ormont is past middle age, the relationship between him and Aminta is superficially similar to the marriage between the young Victor Radnor and the middle-aged Mrs. Burman. But to insist on more than a surface resemblance would be to miss the whole difference between *One of Our Conquerors* and *Lord Ormont*. We are told, in *One of Our Conquerors*, that Victor's living with Mrs. Burman was a wrong against nature. The obvious implication is that the relationship is physically repugnant to Victor, and to nature. No such implication attaches to Aminta's relationship with her husband. Indeed, we are told that during the first days of marriage (the ceremony took place in Madrid and the couple were a long time returning to England) Aminta was supremely happy. As husband to a young girl, the vigorous old lord is no affront to nature. The moral failure in this novel is solely Lord Ormont's pride, with all the consequences it produces: humiliation of Aminta and eventually a break, on her part, for freedom as the unmarried wife of Matey. In many ways, the moral problem is more subtle than it was in *One of Our Conquerors*. Matey and Aminta, when they do run off, do not seem to act in behalf of nature, of the "nature," at any rate, which decreed laws for Victor and Nataly. Apparently, therefore, we are in a dilemma to explain how Matey and Aminta are justified, for justified they are.

The dilemma is only apparent. The explanation is simply that nature is much more subtly conceived in this novel than it was in *One of Our Conquerors*. Nature, in *Lord Ormont*, does not primarily mean eros. It means will. It means individualism in a more complex sense than it ever did before in Meredith's works.

While reading *Lord Ormont*, Henry James wrote to Edmund Gosse: "[Lord Ormont] fills me with a critical rage, an artistic fury, utterly blighting in me the indispensable principle of *respect*." He went on, "Not a difficulty met, not a figure presented, not a scene constituted . . . there are pretty things, but for what they are they come so much too dear. . . . There is another side, of course, which one will utter another day."[18] Just what the unmet difficulties are James did not say. Nor, unfortunately, did he ever put on record a testimonial to the "other side." But given James's own unbounded sense of moral complexity, it is fitting, despite his lack of specific reference, to call to mind here his estimate of *Lord Ormont*.

The central issue should first be approached through Lord Ormont himself. Mary Sturge Gretton has remarked perceptively that Lord Ormont, independently of his injury to his pride, "has lost the power of seeing any woman individually, apart from his general notions as to her sex. His attitude toward the woman he has taken as his wife, though it differs in degree, does not differ in kind from the attitude he has adopted to others."[19] He is guilty, in short, of a terrible error: insensibility to the claims of individualism. The inference is curious. In *Lord Ormont*, Meredith has created a somewhat Jamesian universe in which denial of the social need of another exposes one to personal danger. Lord Ormont's principal form of denial is his refusal to install Aminta as mistress of Steignton, the ancestral home of the Ormonts. In the light of what happens as a result of this refusal, we can understand what must have exasperated James. He, more than any other of Meredith's literary contemporaries, could recognize that Lord Ormont's behavior was, theoretically, an assault upon the very fabric of society. Perhaps James did not regard Ormont's "Coriolanus quarrel with his countrymen" (p. 307) as sufficient motive for so large a threat. If Lord Ormont is to be permitted so symbolic an act (one can imagine James insisting) then he ought to be a more complex, powerful, and influential figure. Instead, Meredith presents him as a brave, simple-hearted soldier who is hardly more than a laughingstock when off the field of glory and who is self-isolated at home. Nobody takes him seriously; consequently, only Aminta, not society, suffers from his intended insult to his countrymen. And even Aminta's suffering is very brief, a short preparation for happiness. Thus Meredith has used the ban on Steignton, which ought—we can suppose James to say—to have had some central significance, proliferating its consequences throughout the circle of characters connected with the Ormonts, merely as a cause for personal disillusion on Aminta's part, as if Lord Ormont had been only another of Meredith's socially harmless egoists rather than a man who would destroy the very forms of society.

The explanation is that Meredith, in the '90's, was more of a romanticist than James was. The fabric of society is hardly ruffled by Lord Ormont's attack; *his* life, by reflex motion, is reduced to tatters. Aminta becomes the instrument of his ruin. And Meredith uses Aminta's social rights, not her private ones, to justify her ruining of Lord Ormont's private world. This intricate pattern of the private and the social, and the moral meaning of the arrangement, are explained by Meredith's romantic doctrine of the will.

Aminta's will has little to do with her intelligence or her sensibility. It is part of her femininity, but it has more to do with her dark complexion and her physical robustness—her affinity with "nature"—than with the cultivated world of society. Like the romantic will traditionally, it is prior to society. Here, too, is a possible reason for James's dissatisfaction. In his world, society is a living matrix, never to be disconnected from the innermost being of its members, and a strong and magnificent individual will is something elicited by the action of society. In Meredith's conception, the individual will, in this case Aminta's, is not only prior to society but operates in such a way as to carry its possessor clear of the tangle of problems and obstacles society would impose.

All this becomes evident in the final portion of the novel. Believing Lord Ormont to be out of England, and curious merely to see Steignton, Aminta travels down in the company of her vulgar, trouble-making aunt, Mrs. Pagnell. Mrs. Pagnell has alerted a fanatical adorer of Aminta, Mr. Morsfield, to the journey, and despite Aminta's effort to escape him, he accompanies aunt and niece right onto the grounds of Steignton. But Lord Ormont has not gone to the Continent. He is in the house, and as he glances out of a window he sees what appears to be defiance of his orders aggravated by brazenness: an invasion of Steignton in which his wife is apparently seconded by the detestable

Morsfield. He sends Matey, his secretary, out to order Morsfield off the grounds and to conduct Aminta back to London.

The trip back is described with colorful detail and is rendered in the best Meredithian manner. But the upshot of it all, as Matey maneuvers bravely and cleverly to throw the infatuated Morsfield and the untrustworthy Mrs. Pagnell off the track, is that he and Aminta recognize that they are in love. Their trip to London is the beginning of a series of events that leads finally to their flight to Switzerland, where Aminta, who once felt that Matey's ambition to set up a school was unmanly, becomes his inspirational partner in the project.

With regard to Aminta's acceptance of Matey's ambition, W. F. Wright's observation is instructive: "Once a little ashamed of him as a prospective teacher—it was he who made her idolize a soldier's career—she now recognizes the romance of his intellectual courage. Again a young woman has come to rediscover freedom and companionship in maturity. For Aminta, as for Keats, life has been a process of 'soul making.' "[20] It is interesting that Wright is reminded of Keats and that he thus suggests the intensely romantic impulse underlying Meredith's conception of Aminta. It is interesting, too, that he speaks of her as "rediscovering freedom," equating this with "a process of soul making." But in the terms we have used here, Aminta has discovered (not rediscovered) freedom and has done so through the power of her will. She will seek her "soul" outside the society of which Steignton is a symbol. And the cause is the humiliation of her willful nature.

In the last scenes, the novel weakens. A number of years have passed, and Matey and Aminta have lived them in Switzerland, conducting their happy, prosperous school. By accident, Lord Ormont, traveling through Europe, comes upon them, but when he does he behaves magnanimously. He not only takes no action against them, but sends his nephew to their school, and shortly afterward dies, leaving Matey and Aminta free to marry. We think of Adam Verver, of Henry James's *The Golden Bowl* (1904), preparing for the more difficult task of living—of leading his unfaithful young wife to American City. We think, too, of Maggie, reclaiming Prince Amerigo through sacrifices which are perfect expressions of individualism and which thus lead to a subtle and pure freedom—within society—and we can see why Lord Ormont's response to Matey and Aminta must have exasperated James.* Yet when we think of Milly Theale, of *The Wings of the Dove* (1902), we imagine that at least the instinct behind the characterization of Lord Ormont ought to have been recognizable to James. On the other hand, this is all the more reason to suppose that he regarded Lord Ormont as an opportunity missed. Too much is imposed upon Lord Ormont. Despite his insensitivity—or perhaps because of it—the mark he leaves on others is never indelible. The frustrations he causes never lie very deeply in another person's being. As for Matey and Aminta, he merely causes them to change their path in life, and as a result they allegedly become happier travelers than they would otherwise have been.

Yet to some extent James has missed Meredith's intention. The best way to get at it will be to compare *Lord Ormont* not with James's works but with Hardy's. Hardy's experience of English life in the '90's was more similar to Meredith's than was James's; yet Hardy's interests are more vividly opposed to Meredith's. Matey Weyburn, who is more central to the ethical theme of the novel than is Lord Ormont, parallels Jude Fawley of *Jude the Obscure*. Matey's ambition to become a schoolteacher is similar to Jude's eagerness to become a scholar. Matey, like Jude, is a boy without means. However, within this very similarity lies the meaningful contrast between the two characterizations. The *degree* of poverty that separates the two boys creates two entirely different social worlds. Poverty, in *Jude the Obscure*, is an authentic social force, a well-articulated engine employed by human cruelty and indifference to crush Jude. Though Meredith was just as aware as Hardy that poverty such as Jude's was a late-nineteenth-century social fact, he no sooner would have dealt with it in a novel than he would, or could, have stripped the universe of all but the subtle intelligence and cultivated sensibility that are the life-substance of James's novels of this period. Matey must have only enough material disability to challenge him, not to crush him, just as he must have, in addition to intelligence and implied sensibility, a kind of military bravery and outlook that, in Meredith's view, are necessary to stiffen character.

* We can only conjecture that it did. James's letter to Gosse was written when he was halfway through the novel. Considering his response to the superior part of the book, however, we can only shudder—or face him out—when we try to imagine how he felt when he arrived at the admittedly inferior conclusion.

Thus the ability to accept a challenge, and triumph, is the key to Matey's character, just as a fated inability to survive the obstacles in his road are the key to Jude's. The greatest challenge Matey faces, ultimately, is the one that Victor Radnor confronted: the problem of good citizenship. Matey says to Aminta, as they prepare to leave for Switzerland (p. 332):

I shall not consider that we are malefactors. We have the world against us. It will not keep us from trying to serve it. . . . I shall have to ask you to strengthen me, complete me. If you love me, it is your leap out of prison. . . . I trust you to weigh the position you lose, and the place we choose to take in the world . . . and if the world is hostile we are not to blame it. In the nature of things it could not be otherwise. My own soul, we have to see that we do—though not publicly, not insolently, offend good citizenship. But we believe—I with my whole faith, and I may say it of you—that we are not offending Divine law. . . . Our union gives us power to make amends to the world.

Commenting on this passage, Mrs. Gretton has said that "the first note and the last, is this of good citizenship. This is the Court of Appeal, the test to which individualistic action has to be referred. It is significant that practically the whole of Meredith's later treatment of Weyburn and Aminta is concerned with their great school and its striking success."[21] We may note, too, that Matey says it is because they do not offend divine law that their desire to be good citizens may yet be recognized. This is the spirit of Puritanism gone tame through too long indwelling in the middle class. Matey appeals to conscience and God, but his highest hope is that the righteous shopkeepers will make a truce with him: recognize that he is after essentially the same thing they are. Herein lies the weakness of the novel, and although Meredith's intention may be, as Mrs. Gretton says, to create for the pair, particularly for Aminta, "a standard that is abstract and non-individual,"[22] the effect misses fire. It suggests uncertainty on Meredith's part as to just what the justification for Matey and Aminta is. The invoking of "Divine law," in a story that has been blandly secular in its intentions and references all along, is sanctimonious and is unworthy of the better things in the novel. The invocation that was so effective in the poetry of the '80's is simply out of place in this story.

The reason why Meredith chose this lame justification is, I suggest, that after having written a romantic novel in which the individual will appears large, authentic, and effective, he could not accept the freedom he had thus envisioned. He still distrusted it. The movement of his novels of the '90's is out of tragic marriage situations into freedom, but years earlier he had shown, in *Beauchamp's Career,* that the will is irrational and hence a poor guide where intricate social maneuvering, as in these marriage situations, is required. Thus the free will had to be placed under the power of something higher than itself for assurance that it would not disclose its irrational power and prove antisocial. But here was Meredith's dilemma. In *One of Our Conquerors,* the "something higher" was nature, decrying the marriage of Victor and Mrs. Burman. The marriage in *Lord Ormont,* however, did not violate nature, and therefore Matey and Aminta could not appeal to nature to justify their act of individual will. Hence the calling upon divinity, despite the lack of any preparation in the story for this appeal, which is made the moment freedom is declared.

Returning to the distinction between Meredith and Hardy, we are put in mind of a further thought, one that has to do with their ways of understanding necessity. In *Tess of the D'Urbervilles* (1891), Hardy, speaking of Tess and Angel Clare, says, "Over them both there hung a deeper shade than the shade which Angel Clare perceived, namely, the shade of his own limitations. With all his attempted independence of judgment, this advanced and well-meaning young man—a sample product of the last five-and-twenty years—was yet the slave to custom and conventionality when surprised back into his early teachings."[23] This is an expression of Hardy's conviction that character—a form of necessity—is, in the well-established sense, man's fate. Meredith, too, believed in necessity, but by the '90's he no longer believed it took the form of character. Matey either creates his own conditions for free action or uses necessity, such as lack of money, as a precondition for free action.

Meredith's confident sense that individuals can make their own destinies, in contrast to Hardy's necessitarianism, is further revealed by a comparison of Aminta with Tess Durbeyfield and Sue Bridehead. At one point in *Lord Ormont* (pp. 198–99) we are told that Aminta regards herself as capable of work and devotion. However, she had been "perverted by her position, and she shook her bonds in revolt from marriage." Similarly, we learn (p. 254) that Aminta has "two kinds of courage—the impulsive and the reasoned." Both inspire her to shake off the bonds of marriage. The impulsive, associated with her will, is the handmaiden of her rational desire to free herself for the devotion and work that Matey has outlined for her. Her courage to be free is more than enough to correct any mistake she made in marrying Lord Ormont. By contrast, Hardy tells us that "chance" throws Tess into the path of Alec D'Urberville at just the moment when the appearance of another man in her life might have meant the beginning of happiness. And once "chance" has occurred, no courage, reasoned or unreasoned, will ever save Tess. In the same manner, Hardy creates the most cruel, seemingly transient reasons for Sue's marriage to Mr. Phillotson, and then builds on her marriage vow in such a way that the vow becomes a commitment leading inexorably to her destruction. There is, in short, no free will in these novels. Truly, when Hardy's stories have concluded, the President of the Immortals has ended his sport with both women. Taking a final glance at Aminta in this comparison, we see that her courage wins divine approval. So does Matey's, though Matey, like the early Angel Clare and the mature Jude, is a young man twenty-five years ahead of his time. Hardy's is a more jealous God than Meredith's. Meredith's seems more like the God who, working through the Evangelical movement, opposed slavery in the colonies and brought about social reform at home.[24]

But all this optimism leaves the major question unanswered. Despite Meredith's encouraging us to see in *Lord Ormont* the workings of divine law, the novel is not credible on such grounds. We therefore feel Meredith is not quite sure what it is that prevents free will from becoming, in strong and confident people like Matey and Aminta, plainly monstrous. Had Matey and Aminta been developed from the first as profoundly religious in instinct, the problem might have been solved. But then we would have had a very different novel, one in which Meredith would have been obliged to advance a new conception of the religious life, like D. H. Lawrence's perhaps. Had that been the case, we might concur in V. S. Pritchett's belief that Meredith, like Lawrence, was "straining to new conceptions of man."[25] But Meredith could not reach very far in this direction so long as what he really meant by "Divine law" was a dubious basis for "good citizenship." He never did arrive at any such conceptions, but he did the next best thing. In his last completed novel, *The Amazing*

*Marriage* (1895), he dropped the entire question of good citizenship
and with it the problem of divine approval. He dropped, in other
words, the barriers preventing him from envisioning the individualist,
the person of free will, as the perfect reconciliation of nature's laws
and society's ideal rules of conduct.

### THE UNFETTERED WILL

There is something gallant in the very structure of *The Amazing
Marriage*, a novel which was written more than a dozen years before
it was published but which was completely and strenuously revised
before it finally appeared in print.[26] As he approached his last fic-
tional work of the period, Meredith's eagerness to perfect the form
of the novel was, like James's, more insistent than ever. Crippled and
nearly deaf when he began the final version of *The Amazing Marriage*,
Meredith nevertheless achieved a vision—of the world he was creating—that was vivid with color and detail. The novel is rich in fresh
themes, problems boldly met, and answers to old questions probed
more deeply. Though it has the serenity of a massive mountain peak,
it is, in conception and execution, a testimony to the energy that
marked his last years as a novelist.

The ambitiousness of structure is immediately revealed by the
carefully rewritten early chapters, in which Meredith creates a kind
of mythic past for the major characters through a narration, full of
symbolic meaning, of the colorful lives and personalities of their
eighteenth-century progenitors. The effort at complex and brilliant
structure is also expressed in Meredith's use of one of his characteristic devices, a tutelary book, recalling "The Pilgrim's Scrip" in *Richard Feverel*, "The Book of Egoism" in *The Egoist*, and the diaries
in *Diana of the Crossways*. The device in *The Amazing Marriage* is
a book called "Maxims for Men," written by Carinthia and Chillon
Kirby's father, a romantic sea captain who, among other things, stole
their mother from under the nose of her legal husband.* Another
structural device in *The Amazing Marriage* is the use of Dame Gossip
as Chorus, Meredith's final effort in his novels to give body and voice

---

* Let it be noted that Chillon, the elder, was not born until enough time had
elapsed for his mother's first husband to die, for Captain Kirby and Chillon's
mother to get married, and for a seemly number of months (eleven) to pass. The
suggestion is that the Captain and his lady lived chastely until free to marry.

to society, though society is no longer the sophisticated sensibility it was in *The Egoist* or *The Essay on Comedy*. None of these devices is so perfectly realized or so effective in shaping the narrative as to make it a triumph of art, but neither is any one of them clumsy or irrelevant. They contribute to the richness of the story, and they are, if not elements pointing forward in the history of the novel, a summation of Meredith's personal history as an experimenter in fiction.

But it is with the principal characters, Lord Fleetwood and Carinthia Jane Kirby, the partners in the "amazing marriage," that Meredith tries most boldly to push ahead in his own intellectual and artistic development. At the same time, it is through them that he gathers up the themes that marked a lifetime of writing. Once again, and for the last time in his novels, he strives to reconcile the claims of nature and society, and to use the affirmation of freedom on the part of individualists as the action revealing the reconciliation. *Lord Ormont* was behind him, but certain problems pertaining to the nature of will and freedom remained to be solved. Boldly, Meredith shifted his ground, gave up measuring and examining the will by the light that society provides. Instead, he conceived a clash between two highly individualistic wills as the situation that would best reveal the nature and character of the phenomenon of will itself, and hence the meaning of freedom.

Carinthia and Lord Fleetwood are the individualists, and they are equally important in this matter of the will. Carinthia's will is shaped by rectitude, virtue, and superior strength, but Lord Fleetwood's is marked by intelligence, perception, and vitality. Unlike Victor and Nataly, or Matey and Aminta, neither Lord Fleetwood nor Carinthia is primarily concerned with society, yet in their pure willfulness, in their unconcern for "good citizenship," in the very privateness of their conflict, they accomplish something of paramount importance to Meredith's conception of society. Through them Meredith shows that far from being threatened by the unbridled will of the individual, society not only has resources to cope easily with individualistic striving, but also provides that individualism with the channels in which it must move if the character in question either is in harmony with nature (as is Carinthia) or is able to seek freedom through methods and means beyond those provided by English middle-class society (as is Lord Fleetwood).

Lord Fleetwood's individualism is clearly established. We are
told (p. 153) that he is "the one living man of his word," and that he
is thus distinguished from "the herd." But his unique characteristic
leads him into marriage with Carinthia Jane, who, at the time, though
a superb vision of nature in humanity (in the tradition of Lucy Desborough of *Richard Feverel* and the girl in "Love in the Valley"), is
nevertheless raw and simple. Meeting her at a ball, and asking her
in a wild, impulsive moment to marry him, Lord Fleetwood goes
through with the ceremony some months later, though the idea now
revolts him. He gave his word he would marry her and he is being
true to it. Carinthia knows nothing of his recoil—the news has been
kept from her by her relatives. She knows only that she loves this
man who asked her to marry him.

She enters marriage serenely and radiantly. The first hours after
the ceremony are spent at a prizefight, to which Lord Fleetwood hur-
ries his bride because his man, Kit Ines, is fighting the protégé of
another nobleman. That night Carinthia is left alone at a local inn,
while her husband takes up the round of his old pleasures. Having
kept his word by marrying her, he feels he is no longer indebted to
her. Toward morning, however, a second wild impulse, the natural
successor to the one that months earlier prompted his proposal, sends
Lord Fleetwood climbing a ladder to Carinthia's window. In her
room, after her first surprise and fright, Carinthia greets him by saying, "It is my husband."

By morning Lord Fleetwood is again in full possession of his arrogant and eccentric independence. The night's escapade means no
more to him than his previous desire for Carinthia. He makes it plain
that, having kept his word, he wants nothing more to do with this
raw girl. He will supply all necessities of her station as Lady Fleetwood, but he insists on living apart from her. Carinthia, for reasons
only partially clear at first (though she believes that his actions to
date signify love), pursues him, determined on an audience. She takes
up residence in Whitechapel, above a greengrocer's shop, where she
is received by the doting family of Madge Winch, who was designated
by Lord Fleetwood as Carinthia's maid but who has become her ally.
From this base Carinthia pursues her husband about London, and
Dame Gossip as Chorus has some of Meredith's most verbally extravagant to-do over the deeds of the "Whitechapel Countess."

Eventually it becomes clear that something besides faith in love has impelled Carinthia to the unheard-of lengths she goes in her attempt to obtain a word with her husband. She is about to have a child, and it is this information she wishes to impart to Lord Fleetwood. The birth of the child, a boy, which takes place in Wales (where, it may be noted, Mary Peacock Meredith went to give birth to her illegitimate son), coincides with a change in Carinthia toward her husband. She no longer loves him; she distrusts him. He, however, begins to soften. He wishes to see the boy, to have his wife and son installed at Esslemont, one of his estates. Above all, he begins to recognize the rare quality of the woman he has married. But it is too late.

The rest of the novel develops Lord Fleetwood with all the skill that made Sir Austin Feverel and Sir Willoughby Patterne such memorable figures when they were at bay. Disappointingly, however, it turns Carinthia from a fresh and credible characterization into "an allegorical personification, a Britomart."[27] Lord Fleetwood tries hard, in some finely written scenes, to acknowledge his wrong, abase his pride, and convince Carinthia of his love. She is unmoved. She has her brother, her child, her friends—particularly the Welsh mine operator, Owain Withan, a dim figure who is eventually bequeathed to her by his dying wife, and whom, at the novel's end, she will marry. Of a husband's love Carinthia, at present, wishes to hear no more. Actually it is her brother, Chillon Kirby, as unabashed and fanatical a military spirit as any Meredith ever created, who is the center of her life. Having recently perfected a new gunpowder,* Chillon is about to leave for Spain, where the Carlist Wars are in progress and where he will fight on the side of the Queen. Carinthia leaves her baby with her sister-in-law, Henrietta, and prepares to accompany her brother. In Spain, at the risk of her life, she is destined to perform memorable deeds as a nurse. Lord Fleetwood, who for years has been seeking an alternative to the unrewarding life of a British aristocrat, and who has made two friends in his search—Gower Wood-

---

* During the period in which Meredith was rewriting *The Amazing Marriage*, a suit was brought by Alfred Nobel, claiming infringement of his patent rights by British munitions manufacturers. The suit was eventually decided in favor of the defendants. It is possible that Meredith's nationalism and protective concern for the British military establishment inspired, at this opportune moment, Chillon Kirby's inventive genius.

seer (a vagrant nature philosopher modeled on Robert Louis Stevenson) and Lord Feltre, a Catholic nobleman—chooses the path advised by the latter. He joins an order of lay brothers where, out of the world he had never conformed to, he dies, leaving Carinthia free, on her return to England, to marry the still dim but allegedly manly Owain Withan.

The flaws in these later developments lie in Carinthia's reasons for turning away from her husband. However, the later absurdities do not cancel the effective characterization of Carinthia that Meredith achieves earlier in the novel. Quite early she is established as a child of nature and therefore as the embodiment of pure volition. She reveals the latter quality throughout the story, and the moments that accentuate it are worth our attention. Early in the novel (p. 40) we are told the curious fact that Carinthia objects to sleep because it robs her of her will. Later, when she is in the first phase of her conflict with Lord Fleetwood—when she has refused his offer that she live at Esslemont, while he lives elsewhere—Henrietta, her sister-in-law, complains (p. 245): "She refuses Esslemont. She insists on his meeting her! No child could be so witless. Let him be the one chiefly or entirely to blame, she might show a little tact—for her brother's sake! She loves her brother? No: deaf to him, to me, to every consideration except her blind will." And much later, after the baby has been born and Lord Fleetwood has become eager to get Carinthia back, he asks her to live at Esslemont *with* him. Carinthia refuses, and Meredith, with perhaps unintentional irony, speaks of her rejection of her husband at this point (p. 348) as "distempered wilfulness."

Significantly, nothing that society can do limits Carinthia's wilfulness. During her reign as the "Whitechapel Countess" she is deaf to social ridicule and censure. Moreover, her indifference signifies that something more primitive than moral sensibility informs her will. We cannot say of her, as F. W. Dupee has said of the women in James's novels of the '90's, that the moral sense leads to individualism and freedom. The contrast with Fleda Vetch, of James's *The Spoils of Poynton* (1897), is particularly illuminating. "To exercise the moral sense, as Fleda insists on doing, is frankly to risk the loss of natural happiness, which is shown to depend on the kind of compromises she refuses to make."[28] Carinthia's natural happiness also depends on compromise, but it is not her moral sense that causes her to risk losing this happiness. It is, strangely, her indifference to happiness—her lack of a real imaginative grasp of it—so that she is quite unaware of risk and possible sacrifice. Fleda, presented with the supreme opportunity to get what she wants, thinks of her duty as something opposed to her desire. For Carinthia, her duty is to get what she desires: her husband's love at first, and freedom to follow her brother later. What kind of a person is it in whom duty and desire are one? In the Christian view, a saint; in Meredith's, a character in whom nature, in a contest of many forces, is the strongest. Duty and desire are not one for every figure in the novel. Certainly they are not for Lord Fleetwood, the mark of whose individualism is his duty to his word and his scorn for everything else, including, ultimately, his own natural desire.

And for what larger end does Carinthia exercise her desire, her free will? Not for happiness, as we saw, but for something at once more simple and profound: to endure. She is like the Carinthian mountains of her birthplace, from which she gets her name and her character. Her expression of self is like theirs. She is self-realized, immobile in terms of the larger activity of the world, towering above those around her but never directing her massive strength against them. In short, though she exercises her free will, she cannot harm or threaten society unless it, through some form or situation, depends on her and she refuses to accept the imposition.

In a colloquy held by Chillon, Carinthia, and Lord Fleetwood, just before the first two leave for Spain, Chillon informs Lord Fleetwood (p. 461) that Carinthia holds to the rite of marriage, "thinks it sacred," but that in other respects "your lordship does not exist for her." Lord Fleetwood answers, "The father of her child must exist for her." At this, Carinthia announces that Henrietta will take care of her boy, adding, "I have my freedom, and am thankful for it, to follow my brother, to share his dangers with him. That is more to me than luxury and the married state. I take only my freedom."

At last "freedom," in Meredith's work, means something other than freedom to be a "good citizen." It means pagan inviolability. Again it is instructive to compare Meredith's heroine with one of James's. Speaking of Maggie, of *The Golden Bowl*, Dupee has said: "Maggie's final success with her marriage would seem to mean that solutions for the gravest problems may be found within the private life itself, without recourse to the courts or the church or even to any established morality."[29] Moreover, the private life is the dimension in which Maggie solves a problem that is as social as it is personal. Carinthia, too, solves her problem without recourse to the courts, the church, or to any established morality. But the ever-present difference between the worlds of James and Meredith is apparent. Not only does "the private life" not mean the same thing in the two novels but neither does freedom. Freedom and the exercise of the will mean for Carinthia glorying in elemental strength. Freedom, for Maggie, is something she must create by entering into carefully made and dangerous social arrangements. Carinthia asks only to be free to follow her brother out of society; Maggie creates, when she creates freedom for herself (i.e., the survival of her marriage), the essential conditions for remaining within society.

Lord Fleetwood offers a different kind of comparison with a character of James. Once Fleetwood learns to love Carinthia, "the reader is forced to recognize that his feeling is more subtle and, in some ways, too delicate for that of his wife."[30] True, but like his wife, he is defined by his individualism. Not only is he faithful to his word, a sardonic expression of individualism in a corrupt world, but, like Carinthia, he has a will. This will, unlike hers, is used to manage others, but like hers it is designed to keep him free of social snares. The one snare that catches them both is their marriage, so any invidious comparison of strength in canceled. And is this marriage, after all, really a snare? Both knew love during its duration, though tragically not at the same time.

The character of James to whom we may compare Lord Fleetwood is Prince Amerigo, of *The Golden Bowl*. James tells us of the Prince:

He knew why he had from the first of his marriage tried with such patience for such conformity; he knew why he had given up so much and bored himself so much; he knew why he had at any rate gone in, on the basis of all forms, on the basis of his having in a manner sold himself, for a *situation nette*. It had all been just in order that his—well, what on earth should he call it but his freedom?—should at present be as perfect and rounded and lustrous as some huge precious pearl. He hadn't struggled nor snatched; he was taking but what had been given him; the pearl dropped itself, with its exquisite quality and rarity, straight into his hand.[31]

In the Jamesian view, freedom is the result of "giving up" a great deal, and in shape and form it is not primordial. It is a finished product, made up of the careful and delicate arrangement of the inner self and of the adjustment of this entity, with equal care and delicacy, to the surrounding complex of social hedges, thorns, and discreet pathways. Lord Fleetwood's freedom, like Carinthia's, is less dependent on a fine preparation of self to receive what the world has to give. Also, unlike Prince Amerigo's guiding principle—which is inner repose and stasis, born out of centuries of knowledge of evil and the social institutions defining self—Lord Fleetwood's governing rule is rapid and erratic motion.

It is worth noting that Lord Fleetwood's conversion to Catholicism and removal to a monastery are as convincing as Matey Weyburn's allusions to divine law are not. Lord Fleetwood's action is a precise and credible consequence of his character. Though Meredith was hardly the man to approve of renunciation of the world,* he unerringly provided the right path for the figure he had created. Meredith once again found a way to provide the individual will with a pathway for action that skirts society. The will, in its free seeking of its own goal, does not threaten society and thus does not require the invocation of "good citizenship." Lord Fleetwood, like Carinthia, has merely remained true to his nonsocial self, and significantly, his ultimate repudiation of society calls for little more than comic horror on the part of Dame Gossip.†

Meredith's achievement is plain. Neither primitive strength (Ca-

* Meredith's own views on the subject were stated in a letter to Frances Forbes-Robertson, who had wavered between marriage and a convent, but had decided finally for marriage. On April 4, 1899, Meredith wrote: "I think you know my view that it is the braver choice to embrace the world than to renounce it. So must I be glad of your putting on the veil of acceptance instead of abnegation. You wavered, I heard; and I can augur well of the man who disposed you to take the way of nature's good old road. Expect merely the commonplace of happiness, accept in conventual spirit what is given, be assured that much of it corrupts, and above all let it be your pride to hold to your courage." (*Letters*, II, 503.)

† The Dame alleges that a mob attacked Calesford, an estate belonging to Lord Fleetwood, when it heard that all the wealth of the young nobleman was passing into the hands of the Church of Rome. According to the Dame's report, however, the only lasting "social" effect of the mob action was talk—renewed talk, all over England, of the Amazing Marriage.

rinthia's) nor complex character (Lord Fleetwood's) need be restricted in the interest of public safety. The will, left to its own devices, works out something socially harmless. The justification for this late discovery was already established in his earliest view of human nature. Like many English nineteenth-century writers, Meredith in his novels shows no developed sense of evil. The daring freedom of will he permits Carinthia and Lord Fleetwood is an arrival, cautiously step by step through *One of Our Conquerors* and *Lord Ormont,* at acceptance of the implications of his own lifelong belief. In a world in which the worst that can be said of human will is that it is liable to error, not evil, and in which nature is always ready to recognize the will as her own offspring, there is little society need fear if that will is allowed its freedom. But when we ask how, in this view, have nature and society been reconciled, the answer quite simply is that they do not need to be. If nature is left to her own devices and society learns to be permissive before the individualism of its members, a practical harmony will be achieved.

Are we not, however, left with a problem more serious than the one with which we began? If error, and the possibility of evil, are rendered innocuous by the ability of the social fabric to resist the will of individuals, how account for moral harm in the world? How account for society's inability to protect its members from suffering that is not self-inflicted? The simplest answer would be that Meredith never did account for such suffering, but we would be negligent, in saying this, if we overlooked his final, and in some ways most ambitious, attempt to do so. He made this attempt by conceiving the will of *society* as an engine which, when erratic, damages more than itself in the larger "society" to which it belongs—the society of nations. The work in which he did this is a unified series of poems entitled *Odes in Contribution to the Song of French History* and published in 1898.

### HISTORY, TRUE LIBERTY, AND SIN

The *Odes,* Meredith's last completed major work, have a multiple significance. Unfortunately, aesthetic triumph is not part of their meaning; however pleasing it would have been to say that Meredith concluded his career with a splendid work of art, the *Odes* contain too much inferior writing to allow us to make the claim. But they do reveal the almost incredible fact that Meredith in his seventieth year was still striving energetically for recognition as a poet, and they tell us much about his final attitude toward form and ideas, much about his response to the climate of the '90's, and much about the closing chapter in his personal drama.

At one point in *The Amazing Marriage* Meredith says (p. 353), "Poetry, however erratic, is less the servant of the bully Present, or pompous Past, than History." There is a suggestion here of Aristotle but more particularly of Meredith's entire career as a poet matching insight and power of conception with the historicist liberals who were his friends. The words quoted are another declaration in favor of the free imagination as a source of truth. They also exhibit a belief that in precise poetic images lie revelations of character (important to Meredith's view of history) not to be achieved through other means. This commitment to poetry explains why Meredith chose to write his last work, the history of France from 1789 to the end of the nineteenth century, as an epic poem. But why did he choose the history of France as his last theme? The answers are many and varied.

Meredith's choice is, first of all, a mark of his recognition of the importance of the French Revolution to all nineteenth-century European history. Secondly, the '90's witnessed new influences of French culture upon English intellectual and artistic life, one sign of which was the publication of Arthur Symons's *The Symbolist Movement in Literature* (1899). Meredith, in the '90's, was too encumbered by his lifelong interests to be fully responsive to this new French influence; he was, however, aware of the importance of France as an idea, and he participated in the fresh interest in France in the way most appropriate for him. He was always eager to be regarded as an artist and a political thinker both, but he regarded artistic craft as something to be acquired through insight and experiment, and history and politics as subjects to be consciously learned. He was always, too, more responsive to intellectual tradition than to the history of form. Thus, while his younger contemporaries of the '90's were acknowledging France as an artistic force, Meredith was paying his tribute through a political and ethical analysis of the nation's history, though rendering it into poetry.

We know Meredith felt strongly that he and others were in France's debt. Le Gallienne tells us that when he visited Meredith in the '90's he found that the chalet at Box Hill, in which Meredith worked, "was furnished mainly with bookshelves, chiefly filled . . . with French and German authors."[32] Lionel Stevenson recounts that Paul Valéry was "impressed by Meredith's accurate knowledge about Napoleon and his empire, and remarked that 'he loved France almost violently.' "[33] With respect to the *Odes*, the most pertinent words are Meredith's own. In a letter to Constantin Photiadès, one of his early biographers, he wrote: "It is true that at all times my heart has beaten for France, and it is not less true that, even up to this day, I have not acknowledged by an adequate testimony the debt that mankind owes her. My *Odes in Contribution to the Song of French History* are an effort in this direction."[34]

The *Odes* had an additional meaning for Meredith, a meaning that has a special drama and poignancy. On July 6, 1898, Meredith wrote to John Morley: "The Odes, including 'France 1870,' printed in your 'Fortnightly,' will be published in September. I want your presence, that I may perceive whether the offer of the Dedication to you would be agreeable. It seems hardly asking you to stand sponsor. . . . At the same time, your knowledge of French History, sympathy with France, and our old friendship, form a sort of plea, with a reminder that I must soon be going."[35]

This letter casts a light backward onto the 1870's, the period in which Meredith, to achieve his own individualism as an artist, had to repudiate Morley the historian, only to desire earnestly ever afterward a renewed closeness with the man whose intellect and historical knowledge he unceasingly admired. Once again, and for the last time, Meredith was seeking the approbation of the unpoetical Morley, while firmly presenting himself in his own role as poet.

How well did Meredith succeed, through the *Odes*, in establishing himself as a historical thinker? Stevenson tells us that "experts testify to the deep insight into historical processes that the *Odes* displayed."[36] Siegfried Sassoon declares, "It has been asserted by distinguished authorities that these odes are among the greatest political poetry ever written. 'It is doubtful,' wrote one of them, 'whether any prose writer has given the essence of Napoleon with such amazing insight. . . . He gives not the mere facts but the essential meaning, the spirit of the facts.' "[37] And G. M. Trevelyan, a historian as well as a student and admirer of Meredith, is similarly unstinting in his praise of the *Odes*.[38]

Thus the work has received strong testimonials. To what extent they are justified is a difficult question to answer. Meredith's conception of history, though by no means antiquated and meaningless, would hardly satisfy modern historians who recognize that historical causation is not easily discussed. On the other hand, the vastness of Meredith's scope, combined with the relative brevity of the form he has chosen, excuses his lack of detail. And, though much of the poetry is simply bad, the boldness and energy with which he drives ahead through passages of clumsy writing to arrive unexhausted at stretches marked by powerful movement and superb lucidity give a borrowed brilliance to the exposition of his thought. Moreover, the best of the *Odes*, the one entitled "Napoléon," is a masterful characterization. It benefits both from Meredith's poetical ability and from the psychological perception that makes the more memorable figures in his novels so forceful.

But the *Odes* have a greater significance than their value as history, whatever the just measure of that value may be. For they return, and now truly for the last time, to the problems posed and left unsolved by the three novels of the '90's. In this final gathering of his forces, Meredith used all he knew of artistic form, history, and ethics to attempt once more to reconcile nature and society through their common incarnation, the individual will.

The *Odes* tell a story, and in the aggregate resemble a novel, or at least a synthesis of operatic eloquence and analytic characterization. The chief actors recall history and at the same time stand inimitably portrayed as privately conceived individuals. And Meredith's major themes are orchestrated together in a last resounding affirmation of their equal importance. The power of nature to inform and shape human society, the role of law in the universe, the ethical meaning of reason, the religious striving that was credible in the poetry of the '80's, the doctrine that work is the condition for salvation, and the idea that the will must remain true to itself—they are all here.

France is personified as a lady of complexities, and in this personification lies Meredith's solution to the problem of how to deal with a society—a nation—as a single entity endowed with will and power. Throughout the drama Meredith skillfully shifts between two conceptions of France: as a creature resembling the human individual and as a sovereign state which is incommensurable with persons in the ordinary sense. Out of this ambivalence arise, for Meredith, answers to the question of how human society can be regarded as a moral force.

In the first ode, titled "The Revolution," France receives a heavenly lover, described as "the young angelical."[39] She does so in 1789. The explanation of how France, crushed so long under the *Ancien Régime,* can respond to such a lover is that nature resurrected her to youth and life, and in fact was quietly nurturing France during the worst years of oppression. In this, the first important idea of the *Odes,* Meredith has returned to the Romantic tradition which says that nature is the source of all strength and virtue in human affairs. The first phase of the Revolution is seen not as a period of conflict and destruction but as a season of rebirth and creativity, depicted in strict nature imagery:

> Read through her launching heart, who had lain long
> With Earth and heard till it became her own
> Our good Great Mother's eve and matin song:
> The humming burden of Earth's toil to feed
> Her creatures all, her task to speed their growth,
> Her aim to lead them up her pathways, shown
> Between the Pains and Pleasures; warned of both,
> Of either aided on their hard ascent.

Revolutionary France makes Earth's song her own and learns thereby that productive toil, and pleasure and pain only in so far as they aid it, mark out the pathway designated by nature's teleology. We may note here, near the beginning of the poem, the epic manner, the Miltonic strain, the long freighted lines moving with grave regularity, solidly joined by enjambment and the interweaving of the two subjects, "Earth" and "France."

But as France moves into the second phase of the Revolution, the life energy derived from Earth is corrupted into a passion for destruction. As the Terror mounts, France is described as drinking of "life's hot flood." And here, significantly, Meredith for the first time discusses seriously the idea of sin. France is regarded compassionately, because in comparison to her enemies', hers was "the appealing sin." But compassionate as he is, Meredith firmly establishes sin as a central theme in the drama, and it is a theme that shapes the rest of the story.

France, in the Terror, has abandoned her heavenly bridegroom, True Liberty. Now Meredith adds the novelistic dimension to the drama. On her downward path France perversely asks

> To have the thing most loathed, the iron lord,
> Controller and Chastiser, under Victory masked.

She asks, in short, for Napoleon. Her "bridegroom of the miracle day," Liberty, though apparently rejected, watches understandingly from above:

> But he, remembering how his love began,
> And of what creature, pitied when was plain
> Another measure of captivity:
> The need for strap and rod;
> The penitential prayers again;
> Again the bitter bowing down to dust.

In commenting upon this passage, we need not separate its intellectual purpose from its prosodic quality. The ellipsis is reminiscent not only of Meredith's earlier poetry but of Browning's work. The repetitive elaboration of the idea of penance is Biblical and appropriate, considering how important this theme will prove to be in the poem.

The second ode, "Napoléon," begins with a description of the man whose name is its title:

> Cannon his name,
> Cannon his voice, he came.
> Who heard of him heard shaken hills
> . . . . . . . . . . . .
> Who looked on him beheld the will of wills.

The characteristic that contrasts Napoleon with France's first lover is immediately established. France's "heavenly bridegroom," True Liberty, was gentle. Liberty is thus not associated with a strong and assertive will, as it was in Meredith's novels of the '90's. It is rather a condition of existence allowing productive and creative pursuits. But Napoleon, who is to be portrayed as the enemy of freedom, is the "will of wills."

The explanation for this apparent shift in Meredith's morality is that Napoleon, by being classified with France—he takes her as his mistress—is no longer simply and literally an individual. France's individualism is a literary convention adopted to make concrete the complex of forces forming a political and social entity. In order that Napoleon may exist in the same realm of discourse that she does, Meredith makes Napoleon's will identical in power and consequences with the will of the state, in this case, France. The individual will is harmlesss in the novels, but the will of a nation, or of its embodiment as here, may be a highly dangerous phenomenon, a threat to the very existence of general freedom.

In anticipation of a later discussion of fate, the laws, and the gods, Meredith explains Napoleon as an inevitable consequence of the Terror and of the equally culpable actions of the nations that made war on Revolutionary France:

> To weld the nation in a name of dread,
> And scatter carrion flies off wounds unhealed,
> The Necessitated came.

At this point the portrait of France, as a woman, is further developed. Fallen from her heavenly lover and having become Napoleon's mistress, she not only is saved by the latter from her tormentors but is raised by him above other nations. Here begins for France, however, a struggle of conscience, significantly equated with reason. She must justify—rationalize—what she has done. France,

> . . . if cold Reason pressed her, called him Fate
> Offering abashed the servile woman's vow.
>
> .  .  .  .  .  .  .  .  .  .  .  .  .
> Till worship of him shone as her last rational state,
> The slave's apology for gemmed disgrace.

We need not dwell on the wordy weakness of the last two lines. It reveals a gap between poetic conception and execution, because of which these lines have an unfinished quality. But their intention is important, for it is carried forward in the rest of the poem.

Since France has made herself a slave, her conscience will not rest.

Returning to an image that occurs in his early nature poetry—in the 1851 volume, Meredith says that "Earth's fluttering little lyre"—the lark, a symbol for the voice of liberty[40]—is still heard in France. Then, in a passage that is operatic rather than novelistic, France struggles between thought (reason) and her worship of Napoleon (sin). Finally she sees her heavenly lover above her and "Knew him her judge, knew yonder the spirit preferred."

The curtains now draw back to reveal the full size of the stage and the magnitude of the drama. England, personified as the "Seaman," begins to dog Napoleon, fighting with money as well as courage.

Soon, however, Meredith returns to the novelistic mode and begins a long analysis of the relations between Napoleon and France. This is the section most often cited when the *Odes* are praised as history. Napoleon's attitude toward France is characterized:

> He, did he love her? France was his weapon, shrewd
> At edge, a wind in onset: he loved well
> His tempered weapon, with the which he hewed
> Clean to the ground impediments, or hacked,
> Sure of the blade that served the great man-miracle.

The opening question is not rhetorical. It is a difficult one and thus not only gives power to the line in which it appears but elicits energy from the lines which contain its answer. The quickening of pace in the second half of the first line and the first half of the second suggests the sword in motion; and the gentler, slower "he loved well" is an ironic introduction to the unexpected "his tempered weapon." Unfortunately, however, the less said about "with the which he hewed" the better. As for the phrase, "the great man-miracle," while not inspired as poetry it recalls the earlier description of True Liberty as "the bridegroom" of the "miracle day."

There follows an amplification of Napoleon's feelings about France:

> He loved her more than little, less than much.
> . . . . . . . . . . . . . .
> Nought save his rounding aim, the means he plied,
> Death for his cause, to him could point appeal.
> His mistress was the thing of uses tried.
> Frigid the netting smile on whom he wooed,
> But on his Policy his eye was lewd.

Thus the abstraction, Policy, has been introduced as another mistress, so that Napoleon becomes the apex of two triangles:

> He deemed nought other precious, nor knew he
> Legitimate outside his Policy.
> Men's lives and works were due, from their birth's date,
> To the State's shield and sword, himself the State.

In the following passage the subject shifts to Napoleon's dealings with people in general:

> The common Tyrant's frenzies, rancour, spites,
> He knew as little as men's claim on rights.
> A kindness for old servants, early friends,
> Was constant in him while they served his ends.

Finally, in a summing up of the characterization, Meredith portrays Napoleon as statesman and despot:

> The statesman steered the despot to large tasks;
> The despot drove the statesman on short roads.
> For Order's cause he laboured, as inclined
> A soldier's training and his Euclid mind.

The end couplet is less than ideal in this passage. But if the couplet has a tinny ring where the sound of heavier metal is wanted, the lines themselves are lean and accurate, and the over-all effect is one of verse properly used for character revelation.

We return, now, to France. To her is given, with poetic if not historic precision, the supreme insight into her master. She

> Perceives him fast to a harsher Tyrant bound;
> Self-ridden, self-hunted, captive of his aim;
> Material grandeur's ape, the Infernal's hound;
> Enormous, with no infinite around;
> No starred deep sky, no Muse, or lame
> The dusty pattering pinions,
> The voice as through the brazen tube of Fame.

But France, though she now sees the truth, suppresses her conscience and continues to dote on Napoleon's victories. She is, for the time being, the captive of her own commitment:

> What wonder, though with wits awake
> To read her riddle, for these her offspring's sake;—
> And she, before high heaven adulteress,
> The lost to honour, in his glory clothed,

Else naked, shamed in sight of men, self-loathed;—
That she should quench her thought, nor worship less
Than ere she bled on sands or snows and knew
The slave's alternative, to worship or to rue!

The turning point in the relations of Napoleon and France is the defeat in Russia. After the debacle, the union between Napoleon and France becomes feverish: the two are desperately attempting to save each other from total ruin. But France, despite fear, is disillusioned beyond the possibility of further self-evasion, and the story, from this point to Waterloo, exhibits France's growing self-confrontation and increasing desire to be rid of Napoleon.

Then, Waterloo. But the liberation it brings is impure, even another form of defeat. France is freed from the oppression of Napoleon "by foreigners who are not the sons of true freedom. She is not set free to rejoin her heavenly lover."[41] And as Meredith relates these developments, the operatic and allegorical quality supersedes the novelistic, which was well-sustained in the two sections concerned with the relations of Napoleon and France.

As this second ode, "Napoléon," nears its conclusion, the tone becomes quietly recitative, and years are spanned. "As the years go by, the liberal movement begins in France in the twenties, the Napoleonic Legend assumes mellow hues of peace and liberty which the real Napoleon hated. The 'young angelical'—the heavenly lover—True Liberty waves aloft again as a hope."[42]

The next ode, "France—December 1870," was actually the earliest to be written. Indeed, it contains the central idea from which Meredith, in the late '90's, developed the entire series. As its title indicates, the ode was composed in December 1870, "when the Germans were round Paris,"[43] and was published in *The Fortnightly* in January 1871. In a letter to Maxse, dated February 27, 1871, Meredith speaks of France as having been "in need of the bitterest of lessons."[44] In this point of view lies the meaning of both "France—December 1870" and of "Alsace-Lorraine," the ode which follows it and concludes the series.

At the very beginning of "France—December 1870," the idea of sin, briefly touched upon in "The Revolution," is made explicit and important. The idea of sin is especially significant in the 1870 ode because it was an idea that had been banished from everything else of significance that Meredith wrote in the '70's. In "France—December 1870," he says:

> She likewise half corrupt of sin,
> Angel and Wanton! can it be?

Then follows an explanation of France's downfall that not only is reminiscent of Meredith's themes of the '70's but explains also the inexorable consequences of her "sin":

> Mother of Reason is she, trebly cursed,
> To feel, to see, to justify the blow;
> Chamber to chamber of her sequent brain
> Gives answer of the cause of her great woe,
> Inexorably echoing thro' the vaults,
> 'Tis thus they reap in blood, in blood who sow:
> 'This is the sum of self-absolvëd faults.'
>
> . . . . . . . . . . . . . . .
> The high strong light within her, tho' she bleeds,
> Traces the letters of returned misdeeds.

The too obviously mannered rhetoric of these lines marks them as the work of one of Meredith's less successful poetic periods. But once again a theme elaborated by inferior lines is important for our understanding of the entire sequence of odes. The events of 1870 are retribution for the eras of both Napoleons. "Reason" makes this clear to France, thus increasing her pain even as it enlightens her.

Meredith next prescribes for France's needs, and as he does we get an early statement of the idea of beneficent law, so important in the poetry of the '80's:

> . . . for Strength she yearns.
> For Strength, her idol once, too long her toy.
> Lo, Strength is of the plain root-Virtues born:
> Strength shall ye gain by service, prove in scorn,
> Train by endurance, by devotion shape.
> Strength is not won by miracle or rape.
> It is the offspring of the modest years,
> The gift of sire to son, thro' those firm laws
> Which we name Gods; which are the righteous cause,
> The cause of man, and manhood's ministers.

This theme is repeated a moment later when Meredith rebukes France for allowing the Church to supplicate for deliverance:

> And now bid hope that heaven will intercede
> To violate its laws in her sore need,
> . . . . . . . . . . . .
> Mother of Reason! can she cheat the Fates?

The question is rhetorical and ironic. But Meredith's purpose is not to rebuke: it is to exhort France to remain true to the faith that she inspired and that Meredith had taken for his own in the '70's—the faith in reason:

> . . . Soaring France!
> Now is humanity on trial in thee:
> Now mayst thou gather humankind in fee:
> Now prove that Reason is a quenchless scroll;
> Make of calamity thine aureole,
> And bleeding head us thro' the troubles of the sea.

The last ode in the series, "Alsace-Lorraine," was written more than twenty years after "France—December 1870." Expectedly, it is richer in connotations, and its poetic density is greater. Like the first two odes, which belong to the same period, it makes wide use of many of Meredith's lifelong themes, those that were still vigorous issues for him in his final years.

It is a poem of restoration—not of lost territory but of national character and strength. As in the first ode, no sooner does Meredith touch on this theme of renewal than he turns to nature imagery. "The Revolution" pictures France gaining energy at the breast of Earth; so "Alsace-Lorraine" depicts a recovered France as a rich countryside alive with the varied activity of nature.

The meaning of this vision is soon amplified. Meredith says of France:

> Her, from a nerveless well among stagnant pools of the dry,
> Through her good aim at divine, shall commune with Earth remake;
> Fraternal unto sororial, her, where abashed she may lie,
> Divinest of man shall clasp; a world out of darkness awake,
> As it were with the Resurrection's eyelids uplifted, to see
> Honour in shame . . .
>
> . . . . . . . . . . . . . . . . .
> For this at our nature arises rejuvenescent from Earth,
> However respersive the blow and nigh on infernal the fall,
> The chastisement drawn down on us merited: are we of worth
> Amid our satanic excrescences, this, for the less than a call,
> Will Earth reprime, man cherish; the God who is in us and round,
> Consenting, the God there seen.

Once more Meredith has enlarged into a theology the idea that nature is beneficent. Not only nature, but "the God there seen"— here unequivocally the God of Wordsworth—forgives sin when we are bent on restoration. The lines expressing this concept distort the clear image in the same angular elliptical way that causes so much of Meredith's didactic verse to march in heavy boots along an uneven road. Yet in comparison to the lightweight oracularity of "France—December 1870," the thought and feeling here at least have substance and mass: the clumsiness seems the result of Meredith's praiseworthy effort to move something heavy and solid through the trained gestures of poetry.

From the beneficent intentions of nature and God to the Goethean-Carlylean doctrine of work is a plausible transition for Meredith. France is praised for having worked hard since her defeat instead of brooding over her "amputated limb," Alsace-Lorraine; for having been determined to pay off the reparations and to rebuild the national honor and strength. But Meredith was not naïve: much of the later part of the poem voices anxiety about the international consequences that would follow should France attempt to regain Alsace-Lorraine by force.

In the earlier part of the ode France is once more presented as a sensate being, if not quite as the alluring maiden who leapt to the embrace of her heavenly lover, True Liberty, in 1789. This lover, incidentally, remains faithful, and is responsive whenever she is. He has never ceased to keep a watchful eye on her. But what he sees in the years following the Franco-Prussian War is not only industry and thrift, the virtues praised in the opening part of the poem. This sensitive, tutelary bridegroom has, in fact, to withhold himself once more, because in the 1870's, Meredith tells us, France flirted dangerously with revived Royalism and Bonapartism.

Meredith scolds France for her recurring worship of Napoleon and declares that she ought to call upon that truer embodiment of saintliness and heroism, Joan of Arc. Recalled in the passages that deal with Joan are all the heroic women of Meredith's novels: women meant to inspire admiration and reverence rather than sensual or even tender love. Joan, in this ode, is not George Bernard Shaw's Joan, humanized as a boyish, simple, but willful revolutionary. She is Vittoria, Princess Ottilia, the later Carinthia Fleetwood, and—if not Meredith's self-effacing French wife, Marie Vulliamy—she is

Hilda de Longueuil, a lady of French background, who, many years younger than he, received a great deal of attention from the widower Meredith in the '90's.[45]

Contrasting Joan with Napoleon, Meredith says:

> She had no self but France: the sainted man
> No France but self.

This is a return to the theme of the poetry of the '80's: the idea that egoism is an unmitigated evil. Meredith's Joan, like Vittoria and Ottilia, has the ability to transform herself subtly into an expression, in accordance with exalted law, of national character and aspiration. And like Carinthia she literally participates in battle for the sake of principle.

Joan, moreover, incorporates in her being the doctrine of work. In the lines that follow, "her" refers to France, and Joan is "the child":

> The child of her industrious;
> Earth's truest, earth's pure fount from the main.

Joan, like France in her best guise, is sprung from Earth, here merged again with work in a mystic union containing history's teleology. Work is not at this point precisely equated with evolutionary purpose, but Meredith believes that productive labor will carry the France of the 1890's to her rightful destiny, and that Joan—her character and her background—symbolizes the necessary spirit for the enterprise.

Lest we confuse the high purpose of productive labor with material ambition, Meredith makes the distinction clear by a disapproving reference to Napoleon III. In embracing what Napoleon III stood for rather than what Joan did, France took a backward step. Napoleon's passion was material greed, therefore regressive, and therefore doomed to fail, because

> In Nature is no rearward step allowed.
> Hard on the rock Reality do we dash
> To be shattered, if the material dream propels.

Nature signifies constant advance, and whatever nature signifies is reality. To step backward is therefore to oppose nature, which in turn is to conflict with reality.

According to Meredith in this ode, defiance of nature is also the disorder of unreason, a thesis which makes us think wistfully of the

less doctrinaire exploration of experience that made his novels of the
'70's so meaningful. But the important distinction must be reiterated.
Meredith, in the *Odes*, is writing about a nation, which may be conceived for poetic purposes as an individual but whose actions have
consequences beyond those of a literal character. In describing how
France endured the era of Napoleon III and also came safely through
the dangerous '70's, marked by the threat of Royalism and Bonapartism, Meredith says:

> She read the things that are;
> Reality unaccepted read
> For sign of the distraught, and took her blow
> To brain; herself read through;
> Wherefore her predatory Glory paid
> Napoleon ransom knew.
> Her nature's many strings hot gusts did jar
> Against the note of reason uttered low,
> Ere passionate with duty she might wed,
> Compel the bride's embrace of her stern groom.
> Joined at an altar liker to the tomb,
> Nest of the Furies their first nuptial bed,
> They not the less were mated and proclaimed
> The rational their issue. Then she rose.

The pattern enlarges and becomes explicit. Ethics and politics
are joined in a thesis that reaches back to the Enlightenment and
forward to the early phase of twentieth-century liberalism. In a
polity establishing true liberty, Meredith has told us here, reason
will flourish. The implication is that reason is a natural plant requir-
ing only proper political conditions for survival and vigorous growth.
This view is no longer prevalent, but in noting that Meredith reveals
the limits of his nineteenth-century mind, we should note also how
firmly he has adopted the outlook of the political thinker, clearly a
necessary achievement given the subject and purpose of the *Odes*.

With reason established, the circle—Earth to polity (or society)
to Earth again—is completed. Initially, it is through the beneficence
of Earth that reason is restored in France. Then,

> Let but the rational prevail,
> Our footing is on ground though all else fail:
> Our kiss of Earth is then a plight
> To walk within her Laws and have her light.
> Choice of the life or death lies in ourselves;
> There is no fate but when unreason lours.

If we are rational, our embrace of nature is an acceptance of her laws, which means, in this continuous circle of ideas, an acceptance of freedom. Once having accepted nature's laws we see in their "light" that we are permitted the grandest choice of all: to live, a choice here contrasted with "fate." Meredith's repudiation of fate is not a rejection of necessity, nor does freedom mean transcendence of necessity. The *Odes* as an entity attempt to reveal the working of necessity—of "law." The fate Meredith rejects is the kind implicit in the concept of original sin and also the kind revealed in Thomas Hardy's novels. What Meredith believes is that through perception of nature's laws and obedience to them man becomes free (for obedience to nature is not bondage) to give his life a rationally inspired pattern.

In another gathering of themes, Meredith says,

> The mother who gave birth to Jeanne;
> Who to her young Angelical sprang;
> Who lay with Earth and heard the notes she sang,
> And heard her truest sing them; she may reach
> Heights yet unknown of nations; haply teach
> A thirsting world to learn 'tis 'she who can.'

The last phrase refers back to a line at the end of "The Revolution." There, in words baldly reminiscent of Carlyle's etymological praise of the able king, but without the praise, Meredith pictured Napoleon regarding himself as "I who can."

The final task for triumphant France is to free herself from the last vestige of desire to recover Alsace-Lorraine:

> She that in History's Heliaea pleads
> The nation flowering conscience o'er the beast;
> With heart expurged of rancour, tame of greeds;
> With the winged mind from fang and claw released;—
> Will such a land be seen? It will be seen;—
> Shall stand adjudged our foremost and Earth's Queen.

In the epithet "Earth's Queen," there are connotations not only of a perfected political form but of artistic and intellectual energy. Meredith, though he could no longer be responsive to and deeply changed by it himself, was well aware of what distinguished the France of the '90's for his contemporaries.

But he could not conclude with even this mild allusion to France as a cultural force. He had to return to political questions and to end the ode by voicing concern and a warning. If France plunges Europe into war over Alsace-Lorraine, both her cultural and political promise will be destroyed. "She," in the following lines, refers to France: "Europe waits; / She chooses God or gambles with the Fates." In conclusion he urges her to "sacrifice in one self-mastering hour," and adds, "The . . . generous find / Renouncement is possession."

Thus at the very end we see that the drama of the will is the drama of the ego we read in Meredith's poetry of the '80's. France must learn not what Meredith told us in the novels of the '90's but what he declared to be true in "The Woods of Westermain." Yet the conclusion is not an abhorred "backward step." Finishing the *Odes,* we recall that it was only by convention that we agreed to envision France as a woman and that the moral drama in which a nation lives is not the same as the one in which an individual has his being. We see, moreover, that the idea of renunciation, however naïve as a proposal for political ethics, is quite meaningful and sophisticated as a suggestion for political strategy. Whether or not Meredith comprehended this, whether or not he recognized that his preachment to France was valuable only insofar as it made an ideal the symbolic mask for the hated word "policy," he had a genuine fear of the World War he did not live to see, and he recognized that the alternative for nations is either to acknowledge the limits they impose on each other or to engage in blow and counterblow, inviting ultimately an enlarged and general holocaust.

This, then, is Meredith's conception of the power of society to harm, to do evil. It is his substitute for that vision of society as a dimension of reality in the lives of individuals that we are given in the novels of Balzac, Stendhal, Flaubert, Hardy, and James. There is curious relevance in the fact that James, after reading Meredith's *Letters,* noted the absence of any reference to Balzac.[46] Meredith's historical curiosity was made to do the moral investigating that the aesthetic power gave rise to in Balzac and James. To satisfy this curiosity Meredith had as his special task to find the grounds for reconciling nature and society. He attempted to do so in the *Odes* by shifting the context of the problem to the international scene. Here, nature counsels liberty in the internal affairs of a nation, reason in international relations. A falling away from these counsels is sin, not error, and thus the historic relations of societies are ultimately judged by God.

Many have quarreled with Meredith's solutions to the ethical and metaphysical problems he raises. Undoubtedly many more will. But even among his contemporaries, those who could not possibly have accepted the answers he offered to the large questions with which he dealt recognized that his faith in his own intellectual and imaginative powers enabled him to range brilliantly over the world he envisioned; enabled him to create characters who live with all the energy that was his own; enabled him to be, in short, intensely individual as an artist. And this, however different their premises, was the same objective sought by his younger contemporaries of the '90's. It is therefore not strange that Oscar Wilde, for example, who hardly shared Meredith's moral vision, and of whom Meredith ultimately strongly disapproved,* could say:

One incomparable novelist we have now in England, Mr. George Meredith. There are better artists in France, but France has no one whose view of life is so large, so varied, so imaginatively true. There are tellers of stories in Russia who have a more vivid sense of what pain in fiction may be. But to him belongs philosophy in fiction. His people not merely live, but they live in thought. One can see them from myriad points of view. They are suggestive. There is soul in them and around them. They are interpretive and symbolic. And he who made them, those wonderful quickly moving figures, made them for his own pleasure, and has never asked the public what they wanted . . . but has gone on intensifying his own personality, and producing his own individual work.[47]

* In 1895 Frank Harris tried to get up a petition for the release of Oscar Wilde from prison. He says: "I was informed . . . that if Meredith headed the petition . . . the Government would grant it. . . . To my astonishment he replied that he couldn't do as I wished. . . . A little later I made it my business to meet Meredith . . . and have it out with him. . . . He defended his want of sympathy. Abnormal sensuality in a leader of men, he said, was a crime, and should be punished with severity. . . . He became emphatic, loud, rhetorical." (*Contemporary Portraits*, 204–5.) Lionel Stevenson, who quotes these words, adds, "If Harris had stopped to remember Meredith's writings he would have realized that the conquest of sensual impulses was the very basis of his whole ethical doctrine." (*Ordeal*, p. 348.) Perhaps so. But Stevenson, too, might be admonished that in Meredith's novels, at least, self-conquest is not always the

Henry James, in another comment on the *Letters,* casts a bright new light on Meredith: "I catch their emanation of something so admirable and, on the whole, so . . . tragic." Then, complaining of the editing of the *Letters,* he asserts that the edition fails "to project the Image (of character, temper, quantity and quality of mind, general size and sort of personality) that such a subject cries aloud for; to the shame of our purblind criticism. For such a Vividness to go a-begging!—"[48]

With the *Odes* in view, we are aware that these estimates of Meredith would not present a complete sense of the man were we to neglect the last image he presented of himself as a political thinker. In 1903, at the age of seventy-five, he gave in *The Manchester Guardian* his opinions concerning "the present position of the Liberal Party." "The article stirred up amazing excitement. Most of the chief London and provincial papers reprinted long passages and many of them discussed it editorially. The Liberals hailed it as courageous and stimulating, the Conservatives smothered it in ridicule. At last Meredith received nation-wide recognition—not as an author but as a political pundit."[49] Here, perhaps, was the origin of the myth, prevalent after Meredith's death, that he was a lifelong, uncomplicated, nineteenth-century Liberal and Radical.

The most suggestive—if ultimately inaccurate—comment concerning the dualistic image of Meredith as artist and social theorist belongs to Henry James. Referring again to the *Letters,* he says,

The whole aesthetic range, understanding that in a big sense, strikes me as meagre and short; he clearly lived even less than one had the sense of his doing in the world of art. . . . He was *starved,* to my vision, in many ways—and that makes him but the more nobly pathetic. In fine the whole moral side of him throws out some splendidly clear lights—while the "artist," the secondary Shakespeare, remains curiously dim.[50]

George Bernard Shaw had his word about Meredith, too, and it is the one which suggests our final insight into the figure Meredith presents. Recounting a visit he had paid to Box Hill, Shaw said: "He

---

simple ethical decree. At his best, Meredith has a perceptiveness and range of sympathy that make Harris's request plausible. Meredith's response to that request was the response of Meredith the public figure, the friend of statesmen, the oracle of good citizenship, not of the Meredith who wrote *Beauchamp's Career* or *The Amazing Marriage.*

had supported the reactionary candidate in a recent election, imagining that he represented the principles of the French Revolution, and Meredith was apologetic when I explained to him that my Fabianism was the latest thing. He was a relic of the Cosmopolitan Republican Gentleman of the previous generation."[51]

While enjoying the image Shaw presents us, we note something other than comic in Meredith's fumbling, at the end of the century, for the principles of the French Revolution. Meredith was expressing the two sides of his nature: the romantic and the enthusiast of reason. Reason is the hinge that connects Meredith the political thinker with Meredith the artist. The adherent of reason, in his view, is the safe leader of men, but this adherent, in his novels, is fascinatingly ambivalent and indeed gives way in the '90's, in the decade of Nietzsche in England, to the romantic man of will. If Meredith failed to recognize that Fabianism was the latest thing, perhaps the explanation is that he was not so much a political participant, in any of the restrictive meanings of the term, as a man for whom acceptance of social responsibility meant exercise—in the light of his own needs—of moral and critical imagination. Despite all that has been said, it was the novel, and to a lesser extent the poem, that was his field of action and of thought. And in the '90's, the principles of the French Revolution were still more useful to him for creating the moral dimension of his art than were those of Fabianism. Shaw's comment on Meredith's political ineptitude suggests something of central importance: however eager Meredith was to be known as a historian, as a "political pundit," or for that matter as a military strategist, his commitment was to art, not to history or politics or military science. However eagerly he attempted to speak from other points of view, it is as an artist-moralist that he made his claim for survival, and it is as such that we see him now.

# *Appendix* *

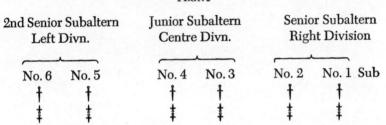

FRONT

2nd Senior Subaltern     Junior Subaltern     Senior Subaltern
Left Divn.           Centre Divn.        Right Division

No. 6    No. 5       No. 4    No. 3      No. 2    No. 1   Sub

Early morning—battle beginning—trumpet sounds: Boot & Saddle (cheery sound)—no sound for parade or inspection—all ready—Captain of battery & 2nd—command 'Trot march': in direction of firing: couple of regiments in mist to right: come to sharp ridge:—smoke: shots—command 'Action front':—sergeant dismounts from horse, corporal on waggon, bombardiers 2 gunners on gun—limbers:—gunners down—sergeant down—leading driver snatches rein to hold horse—gunners on each side Trail of gun, unhook Trail from limber, drop trail—shakes earth—command 'with shrapnel, load: what range? where enemy?—'Range 700 yards—with shrapnel'—Young Downes perceives enemy close & shouts: "Case!"—Men sure to obey subaltern. "Case LOAD." Downs [sic] loads own gun. "Ready. Fire from right of Divisions": Men are falling by gun: 2 guns firing case scatter enemy. enemy come (on?) shrapnel firing guns: Commanding officer shouts "Rear, limber up": only (the?) right division guns can execute order: others will not sacrifice limbers to attempt to save guns. Captain sees guns in enemy's hands—says to 2nd subaltern: "Mr. B. will you disgrace me?" B. hesitates. Downes dashes forward, shoots and sabres enemy: his men follow, gunners & bombardiers, & rescue guns. Limbers drive up, hook on.

---

* This material is given just as it appears in Meredith's manuscript. In addition, in the left margin is the sentence "Limbers drive on" when unhooked.

# Notes

CHAPTER I

1. Stevenson, *Ordeal*, p. 60. Complete names, titles, and publication data will be found in the Bibliography, pp. 237–43.
2. *Ibid.*
3. Meredith is not "anti-scientific" either in his portrait of Sir Austin or in anything else that belongs to the record of his opinions in the '50's. His artistic and ethical criticism is directed only against those who see science as necessarily materialistic. In this respect Meredith was ahead of his time. As Jacques Barzun has observed (*Darwin*, p. 96), "The fifties and the sixties saw [the] heyday [of mechanistic theorizing] among the thinking part of the world. Already in the seventies there were strong countercurrents, which won recognition in the eighties and nineties, and which show there was nothing necessary in the union of science and materialism."
4. Samuel Lucas, writing in *The Times* for October 14, 1859 (see Forman, pp. 51–70), pointed out that the System could not be blamed for the tragedy. However, Lucas therefore concluded that *Richard Feverel* is poor in structure, a conclusion which neither follows logically from his analysis of the System nor is confirmed by a close reading of the novel.
5. Unpublished letter, dated 1859, in the Yale University Library. Also quoted by Sassoon, p. 26.
6. Crum, p. 61.
7. *Feverel*, pp. 520–23.
8. It is interesting that in Meredith's earliest work, the volume of poems published in 1851, no fewer than ten poems contain the idea of rebirth as a major or secondary theme. These poems are "The Wild Rose and the Snowdrop," "The Death of Winter," "Twilight Music," "Song" ("Should thy love die"), "Pastorals" (IV and VII), "Sorrows and Joys," "Song" ("No, no the falling blossom is no sign"), "Pictures of the Rhine," "To a Nightingale," and "Invitation to the Country."
9. See Galland, p. 135.
10. For a discussion of the Young England Movement, see Woodward, pp. 108–12.
11. Stevenson, *Ordeal*, pp. 19–21.
12. Sassoon, p. 5.
13. Clodd, "Recollections," p. 21.
14. Woodward, p. 108.
15. *Ibid.*
16. J. B. Priestley (pp. 21–22) effectively dismisses the notion that economic need is sufficient as a cause to explain Meredith's weekly "apostasy," but is unable to suggest an alternative cause. Hammerton (p. 14)

proposed the odd notion that the gusto and verve with which Meredith expressed Tory sentiments were proof only of his desire to do a conscientious job for his employers and did not indicate anything about what he really believed. Lionel Stevenson stated flatly (*Ordeal*, pp. 85–86) that Meredith, despite the independence of many of his views, regarded himself as a Conservative. This opinion, though it has more basis in reality than contrary ones, seems to me an oversimplification. Jack Lindsay, the most recent commentator on the matter and the one who undoubtedly found it least congenial to his thesis, merely explained curtly that Meredith's "literary earnings were slight; he had to turn to journalism" (p. 101); thus Lindsay by-passes rather than solves the problem. Lindsay presents Meredith as a kind of intuitive Marxist who hailed the "class-struggle" and championed the proletariat, a thesis that violates many facts.

17. In his *Ipswich Journal* articles (Hammerton, pp. 14–15), Meredith attacked John Bright and other leaders of the "Manchester School." But he was not always to regard the commercial classes—the leaders of business and industry—as the enemy. By the end of the century, as we shall see, his attitude toward them had changed remarkably.

### CHAPTER II

1. Stevenson, *Ordeal*, p. 344.

2. Jacques Barzun, in commenting upon the latter part of the nineteenth century (*Darwin*, p. 100), has noted that "War became the symbol, the image, the inducement, the reason, and the language of all human doings on the planet. No one who has not waded through some sizable part of the literature of the period 1870-1914 has any conception of the extent to which it is one long call for blood."

3. Stevenson, *Ordeal*, p. 141.

4. Ross, pp. 51–53.

5. This and subsequent quotations in this paragraph are from Meredith's unpublished letters in the Yale University Library; the first excerpt is from a letter dated 1859, the others from letters dated 1860.

6. Ross, p. 50.

7. Meredith is quite explicit about this. Ten of the twenty-one chapters which describe the Harringtons at Beckley Court have headings that signify a war is in progress. These chapters and their headings are as follows: XIV, "The Countess Describes the Field of Action"; XV, "A Capture"; XVI, "Leads to a Small Skirmish Between Rose and Evan"; XXI, "Tribulations and Tactics of the Countess"; XXVII, "Exhibits Rose's Generalship"; XXIX, "Prelude to an Engagement"; XXX, "The Battle of the Bull-Dogs. Part I"; XXXI, "The Battle of the Bull-Dogs. Part II"; XXXV, "Rose Wounded"; and XXXVII, "The Retreat from Beckley."

8. Eliot, *The Mill on the Floss*, I (Cabinet edition, Vol. XVII), 254. Hereafter multi-volume works within a numbered edition will be referred to simply by I, II, etc. The edition numbering is given in the Bibliography.

9. All references to *Modern Love* will be to the text as it appears in *Poetical Works*. Numbers refer, respectively, to stanza and page.

10. See, for example, C. Day Lewis, *Image*, pp. 58–59, and 85; E. C. Wright, p. 7; and N. Friedman, pp. 9 and 24. Friedman, who is concerned with major "image-clusters" in *Modern Love*, finds that one such cluster is made up of "murder-knife-wound-blood" images. See pp. 17–18.

11. Browning, *Personae*, p. 17.

12. *Ibid.*, p. 22.

13. Of course *The Ring and the Book* also appeared in the '60's, and this great work tells a very different story of an unhappy marriage than does "James Lee." Like *Modern Love*, *The Ring and the Book* concerns conflict and violence, but Browning's purpose was again different from Meredith's. *Modern Love* explores what Meredith believes is the human condition; *The Ring and the Book* has to do with the fascinating way in which the "truth" changes as the point of view shifts.

14. *Virtue*, p. 36.

15. *Ibid.*, p. 40.

16. *Ibid.*, pp. 32–33, 50.

17. Quoted in Le Gallienne, *Meredith*, p. 123.

18. Henderson, p. 73.

19. See Stevenson, *Ordeal*, pp. 265, 289.

20. See, for example, Annan, p. 52.

21. Quotations from R. Semmes, *The Cruise of the Alabama and the Sumter* (New York: 1864), pp. 232–34.

22. *Letters*, I, 200.

23. See *Letters*, II, 529; also Stevenson, *Ordeal*, p. 131; and Lindsay, pp. 75–76.

24. Compare with Swinburne's poem "A Song of Italy."

25. "Correspondence from the Seat of War in Italy," *Miscellaneous Prose*, Memorial ed. XXIII, pp. 174–75.

26. *Ibid.*, p. 188.

27. That is, not to dueling as such. There are, however, many references to fencing and boxing—i.e., sports, the democratic substitute for dueling. In *Lord Ormont and His Aminta*, one of Meredith's novels of the '90's, a man is killed at swordplay. But the death occurs at a fencing parlor, and only the participants, neither of whom is a hero, know that the swords are unbuttoned. The world is immediately told that a terrible accident has occurred.

28. Not as a man, at any rate. At the end of his career Meredith did endow a sympathetic character with chivalric qualities, but that character was a woman. See discussion of *The Amazing Marriage*, pp. 189–97.

29. Howe, p. 94. As Miss Howe says, Meredith, in *Beauchamp*, called for a strong navy. Elsewhere, particularly in his letters, he was equally vociferous about the need for a well-trained army.

30. Stevenson, *Ordeal*, p. 280.

31. *British History*, p. 363.

32. *Letters,* II, 362–63.

33. Unpublished letters in the Yale University Library. Seymour Trower was the friend to whom the second letter, dated August 2, 1905, was addressed.

34. Stevenson, *Ordeal,* p. 347.

35. *Letters,* II, 618.

36. *Poetical Works,* Notes (Trevelyan), p. 607.

37. *Ibid.,* p. 458.

38. *Victorian Temper,* p. 175.

39. *James,* p. 249.

40. Howe, p. 163. This work, an account of the many kinds of interest engendered in novelists by empire, makes clear how comparatively minor Meredith's contribution was. Alongside others Miss Howe discusses, Meredith seems hardly a "novelist of empire" at all.

41. See "Outside the Crowd," *Poetical Works,* pp. 456–57. See also Trevelyan's note, *ibid.,* p. 608.

42. "Shooting Niagara," p. 621.

43. *Poetical Works,* p. 543.

44. Littmann, pp. 229, 230. Meredith quotations are from *Poetical Works,* pp. 329, 407, 421, 394, 401, 240, 423, 449.

45. *Ordeal,* p. 280.

46. "Sir Leslie Stephen," p. 187.

47. These manuscripts are in the Yale University Library. I have attempted to date them by comparing the calligraphy with that of earlier and later manuscripts of established date.

48. See Appendix for this sketch.

49. An observation by Lionel Stevenson (*Ordeal,* p. 344) may be apropos, though it does not take account of motives that we discussed in connection with *Evan Harrington* and *Vittoria*: "[Meredith's] fascination with warfare and distant countries revealed a sense of unfulfillment in his own experience: he felt that he ought to have been a fighter or an explorer." It should be noted that Stevenson makes this observation while discussing Meredith in his later years.

50. Sandra Belloni is "Vittoria" as a younger girl.

51. *Friedrich II,* p. 133.

52. *Letters,* I, 207–08.

53. *Poetical Works,* p. 433. Subsequent quotations are from *Poetical Works,* pp. 396, 605, 524, 433, 476.

54. *Letters,* II, 509.

55. Unpublished letter, dated April 29, 1907, in the Yale Library.

56. See Hammerton, p. 49.

CHAPTER III

1. John Morley, of whom we shall hear again, described the period as one in which each controversialist was eager to have it thought "he wore the colours of the other side . . . when the theologian would fain pass

for the rationalist." (*Voltaire*, p. 8.) Leslie Stephen, who will also figure here, complained that "reason" had been used on all sides of philosophical debates (p. 859). It would seem from Morley's comment, and by implication from Stephen's, that it was the theologian who was guilty of misappropriating the title "rationalist." But consider A. W. Benn's definition of rationalism, proposed at the beginning of his impressive work on the subject: "Rationalism might be defined as the method and doctrine of those who . . . make reason the supreme regulator of their beliefs . . . who try to think and speak in terms to which fixed and intelligible senses are attached." Though Benn was no friend of theology or metaphysics, there is nothing in his definition which a Christian or a non-Christian metaphysician could not, with enough sophistication, apply to his own position. It may also be noted that the nontheological disputants, at war with each other, could all claim standing room under Benn's umbrella. The confusion, in short, was not the fault of theologians or any other particular group, but was caused by the unexamined difficulties inherent in the words "reason" and "rationalist." We should also note that the *one* meaning of rationalism *not* usually intended by the people we have been discussing was the technical one. They were not rationalists in the tradition of Descartes, Leibnitz, and Kant. Indeed, rather than being interested in a priori conditions for knowing, most of them, as we shall see, were concerned with getting at the reality of the external world, a reality they assumed to be in no way dependent on the knower. Rationalism, for the group we are considering, meant "common sense," obeying one's intellect rather than one's emotions, and examining carefully the evidence provided by the external world—the source of one's "experience."

2. *Modern Love*, XLVIII, p. 154.

3. Lionel Stevenson has said that as the '70's began Meredith "was going through a serious revaluation of his own beliefs, making for the first time a synthesis of his opinions on science, religion, and the structure of society." Stevenson adds that Meredith, giving up his employment on *The Ipswich Journal* about this time, "could ruminate with more leisure" on what he had learned of politics and international affairs while he was a journalist. Stevenson concludes that as a result Meredith formed "a more coherent and more radical outlook." (*Ordeal*, pp. 176–77). More coherent it certainly was, but whether it was actually more "radical" is a question that will need to be considered at some length.

4. Morley, Stephen, and Maxse were members of the *Fortnightly* group, described by E. M. Everett (in an elliptical quote from Morley: see p. 226, n. 17) as "the party of humanity." To what extent Meredith can be identified with this group is a question under discussion here. For some indications of what "rationalism" meant to Meredith's friends, see Everett, pp. 23, 292; Morley, *Compromise*, pp. 11–12, "Mr. Mill's Autobiography," p. 1; Stephen, p. 859; Annan, p. 189. For Meredith's relationship with these men and their ideas, see Everett, p. 70; Stevenson,

*Ordeal,* pp. 171, 186; Lindsay, p. 224; Meredith, *Letters,* I, 201n. A brief glimpse of what rationalism signified to Meredith is contained in a letter to his first son: "My aim . . . is never to take counsel of my sensations, but of my intelligence. I let the former have free play, but deny them the right to bring me to a decision." (*Letters,* I, 213.)

5. Whether *Harry Richmond* is structurally a triumph is, for me, a vexed question. Most critics and scholars have praised the book's style and construction. Virginia Woolf: "The story bowls smoothly along the road which Dickens [had] already trodden of autobiographical narrative. . . . For that reason, no doubt, the author has curbed his redundance and pruned his speech. The style is the most rapid possible. It runs smooth, without a kink in it." ("Novels of Meredith," p. 249.) Stevenson speaks of the book's firmly built plot. (*Ordeal,* p. 181.) J. B. Priestley says (p. 157): "The form compels him to slow up the action and join together most of his customary loose ends." Arthur Symons calls attention to the "painstaking perfection and strenuous realism of the character drawing" and to the "superb intellectual quality of the book." (Quoted by Hammerton, p. 214.) R. H. Hutton stands alone, it almost seems, in insisting on *Harry Richmond*'s "manifold retardations," caused by its want of "narrative-flow" and of "simplicity of style," and the lack "of clear relation between the different parts" of the tale (p. 79).

6. Only Galland has given proper emphasis to the importance of these works (p. 300): "The three novels, *Harry Richmond, Beauchamp's Career,* and *The Egoist,* written between 1866 and 1878, correspond to the full maturity of the artist and count among his great masterpieces. . . . We can take this period for the most magnificently rich of this creative life."

7. *Ordeal,* p. 181.

8. Introduction to James, *Princess,* p. x. Trilling calls this kind of hero "The Young Man from the Provinces." Most of Meredith's heroes do not fit this description because they do not travel very far, physically or spiritually, from their place of origin. The great centers of power do not attract them. They are perhaps fearful of showing too much ambition, or are too concerned with altruism to give themselves up frankly to the drive for success that Meredith, on the other hand, carefully includes among their characteristics. Harry Richmond, though different in many ways from the Young Man from the Provinces, does, among Meredith's heroes, come closest to the type.

9. Meredith's characterization of Princess Ottilia brings to mind an observation of G. M. Young (p. 4) concerning the women in George Eliot's novels: "The pagan ethic which . . . carried into the next, the agnostic, age the evangelical faith in duty and renunciation, was a woman's ethic. . . . [George Eliot] is the moralist of the Victorian revolution." Meredith's heroines are not always distinguished by their "faith in duty and renunciation," but Princess Ottilia, despite her royal trappings and

problems, is closer to Maggie Tulliver or Dorothea Brooke than any of his others.

10. There is an interesting parallel between these words Meredith uses to describe the Princess (II, 350) and certain observations made by John Morley. In *On Compromise,* he said (p. 164): "You must have authority, and must yet have obedience. The noblest and deepest and most beneficent kind of authority is that which rests on an obedience that is rational and spontaneous." And in an earlier essay, devoted to Mill, Morley had used almost the same words: "The noblest . . . authority is that which rests on an obedience which is rational, deliberate, and spontaneous." ("Liberty," p. 241.) Indeed, the idea is Mill's.

11. Meredith was quite close, in this regard, to friends like Morley, Maxse, and Stephen. Noel Annan, speaking of the period we are discussing, has said (p. 159): "The middle class rationalists apprehended that the political reforms they desired could be achieved within a framework of Liberalism . . . they could be achieved so long as public opinion was assured that rationalists were not agitators or subversive." The real difference between Meredith and his friends, as we shall see, had to do with how the artist should treat within his work even the seemingly mild doctrine of reform. It was not the content of the doctrine but the very conception "doctrine" that became an issue.

12. See *David Copperfield,* I, 400–01. With G. M. Young's observation in mind (see note 9, above), we find it interesting, too, that both David and Harry are taught by women to identify "reasonable" with "moral" behavior.

13. This effectively controlled complication of the story bears out E. M. Forster's contention (pp. 89–92) that Meredith was supremely capable in creating plots (a contention made in the course of severely limited praise of Meredith).

14. Meredith may have had something like this in mind when he complained to Jessop that the British reading public would not let him probe deeply into humanity and that therefore *Harry Richmond* misses profundity (Stevenson, *Ordeal,* p. 178). Whether or not it was fair to place so much blame on his public and so little upon himself is a question. But there is no difficulty in deciding that the fault in the novel lies in the characterization of Harry, not of Roy.

15. With respect both to the general thesis of this chapter and to the point just made, an author's aside (appearing in the course of the story) is of interest: "My people . . . are actual, yet uncommon. It is the clockwork of the brain that they are directed to set in motion, and . . . the conscience residing in thoughtfulness which they would appeal to" (II, 553). Meredith has indicated here just how intellectual is his method. As we shall see, however, the success of Beauchamp as a character depends on more than the above.

16. G. M. Trevelyan called it the outstanding political novel of the

nineteenth century. (See *British History*, p. 343n.) He does not, however, seem to have meant much more than that it colorfully and shrewdly dissects the various parties of the '60's. Jack Lindsay similarly praised it (pp. 203–223), but for reasons even more restrictive, and certainly less accurate, than Trevelyan's.

17. Dr. Shrapnel supplies some of the best of these definitions (I, 294): "The Tories of our time walked, or rather stuck, in the track of the Radicals of a generation back. Note, then, that Radicals, always marching to triumph, never taste it; and for Tories it is Dead Sea fruit. . . . Those Liberals, those temporisers, compromisers, a concourse of atoms! glorify themselves in the animal satisfaction of sucking the juice of the fruit, for which they pay with their souls. They have no true cohesion, for they have no vital principle." Elsewhere, Beauchamp himself apostrophizes the Whigs, who are spiritually present in the novel among some of the older gentry (I, 221): "The Whigs preached finality in Reform. It was their own funeral sermon." With respect to Dr. Shrapnel, it is a curious fact that Morley had been known to talk like him. In a leading article in *The Fortnightly* Morley had said: "Wherever you come to a real difficulty, to an organic question, the Tory and the parliamentary liberal are of one accord. . . . Opposed in full front to both is the party of active humanity, of political initiative, of the republic in its true sense." ("England," p. 480.) What makes this fact interesting is that Dr. Shrapnel is in many ways a comic figure.

18. A reason why Meredith's detailed attention to party differences made an impression on readers, at least during the '70's, is suggested by D. C. Somervell's observation, offered in a different connection (p. 79): "Only after 1868, with the emergence of Gladstone and Disraeli as indisputable leaders of their respective parties, does the strife of parties become once again a strife of policies and principles." In other words, by paying a great deal of attention to political distinctions Meredith caught the spirit of the times in one of its freshest manifestations.

19. See, for example, Lindsay, pp. 203–23.

20. *Letters*, I, 232–33.

21. *Ibid.*, p. 224.

22. *Ibid.*, pp. 225–26. William Maxse Meredith left blank the name of the person to whom this letter was addressed. Lionel Stevenson identified the letter as one written to Morley.

23. *Ibid.*

24. *Ibid.*, p. 241.

25. Unpublished letter, dated October 13, 1874, in the Berg Collection.

26. And modeled upon Meredith's estimable Tory friend, William Hardman. One of Blackburn Tuckham's characteristic ideas is that education will only increase the possibility of revolution. He says (I, 284): "The best education for the people is government." It is interesting to note that he contrasts more directly with George Eliot's Radical than with any of

Meredith's. Felix Holt does not want to give the people political power *until* they have education.

27. If we look closely at some of the "radical" ideas held by Nevil and Dr. Shrapnel, we see why, even when they are attributed to the '60's or '70's, they signify nothing that should have aroused fear, anger, or other deep emotion in conservatives of the period. At one point Dr. Shrapnel says (II, 328): "Society is our one tangible gain, our one flooring and roofing in a world of most uncertain structures built on morasses. Toward the laws that support it men hopeful of progress give their adhesion." Compare these words, incidentally, with something Meredith wrote to his son, Arthur: "Society is a wanton hypocrite, and I would accommodate her in nothing: though for the principle of Society I hold that men should be ready to lay down their lives." (*Letters*, I, 237.) On economic "radicalism," here is Dr. Shrapnel speaking (I, 122): "[Capital] is the villain . . . [but] let him live, for he too comes of blood and bone. He shall not grind the faces of the poor and helpless—that's all." It is a sentiment with which enlightened manufacturers, Tory reformers, and even Tory spokesmen of the period could agree, and can hardly be thought of as threatening to any of the characters we meet in the novel. As for Nevil's own Radical platform when he stands for Parliament, it is mild indeed. He wants museums to open on Sundays, he makes unspecified references to the "land question" (I, 104), and, as W. F. Wright says (p. 123), "He would make politics a frank contest of issues in which reason could examine facts and dispassionately choose the best." Even in the '60's and '70's most men recognized that such ideas did not threaten the fabric of society. In the novel itself, Tories Seymour Austin, Stukely Culbrett, and Blackburn Tuckham are the most articulate and perceptive in pronouncing Nevil harmless. It may be added that Nevil displeases his fellow Radicals because "he won't go against the game laws for them, and he won't cut down the army and navy" (I, 213). Thus, like Maxse, he is quite ready to identify himself with the aristocracy on a number of controversial issues. Indeed, like so many other Britons of the period, Nevil would have been inclined to see power pass back into the hands of the aristocracy if only it would show itself capable of ruling. Early in the novel he makes it plain he does not attack hereditary aristocracy as an institution, only those of its families that do not produce leaders. Later (I, 310): "I respect a true aristocracy. . . . I say that is no aristocracy, if it does not head the people in virtue—military, political, national: I mean the qualities required by the times for leadership." And Dr. Shrapnel (II, 324): "Where kings lead, it is to be supposed they are wanted. Service is the noble office on earth, and where kings do service let them take the first honours of the State." There is certainly more of Carlyle in both assertions than of any "Radical," if the *Fortnightly* group represented Radical thought in the '60's and '70's. Dr. Shrapnel, it should be added, is a Radical who believes in God and prayer, a fact that sharply distinguishes him from such Radicals as Leslie Stephen and Maxse. Dr.

Shrapnel says (I, 322): "Prayer . . . is the soul's exercise and source of strength. . . . Cast forth the soul in prayer, you meet the effluence of the outer truth, you join with the creative elements giving breath to you." Indeed, in these lines at least, Meredith achieves a tone that is reminiscent of no one so much as D. H. Lawrence. In the sense, then, that Lawrence was a radical, Dr. Shrapnel is, too. But he is not, let us repeat, a radical in the sense Meredith's friends were radicals.

28. *Almost* persuaded, that is, despite evidence to the contrary. This evidence depends on nothing less than the fact that Nevil at one point (II, 417) actually won approval of Cecilia's *reason*: "Had Beauchamp appeared at Mount Laurels, Cecilia would have been ready to support and encourage him, boldly. Backed by Mr. Austin, she saw some good in Dr. Shrapnel's writing, much in Beauchamp's devotedness. . . . He shone clear to her reason at last: partly because her father in his opposition to him did not, but was on the contrary unreasonable, cased in mail, mentally clouded."

29. The opinions of the "sweet-faced girl" (I, 296) are especially interesting because they bear a remarkable resemblance to utterances contained in a letter Meredith wrote to Maxse in 1865. (See *Letters*, I, 170.)

30. The first to protest was Meredith's wife, who pleaded with him to change the conclusion. He replied that there was no other possible end for Beauchamp. For other objections to the ending, see Stevenson, *Ordeal*, p. 198; Priestley, p. 146; Sassoon, p. 129; Hammerton, pp. 216–17. Lindsay's interpretation (p. 220), though approving of the conclusion, does not seem to me to do justice to the facts: "But [Beauchamp] cannot advance to mass-struggle. He dies in an individual act of heroism, which expresses his anguished desire for union with the common people but which also kills him, returning him to romantic loss. He dies saving a worker's child from drowning. Shrapnel and Romfrey are linked in the thought over his corpse: 'This (*the muddy urchin*) is what we have in exchange for Beauchamp!' But though Meredith in one sense means this phrase ironically, tragically, he is also pointing simply to the solution that has evaded Beauchamp. There can be no irony in the end of such a man; the saved child is the future for which he has striven; the child is the working class with whom the next word [sic] lies." E. M. Everett, in my opinion, has come closest to the significance of the ending (p. 267): "That [Beauchamp] sacrificed his life to save a worthless waif, 'an insignificant bit of mudbank life,' suggests inevitably the quixotism of the radical heroics. 'This is what we have in exchange for Beauchamp!' Meredith says, calling attention to the rescued child—and to many things besides. For Beauchamp's friends—and for the world—it was a sorry exchange. But the Comic Spirit was the spirit of detachment, detachment too rare among the *Fortnightly* group."

31. Eliot, I, 221.
32. Pattison, p. 361.
33. Broderick, p. 185.
34. *Culture and Anarchy*, pp. 72–108.

35. Politics are dealt with again in an inferior work, *The Tragic Come-dians* (1880), but even less concretely than in *Beauchamp*. Passion, on the other hand, is presented with an awkward and exaggerated display of energy.

36. G. M. Trevelyan has sensed the experimental nature of Meredith's work and has, as a consequence, put Meredith in good company: "Mill taught that what was needed in the England of that day was a change of attitude in the direction of freedom to express new ideas in word and action . . . the mid-Victorian literature,—represented by Matthew Arnold, George Eliot, the Brownings, and Meredith, . . . —was instinct with the principle of freedom and experiment, always within the limits imposed by sound learning and the social sense." (*British History*, pp. 341–42.)

37. This is a conventional short title for *On the Idea of Comedy and the Uses of the Comic Spirit*. Delivered as a lecture on February 1, 1877, the *Essay* appeared in print in April of that year in *The New Quarterly Magazine*.

38. J. B. Priestley, without specifically mentioning the *Essay* and the great comic work which followed it—*The Egoist*—has made an observation (p. 140) which tends to confirm my thesis that Meredith's career had always pointed toward the creation of these two works: "His whole phi-losophy . . . would urge him towards Comedy, because . . . that phi-losophy gives the highest place to the intellect."

39. A number of critics have commented upon "common sense," "the comic spirit," and "society" in Meredith's view. See, for example, Priest-ley, pp. 117–18; Curle, pp. 232–33. And Lindsay for once does not have to distort Meredith's meaning in order to talk about him: "It [the comic spirit] is earthy, the ceaseless correction of idealist abstraction, but it has nothing of Peacockian detachment or Carlylean contempt-of-earth, for it owns a universalizing quality—civilization being founded on common sense, on rationality—and it thus unites men as well as intensifying their individual apprehensions of the concrete world of experience. It is the 'spirit form of our united social intelligences' " (p. 233).

40. See "The Idea of Comedy," *New Statesman*, p. 409 (Signed H.C.H.).

41. "Meredith on Comedy," p. 314.

42. An indication of how similar Meredith's thinking could sometimes be to the *Fortnightly* group's is provided by the fact that his equation of "common sense" and "reason" (or "rationalism"—they are all the same for him) was also made by Mark Pattison (p. 343), a member of the group, when he reviewed Leslie Stephen's *History of English Thought in the Eighteenth Century*: "Writing of the eighteenth century—the rationalist century—Mr. Stephen is eminently rational; he applies the standard of common sense to every opinion that offers. We have no *à priori* system thrust upon us at every turn."

43. Introduction to *The Egoist*, pp. xiv–xv. Mary Henderson's obser-vation (p. 153) seems to me more accurate: "To Meredith Egoism is what

Original Sin was to our forefathers, an initial condition common to all and only to be outgrown by much prayer and fasting." Insofar as Meredith may at times have been interested in evolutionary theory, he was probably in agreement with Morley's view of it, which not only connected nature and civilization but denied fatalism with regard to the future. For Morley's approach, see for example "Mill on Religion," pp. 649–51.

44. Early in *The Egoist* (I, 4) Meredith tells us that comedy corrects the *vestiges* of rawness and grossness to be found among us: "She is the ultimate civilizer." Richard Le Gallienne (p. 52) sees the goal of Meredith's comedy as the abstraction, Truth, but at the same time Le Gallienne's language seems to acknowledge that there is something retrograde in the movement Meredith envisages: "Truth, indeed, life as it is, is the one great desire of the comic muse, and to whip men *back* to that does she carry her lash of laughter [italics mine]." Priestley (pp. 112–13) solves the contradiction by equating "progress" with "reform" rather than with novelty.

45. It is significant that in *The Egoist* Meredith alludes, with comic skepticism, to evolutionary theory. At one point he says that science has given us a tail, without removing our egoism. "We have little to learn from the apes." Rather, he concludes (I, 2–3), art "is the specific." And comedy, born of our united social intelligence, is the key to "the Book of Egoism." Surely these thoughts agree with the assertion in the *Essay* that it is man's present, not his future, that interests the comic spirit. Art is concerned with what can be envisioned *now*; it creates the present, for it is the only human enterprise that can capture the spirit and sense of the immediate.

46. Stevenson, *Ordeal*, p. 217.

47. Lionel Stevenson compares Sir Willoughby to the Countess de Saldar, of *Evan Harrington*. (*Ordeal*, p. 217.) Though Stevenson does not stress the fact that sexuality is the basis of Sir Willoughby's character, his comparison is interesting because in terms of sexuality the Countess was the most successful figure that Meredith had created before he wrote *The Egoist*.

48. He said so in the *Essay*, providing another important link between it and *The Egoist*. In two letters, written ten years apart, Meredith also made clear how highly he regarded Molière. In the first, dated October 6, 1876, he asked his friend, Bonaparte Wyse, to tell him of "any essay or notice" about Molière he knew of. Meredith concluded: "I am going to deliver a lecture on him as the grand and unique illustrator of comedy." And on December 31, 1886, he wrote to Havelock Ellis: "Molière is the only writer of pure comedy, so rare is it." (Unpublished letters, Yale University Library.) Among others (see Henderson, p. 163), W. E. Henley has observed the connection between *The Egoist* and the works of Molière: "It [*The Egoist*] is an attempt at art by an elderly apprentice of genius. It is the material for a perfect comedy—not of intrigue; d--n intrigue; intrigue is not comic—but of character—the missing link between Art and Nonsense. An Inorganic 'Misanthrope.' The devil will surely damn him hot and deep. I hate and admire him." (See Stevenson, *Ordeal*, p. 233.)

49. Even as we read, in the *Essay*, Meredith's description of Alceste (pp. 22–23), we get a prevision of Sir Willoughby, not yet created when the *Essay* was written.

50. In collaboration with Alfred Sutro, Meredith wrote a dramatization of *The Egoist* in 1898. The play, however, was never produced. For comments upon the dramatic nature of the novel, see Granville-Barker, p. 183; Priestley, p. 152; Stevenson, *Ordeal*, p. 225; Galland, p. 378. Not to be overlooked either is Meredith's explicitness about his intentions. The full title of the novel is *The Egoist, A Comedy in Narrative*.

51. Another aspect of Meredith's presentation of Clara, not stressed here, is indicated by an observation of Lionel Stevenson: "When conveying the wishes and fears of his central characters, Meredith often used a technique not unlike that which in the twentieth century came to be called the 'stream of consciousness.' He showed that the process of thinking was a confused sequence of images and almost formless concepts, rather than the organized reasoning that previous novelists had chronicled." (*Ordeal*, p. 229.)

52. Cf. Galland, p. 390.

53. The description of Vernon by Mrs. Mountstuart Jenkinson (I, 11) undoubtedly hits off Meredith's own picture of Stephen. Meredith says that her words, "He is a Phoebus Apollo turned fasting friar," painted "the sunken brilliance of the lean long-walker and scholar at a stroke." At one point (I, 85), Vernon says that he is thirty-two and has not yet tried anything; therefore he intends to leave Patterne Hall, take himself to London, and try journalism. All this is reminiscent of Stephen, for whom Cambridge had been what Patterne Hall is to Vernon, and who gave up his fellowship to go off to London and journalism. Cf. Stevenson, *Ordeal*, p. 231.

54. *Lighthouse*, p. 51.

55. Though V. S. Pritchett does not refer specifically to this portrait, it may have been in his mind when he said, "What distresses us is that Meredith does not know when he is vulgar." And: "He has gone to the intellect and its pride to seal off the wounds of life, as a young man will before he learns that the brain will do nothing for us." ("Meredith," p. 207.) Perhaps the same was true of Stephen. Jack Lindsay (p. 225) notes "fear elements" in Stephen causing him to avoid conflicts that could not "be stated in terms of an abstract rationalism."

56. We may note that Sir Willoughby had visited America, as had Morley, and that Willoughby was a student of Darwin, as was Morley. However, to do anything more than note these coincidences would be carrying speculation too far. Something of much more interest has been recorded by Lionel Stevenson: in 1889 Meredith talked about writing a novel to be called *The Journalist*, in which he intended to depict Morley as one of the main characters. Meredith apparently did write it, but he left orders that it was not to be published until after his death, and "there is a story to the effect that he eventually made his friend Dr. Plimmer burn it in his presence." (*Ordeal*, pp. 283–84.) Why Meredith, who saved

so many drafts and unfinished sketches of stories, should have insisted on burning the one in which Morley was a main character is a question to which we have no direct answer. In a way, however, our entire discussion of the relations between Meredith and Morley is an answer.

57. Though Meredith and Morley remained friends till the end, it is a fact that after the '70's, as Morley became more and more involved in political life, they saw relatively little of each other. There is a plaintive and sad note in a letter Meredith wrote to James Cotter Morison on May 6, 1879: "Marriott gave me a good account of Morley some time back, and that, as I never see him now, refreshed me." (*Letters*, I, 299.)

58. In 1867, on the occasion of Morley's trip to America, Meredith addressed two relatively minor poems to him ("To J. M." and "Lines to a Friend Visiting America").

59. A rounded sketch of his ideas can be obtained from his letters. On March 2, 1880, he wrote to Maxse: "The Liberal chiefs here have ruined the cause for twenty years. The only hope, it seems to me, is that Radicalism should be avowed, and the sham medium done away with." (*Letters*, I, 306.) We recognize these as sentiments Dr. Shrapnel (and Morley) had expressed some years earlier, and which Meredith, at the time, had treated with comic skepticism. On July 22, 1887, Meredith wrote the following words, clearly forming a rationalist credo, to G. P. Baker: "Close knowledge of our fellows, discernment of the laws of existence, these lead to great civilization. I have supposed that the novel, exposing and illustrating the natural history of man, may help us to such sustaining roadside gifts." (*Ibid.*, II, 398.) As for some of the specific political currents affecting him in the '80's, we get an idea of these from a letter he wrote in his role as publisher's reader to Chapman and Hall, a role he continued to fill until 1894. The letter is addressed to Frederick Chapman and reads in part: "Essays by Scrutatis, a small volume. These are tersely written tending to enlarged modern views in politics: so far Socialistic that he is for the Nationalization of Land; the putting of much into the hands of the state—which is opposed to English feeling, although there are signs of English reason awakening to some idea of the necessity." (Unpublished letter dated October 3, 1887, Yale University Library.) But as he got older, the tone of Meredith's statements underwent a remarkable change. It did not so much become more conservative as it did more independent and disinterested. It marked, actually, a return in Meredith's old age to the point of view that had characterized his most creative and intellectually strongest period: the 1870's. Thus, in a letter to H. W. Nevinson dated June 7, 1904, Meredith said rather sadly: "Generally I am with the Liberals, but I do not always take Party views. The independent person is not held to be worth a hearing in times of excitement." (Letter in Berg Collection.) In an interview with Nevinson, published in *The Daily Chronicle* later in the same month, Meredith made statements which underline many of the things we said in our discussion of his work in the '70's, particularly in our consideration of *Beauchamp*. At one point in the interview he was

quoted as saying, "John Stuart Mill called the Conservatives 'the stupid party,' but that was unfair. Many of their leaders are personal friends of mine. I know them well and find plenty of brains among them." (Printer's proof of article, Berg Collection.) Thus did he confirm, at the very end of his life, that he regarded the portraits of Blackburn Tuckham, Stukely Culbrett, and Seymour Austin to be authenticated by his experience in the world. Later in the interview he spoke of the relation between art and society in a way that not only recalls *Beauchamp* but strongly suggests what might have been the beliefs out of which that work grew: "I remember: when you [*The Daily Chronicle*] became a halfpenny paper I told you that you must be democratic in politics but maintain an aristocracy of literature. In politics you cannot be too democratic, for we see through History that no governing class has legislated for the needs of the supporting class below, except when shaken and in alarm: but all art is aristocratic in so far as it aims only at the very highest, and must be content with nothing less. Popularity and democratic opinion have nothing to do with literature."

60. In 1906 John Morley paid Meredith one of the infrequent visits that marked the later years of their friendship. Writing about that visit, Morley said: "He quarreled a little with his literary fate. I tried to comfort him in the reminder that he had now at last arrested the imagination of some of the best intelligences of his time, by a gallery of creations some of whose names had gained a place among the most familiar in fiction. My solace did not move him, for his poetry had found no large audience, and it was as oracle from the tripod of the poet that he would have chosen to sway his age." (*Recollections*, I, 49.)

CHAPTER IV

1. Page references for Meredith's poems will be to the 1912 edition of *The Poetical Works of George Meredith*, edited by G. M. Trevelyan. This single volume is as nearly definitive a collection of Meredith's poetry as any in existence.

2. We could dignify Meredith's unsuccessful image by calling it an example of attempted synesthesia. William Empson (pp. 16–18) points out that Swinburne often uses devices that seem to aim at synesthesia, and it is interesting that not only were Swinburne and Meredith close at various periods of their lives, but critics have attempted to detect influences of Swinburne upon Meredith.

3. Cf. Trevelyan, *Poetry and Philosophy*, p. 162.

4. Beach, *Concept*, p. 477.

5. *Poetical Works*, Notes, p. 597.

6. *Concept*, p. 491.

7. *Ibid.*, p. 495.

8. *Poetical Works of Arnold*, p. 5.

9. Unpublished letter in the Berg Collection.

10. "Maud," Part I: IV, iv, p. 201.

11. This poem was first printed as stanza vi of a long poem called "In

the Woods," which appeared in *The Fortnightly Review*, August 1870, pp. 179–83. The version given here, which is much altered from the original, was printed as a separate poem in *Ballads and Poems of Tragic Life* (1887).

12. The poem referred to here is composed of the verses that remained from the original longer version, first published in *The Fortnightly Review*, after Meredith had divided that version into a number of separate poems. Besides "Whimper of Sympathy," two other poems, "Woodland Peace" and "Dirge in Woods," were part of the original work. The remaining stanzas, from which the selection quoted here was taken, were included by Trevelyan in *A Reading of Earth* (1888) under the title Meredith had given the whole in 1870.

13. "In Memoriam," LV, p. 176.

14. *Songs Before Sunrise*, pp. 166, 173. Cf. Roppen, p. 205.

15. Beach, *Concept*, p. 23. The observation, of course, has been made by many, including Alfred North Whitehead and R. G. Collingwood.

16. *Ibid.*, p. 184.

17. *England*, p. 110.

18. But the attitude Meredith expresses toward individualism in his poetry does not tell the whole story. In his novels of the '90's, Meredith's conception of individualism took a new turn. See pp. 165–216.

19. Lines 1–12, p. 884.

20. *Concept*, p. 47.

21. Warren, pp. 237–38.

22. Unpublished letter, dated July 9, 1851, in the Berg Collection.

23. "The Tables Turned," ll. 21–24, p. 481.

24. "In Memoriam," LVI, p. 176.

25. *Evolution*, p. 224.

26. *Poetry and Philosophy*, pp. 113–15.

27. *Concept*, p. 499.

28. *Poetry and Philosophy*, p. 119.

29. See for example Beach, *Concept*, p. 471, and Roppen, pp. 220, 223.

30. *Concept*, p. 476.

31. *Letters*, I, 33.

32. *Concept*, p. 480.

33. This and the following quotations from *Understanding Poetry* appear on pp. 368, 369, 371–72.

34. Indeed, what I have quoted does not give the full effect of their concentration on this one idea and the line that expresses it. They add to their own discussion of the fourteenth line of "Lucifer" a phonetic analysis made by Chard Powers Smith, who asserts that because the accented vowels in Meredith's line all arise from approximately the same location in the vocal apparatus, the line is "musically all of a piece." (*Pattern and Variation in Poetry*, pp. 57–59; quoted on pp. 372–73.)

35. However, Jack Lindsay notes (p. 370n) that Yeats, in the '90's, was reading Meredith with admiration. He quotes Yeats: "[The poems] are certainly very beautiful, and have far more serenity and suavity than I

had expected. [*Love in the Valley*] . . . is full of a curious intricate richness."

CHAPTER V

1. Ensor, p. 304.
2. *The '90's*, pp. 136–37.
3. Ensor, p. 304.
4. *Meredith*, p. 44.
5. Sassoon, p. 210.
6. *James*, p. 161.
7. It also ran as a serial in *The Fortnightly* from October 1890 to May 1891.
8. Unpublished letter, Yale University Library.
9. *The '90's*, p. 208. There is, in particular, a compelling parallel between Meredith's prose-song of the city and W. E. Henley's *London Voluntaries* (published in 1892 as *The Song of the Sword and Other Verses*). Jerome H. Buckley has said of this collection that it was the first English poetry to treat London not merely as background but as a sentient creature—the first to adapt "English verse to the depiction of the metropolis as a great organism throbbing with its own vitality." (*Henley*, p. 185.) Meredith, too, in *One of Our Conquerors*, depicted London as a vivid being, with a life and active personality—however ambiguous—of its own.
10. Unpublished notebooks and manuscript sheets, Yale University Library.
11. The passages that discuss Victor's participation in business activities are singularly plain and straightforward in praise of him. See, for example, p. 201.
12. The very essence of Meredith's conception of Victor forms a striking parallel with an estimate of Joseph Chamberlain that Meredith was later to make: "He is merely the man of a tremendous energy acting upon one idea . . . altogether at the mercy of the idea animating him." (Letter to the Croydon electors, 1906; quoted by Henderson, p. 141. See also Lindsay, p. 285.)
13. *Art and Substance*, pp. 189–90.
14. Lindsay, p. 285.
15. Priestley, pp. 184–85.
16. *James*, p. 174.
17. Lionel Stevenson tells us that Meredith let it be known that Lord Ormont was modeled upon the Earl of Peterborough, "a brilliant general of the time of Queen Anne and a headstrong, tactless man who was repeatedly in disgrace with the government. Late in his life Peterborough secretly married a lovely young actress, Anastasia Robinson, and the public believed her to be his mistress until he acknowledged her as his wife, not long before he died." Stevenson suggests that Meredith also drew upon the life of the Earl of Cardigan, "leader of the Light Brigade . . . at the Battle of Balaklava." Lord Cardigan, at the age of sixty-three, was married at

Gibraltar to a very young lady. Lord Ormont was married to Aminta at the British Embassy in Madrid. See *Ordeal,* pp. 313–14.

18. James, *Letters,* I, 219.
19. Gretton, p. 209.
20. *Art and Substance,* p. 101.
21. Gretton, p. 216.
22. *Ibid.*
23. *Tess,* p. 302.
24. Buckley, *Victorian Temper,* pp. 9, 118, 119; Annan, pp. 4, 7, 110, 116.
25. "Pagan," p. 792.
26. Stevenson, *Ordeal,* pp. 308–9.
27. W. F. Wright, p. 100.
28. Dupee, p. 166.
29. *Ibid.,* p. 231.
30. Gretton, p. 231.
31. *Golden Bowl,* I, 358.
32. *The '90's,* p. 44.
33. *Ordeal,* p. 317.
34. Letter dated September 19, 1908. Present whereabouts of this letter unknown.
35. *Letters,* II, 495.
36. *Ordeal,* p. 334.
37. Sassoon, p. 240.
38. *Poetry and Philosophy,* pp. 209–18.
39. This and subsequent quotations from the *Odes* are from Meredith's *Poetical Works*: "The Revolution," pp. 468–77; "Napoléon," pp. 477–96; "France, 1870," pp. 497–504; "Alsace-Lorraine," pp. 505–20.
40. G. M. Trevelyan has supplied the meaning of this symbol. Elsewhere he tells us he received from Meredith himself the explication of difficult matters in the *Odes*. See *Poetical Works,* Notes, pp. 610–12.
41. *Ibid.,* p. 611.
42. *Ibid.*
43. *Ibid.*
44. *Letters,* I, 223.
45. See Stevenson, *Ordeal,* p. 290. Also there is in the Yale University Library a letter from Meredith to his son William, in which the father, evidently having received a resentful letter from William, assures him with hurt dignity that his interest in Hilda de Longueuil is only the interest of an old man in a young friend.
46. James, *Letters,* II, 254.
47. "The Soul of Man," p. 169.
48. James, *Letters,* II, 249–50.
49. Stevenson, *Ordeal,* p. 340.
50. James, *Letters,* II, 251.
51. Quoted by Stevenson, *Ordeal,* p. 346.

# Bibliography

## WORKS BY GEORGE MEREDITH

*The Adventures of Harry Richmond.* Memorial ed. IX and X. London: Constable and Co., 1910.

*The Amazing Marriage.* Memorial ed. XIX. 1910.

*Beauchamp's Career.* Memorial ed. XI and XII. 1910.

*Celt and Saxon.* Memorial ed. XX. 1910.

"Correspondence from the Seat of War in Italy," *Miscellaneous Prose.* Memorial ed. XXIII. 1910, pp. 163–213.

*The Cruise of the Alabama and the Sumter: From the Private Journals and Other Papers of Commander R. Semmes.* (Introductory and concluding chapters by Meredith.) New York: Carleton; London: Saunders, Otley, and Co., 1864.

*Diana of the Crossways.* Memorial ed. XVI. 1910.

*The Egoist.* Memorial ed. XIII and XIV. 1910.

*Evan Harrington.* Memorial ed. VI. 1910.

*Farina.* Memorial ed. XXI. 1910.

*Letters.* Collected and edited by William Maxse Meredith. Memorial ed. XXVIII and XXIX. New York: Charles Scribner's Sons, 1912.

*The Letters of George Meredith to Alice Meynell: With Annotations Thereto, 1896–1907.* London: The Nonesuch Press, 1923.

*Lord Ormont and His Aminta.* Memorial ed. XVIII. 1910.

"On the Idea of Comedy and of the Uses of the Comic Spirit," *Miscellaneous Prose.* Memorial ed. XXIII. 1910, pp. 3–55.

*One of Our Conquerors.* Memorial ed. XVII. 1910.

*The Ordeal of Richard Feverel: A History of a Father and Son.* Memorial ed. II. 1909.

*The Poetical Works of George Meredith: With Some Notes by G. M. Trevelyan.* London: Constable and Co., 1912.

*Rhoda Fleming.* Memorial ed. V. 1910.

*Sandra Belloni.* Memorial ed. III and IV. 1910.

*The Shaving of Shagpat: An Arabian Entertainment.* Memorial ed. I. 1909.

*Short Stories.* Memorial ed. XXI and XXII. 1910.

"Sir Leslie Stephen, K.C.B.," *The Author,* XIV (April 1904), 187.

*The Tragic Comedians.* Memorial ed. XV. 1910.

*Up to Midnight: A Series of Dialogues Contributed to the Graphic.* Boston: Luce, 1913.

*Vittoria.* Memorial ed. VII and VIII. 1910.

OTHER WORKS

Aiken, Henry D. *The Age of Ideology.* New York: The New American Library, 1956.

Annan, Noel. *Leslie Stephen: His Thought and Character in Relation to His Time.* Cambridge, Mass.: Harvard University Press, 1952.

Arnold, Matthew. *Culture and Anarchy.* New York: Macmillan and Co., 1883.

——. *England and the Italian Question.* Introduction and notes by Merle M. Bevington. Durham, N.C.: Duke University Press, 1953. Reprinted from original edition, London: Longman, Green, Longman, and Roberts, 1859.

——. *The Poetical Works of Matthew Arnold.* Edited by C. B. Tinker and H. F. Lowry. London: Oxford University Press, 1950.

Bailey, Elmer Barnes. *The Novels of George Meredith: A Study.* New York: Charles Scribner's Sons, 1907.

Barzun, Jacques. *Darwin, Marx, Wagner: Critique of a Heritage.* Boston: Little, Brown, and Co., 1946.

——. *Romanticism and the Modern Ego.* Boston: Little, Brown, and Co., 1944.

Beach, Joseph Warren. *The Comic Spirit in George Meredith: An Interpretation.* New York: Longmans, Green, and Co., 1911.

——. *The Concept of Nature in Nineteenth-Century English Poetry.* New York: Pageant Book Co., 1956.

Benn, Alfred William. *The History of English Rationalism in the Nineteenth Century.* 2 vols. London, New York: Longmans, Green, and Co., 1906.

Boner, Harold A. *Hungry Generations: The Nineteenth-Century Case Against Malthusianism.* New York: King's Crown Press, 1955.

Broderick, George C. "What Are Liberal Principles?" *The Fortnightly Review,* XIX N.S. (Feb. 1, 1876), 174–91.

Brooks, Cleanth, and Robert Penn Warren. "Lucifer in Starlight," *Understanding Poetry.* Rev. ed. New York: Henry Holt and Co., 1950, pp. 367–73.

Browning, Robert. *Dramatis Personae.* London: Chapman and Hall, 1864.

——. *Men and Women.* London: Chapman and Hall, 1855.

——. *The Ring and the Book.* Works, Riverside ed. III. Boston and New York: Houghton Mifflin and Co., 1895.

Buckley, Jerome Hamilton. *The Victorian Temper: A Study in Literary Culture.* Cambridge, Mass.: Harvard University Press, 1951.

——. *William Ernest Henley: A Study in the "Counter-Decadence" of the Nineties.* Princeton: Princeton University Press, 1945.

Cantimori, Delio. "Italy in 1848," *The Opening of an Era: 1848.* Ed. by François Fejtö. London: Allen Wingate, 1948, pp. 114–42.

Carlyle, Thomas. *The French Revolution.* New York: Random House, n.d.

——. *History of Friedrich II of Prussia, Called Frederick the Great.* 8 vols. *Works,* Centenary ed. XII–XIX. London: Chapman and Hall, 1898.

——. "Shooting Niagara: And After?" *Critical and Miscellaneous Essays.* Works, Ashburton ed. XVII. London: Chapman and Hall, 1883, pp. 587–627.

Chambers, E. K. "Meredith's Modern Love," "Meredith's Nature Poetry," *A Sheaf of Studies.* London: Oxford University Press, 1942, pp. 71–91.

Chislett, William, Jr. *George Meredith: A Study and an Appraisal.* Boston: R. G. Badger, 1925.

Clodd, Edward. "George Meredith: Some Recollections," *The Fortnightly Review,* LXXXVI N.S. (July 1909), 19–31.

——. "Meredith's Conversations with Clodd," I and II: From a correspondent, *The Times Literary Supplement* (May 8 and May 15, 1953), 308 and 324.

Collingwood, R. G. *The Idea of History.* Oxford: The Clarendon Press, 1946.

——. *The Idea of Nature.* Oxford: The Clarendon Press, 1949.

Crees, J. H. E. *George Meredith: A Study of His Works and Personality.* Oxford: B. H. Blackwell, 1918.

Crum, Ralph B. *Scientific Thought in Poetry.* New York: Columbia University Press, 1931.

Curle, Richard H. P. *Aspects of George Meredith.* London: George Routledge and Sons, 1908.

Day Lewis, Cecil. "George Meredith and Responsibility," *Notable Images of Virtue.* Toronto: The Ryerson Press, 1954, pp. 27–52.

——. *The Poetic Image.* London: Jonathan Cape, 1947.

Dickens, Charles. *Great Expectations.* Works, Roxburgh ed. XLI and XLII. Boston: Estes and Lauriat, 1892.

——. *The Personal History of David Copperfield.* Works, Roxburgh ed. XXXVI–XXXVIII.

——. *A Tale of Two Cities.* Works, Roxburgh ed. XXVII and XXVIII.

Drinkwater, John, ed. *The Eighteen-Sixties: Essays by Fellows of the Royal Society of Literature.* Cambridge, England: Cambridge University Press, 1932.

Dupee, F. W. *Henry James: His Life and Writings.* New York: Doubleday and Co., 1956.

Eliot, George. *Adam Bede.* 2 vols. Boston: Dana Estes and Co., n.d.

——. *Felix Holt.* 2 vols. Boston: Dana Estes and Co., n.d.

——. *The Mill on the Floss.* Works, Cabinet ed. XVII and XVIII. Edinburgh and London: William Blackwood and Sons, n.d.

Ellis, S. M. *George Meredith: His Life and Friends in Relation to His Work.* London: Grant Richards, 1919.

Empson, William. *Seven Types of Ambiguity.* New York: Meridian Books, 1955.

Ensor, R. C. K. *England: 1870–1914.* Oxford: The Clarendon Press, 1936.

Everett, Edwin Mallard. *The Party of Humanity: The Fortnightly Review and Its Contributors, 1865–1874.* Chapel Hill: The University of North Carolina Press, 1939.

Faverty, Frederic E. *et al. The Victorian Poets: A Guide to Research.* Cambridge, Mass.: Harvard University Press, 1956.

Fitzgerald, Edward. *The Rubáiyát of Omar Khayyám.* Works, I. New York and Boston: Houghton, Mifflin, and Co., 1887.

Forman, Maurice Buxton, ed. *George Meredith: Some Early Appreciations.* New York: Charles Scribner's Sons, 1909.

Forster, E. M. *Aspects of the Novel.* New York: Harcourt, Brace, and Co., 1954.

Friedman, Norman. "The Jangled Harp: Symbolic Structure in 'Modern Love,'" *Modern Language Quarterly,* XVIII, No. 1 (March 1957), 9–26.

Galland, René. *George Meredith: Les Cinquante Premières Années.* Paris: Les Presses Françaises, 1923.

Gissing, George. *Denzil Quarrier.* London: Lawrence and Bullen, 1892.

——. *The Whirlpool.* London: Lawrence, 1897.

Granville-Barker, Harley. "Tennyson, Swinburne, Meredith—and the Theatre," *The Eighteen-Seventies: Essays by Fellows of the Royal Society of Literature.* Ed. by Harley Granville-Barker. Cambridge, England: Cambridge University Press, 1929, pp. 161–91.

Gretton, Mary Sturge (Henderson). *The Writings and Life of George Meredith: A Centenary Study.* London: Oxford University Press, 1926.

Haight, Gordon. "George Meredith and the Westminster Review," *Modern Language Review,* LIII (January 1958), 1–16.

Hammerton, J. A. *George Meredith in Anecdote and Criticism.* London: Grant Richards, 1909.

Hardy, Thomas. *The Dynasts: An Epic Drama of the War with Napoleon.* 2 vols. London: Macmillan and Co., 1954.

——. *Jude the Obscure.* New York: Harper and Brothers, 1923.

——. *Tess of the D'Urbervilles.* New York: Harper and Brothers, 1891.

Harris, Frank. "George Meredith," *Contemporary Portraits.* New York: Mitchell Kennerly, 1915, pp. 198–218.

Henderson, M. Sturge. *George Meredith: Novelist, Poet, Reformer.* New York: Charles Scribner's Sons, 1907.

Howe, Susanne. *Novels of Empire.* New York: Columbia University Press, 1949.

Hughes, H. Stuart. *Consciousness and Society: The Reorientation of European Social Thought, 1890–1930.* New York: Alfred A. Knopf, 1958.

Hutton, R. H. "The Adventures of Harry Richmond," *The Spectator,* XLV (January 20, 1872), 79–80.

"The Idea of Comedy," *The New Statesman,* XIV (January 10, 1920), 408–9. Article signed "H.C.H."

James, Henry. *The Awkward Age.* New York ed. of the Novels and Tales, IX. New York: Charles Scribner's Sons, 1922.

——. *The Golden Bowl.* New York ed. XXIII and XXIV.

——. *Letters,* 2 vols. Ed. by Percy Lubbock. New York: Charles Scribner's Sons, 1920.

———. *Notebooks*. Ed. by F. O. Matthiessen and Kenneth B. Murdock. New York: Oxford University Press, 1947.

———. *The Princess Casamassima*. 2 vols. Introduction by Lionel Trilling. New York: The Macmillan Co., 1948.

———. *The Spoils of Poynton*. New York ed. X.

———. *What Maizie Knew*. New York ed. XI.

———. *The Wings of the Dove*. New York ed. XIX and XX.

Jerrold, Walter. *George Meredith: An Essay Towards Appreciation*. London: Greening and Co., 1902.

Le Gallienne, Richard. *George Meredith: Some Characteristics*. London: Elkin Matthews, 1890.

———. *The Romantic '90's*. New York: Doubleday, Page, and Co., 1925.

Lindsay, Jack. *George Meredith: His Life and Work*. London: The Bodley Head, 1956.

Littmann, Hildegard. *Das Dichterische Bild in der Lyrik George Merediths und Thomas Hardys*. Bern: published dissertation, 1938.

Loewenberg, J. *Dialogues from Delphi*. Berkeley and Los Angeles: University of California Press, 1949.

Merz, John Theodore. *A History of European Thought in the Nineteenth Century*. 4 vols. Edinburgh and London: William Blackwood and Sons, 1907–1914.

Mill, John Stuart. *Utilitarianism, Liberty, and Representative Government*. London: J. M. Dent and Sons, 1910.

Mooney, E. A., Jr. Introduction to *The Egoist*. New York: Random House, 1951, pp. vii–xix.

Morley, John. "Mr. Mill's Autobiography," *The Fortnightly Review*, XV N.S. (Jan. 1, 1874), 1–20.

———. "England and the War," *The Fortnightly Review*, VIII N.S. (Oct. 1, 1870), 479–88.

———. "Mr. Mill's Doctrine of Liberty," *The Fortnightly Review*, XIV N.S. (Aug. 1, 1873), 234–56.

———. "Mr. Mill's Three Essays on Religion," *The Fortnightly Review*, XVI N.S. (Nov. 1, 1874), 634–51.

———. *On Compromise*. Works, III. London: Macmillan and Co., 1903.

———. *Recollections*. 2 vols. New York: The Macmillan Co., 1917.

———. *Voltaire*. Works, VII. London: Macmillan and Co., 1921.

Pattison, Mark. "The Age of Reason," *The Fortnightly Review*, XXI N.S. (March 1, 1877), 343–61.

Petrie, Sir Charles. *The Chamberlain Tradition*. London: Lovat Dickson, 1938.

Petter, Guy B. *George Meredith and His German Critics*. London: H. F. and G. Witherby, 1939.

Photiadès, Constantin. *George Meredith: Sa Vie, Son Imagination, Son Art, Sa Doctrine*. Paris: Librairie Armand Colin, 1910.

Priestley, J. B. *George Meredith*. London: Macmillan and Co., 1926.

Pritchett, V. S. "The Didactic Pagan," *New Statesman and Nation*, LII, No. 1344 (Dec. 15, 1956), 792.

——. "Meredith," *Books in General*. London: Chatto and Windus, 1953, pp. 197–208.

Roppen, Georg. *Evolution and Poetic Belief: A Study in Some Victorian and Modern Writers*. Oslo: Oslo University Press, 1956.

Ross, Janet. *The Fourth Generation*. New York: Charles Scribner's Sons, 1912.

Ruskin, John. *The Stones of Venice*. 3 vols. London: Smith, Elder, and Co., 1851–53.

Somervell, D. C. *English Thought in the Nineteenth Century*. London: Methuen and Co., 1950.

Sassoon, Siegfried. *Meredith*. New York: The Viking Press, 1948.

Seeley, J. R. *The Expansion of England*. Boston: Roberts Brothers, 1883.

Sencourt, Robert E. *The Life of George Meredith*. New York: Charles Scribner's Sons, 1929.

Shaw, George Bernard. "Meredith on Comedy," *The Saturday Review*, LXXXIII, No. 2161 (27 March, 1897), 314–16.

Spencer, Herbert. *Education: Intellectual, Moral, and Physical*. New York and London: D. Appleton and Co., 1909.

Stephen, Leslie. "An Agnostic's Apology," *The Fortnightly Review*, XIX N.S. (June 1, 1876), 840–60.

Stevenson, Lionel. *Darwin Among the Poets*. Chicago: The University of Chicago Press, 1932.

——. *The Ordeal of George Meredith*. New York: Charles Scribner's Sons, 1953.

Stone, James. "Meredith and Goethe," *University of Toronto Quarterly*, XXI (January 1952), 157–66.

Swinburne, Algernon Charles. *Poems and Ballads*. Works, Bonchurch ed. I. New York: Gabriel Wells; London: William Heinemann, 1925.

——. "A Song of Italy," "Ode on the Proclamation of the French Republic," *Songs Before Sunrise*. Works, Bonchurch ed. II.

Symons, Arthur. *The Symbolist Movement in Literature*. New York: E. P. Dutton and Co., 1958.

Tennyson, Alfred Lord. *The Complete Poetical Works*. Cambridge ed. Boston: Houghton Mifflin Co., 1898.

Thackeray, William Makepeace. *The Virginians*. Works, Biographical ed. X. New York and London: Harper and Brothers, 1899.

Tindall, William York. *Forces in Modern British Literature: 1885–1956*. New York: Vintage Books, 1956.

——. *The Literary Symbol*. Bloomington: Indiana University Press, 1955.

Tinker, Chauncey B. "Meredith's Poetry," *Essays in Retrospect*. New Haven: Yale University Press, 1948, pp. 83–89.

# Bibliography

243

Trevelyan, George Macauley. *British History in the Nineteenth Century*. London: Longmans, Green, and Co., 1934.

——. *The Poetry and Philosophy of George Meredith*. London: Constable and Co., 1907.

Trilling, Lionel. "Freud and Literature," "The Sense of the Past," "Manners, Morals, and the Novel," and "The Meaning of a Literary Idea," *The Liberal Imagination*. New York: The Viking Press, 1950, pp. 34–57; 181–97; 205–22; 281–303.

——. *Matthew Arnold*. 2nd ed. New York: Columbia University Press, 1949.

Warren, Robert Penn. "A Poem of Pure Imagination: An Experiment in Reading," *Selected Essays*. New York: Random House, 1958, pp. 198–305.

Webb, Robert K. *Harriet Martineau: A Radical Victorian*. New York: Columbia University Press, 1960.

Wilde, Oscar. "The Decay of Lying," *Intentions*. Works, X. New York: Lamb Publishing Co., 1909, pp. 7–63.

——. "The Soul of Man Under Socialism," *Works*, I. London, New York: A. R. Keller and Co., 1907, pp. 121–85.

Williams, Raymond. *Culture and Society, 1780–1950*. London: Chatto and Windus, 1958.

Woodward, E. L. *The Age of Reform: 1815–1870*. Oxford: The Clarendon Press, 1946.

Woolf, Virginia. *To the Lighthouse*. New York: Harcourt, Brace, and Co., 1927.

——. "The Novels of George Meredith," *The Second Common Reader*. New York: Harcourt, Brace, and Co., 1932, pp. 245–56.

Wordsworth, William. *The Poetical Works*. New York: Oxford University Press, 1933.

Wright, Elizabeth Cox. "The Significance of the Image Patterns in Meredith's *Modern Love*," *The Victorian Newsletter*, No. 13 (Spring 1958), 1–9.

Wright, Walter F. *Art and Substance in George Meredith: A Study in Narrative*. Lincoln, Nebraska: University of Nebraska Press, 1953.

Young, G. M. *Victorian England: Portrait of an Age*. 2nd ed. London: Oxford University Press, 1953.

# Index

(c) indicates character in a work discussed